JOURNEYS TO IMPOSSIBLE PLACES

Simon Reeve is an author and adventurer who has travelled to more than 130 countries, making multiple award-winning TV series exploring and explaining the world. They include *The Americas, Indian Ocean, Tropic of Cancer, Equator, Sacred Rivers, Caribbean, Tropic of Capricorn, Russia, Mediterranean, Colombia, Australia* (Winner of the British Travel Press Award for Broadcast Travel Programme) and *The Lakes*.

Simon has received a One World Broadcasting Trust Award for 'an outstanding contribution to greater world understanding', the prestigious Ness Award from the Royal Geographical Society, and the John Tompkins Natural History Award from the International Moving Image Society 'for extraordinary achievements' in the field of natural wildlife and history filmmaking. His books have been in both the *Sunday Times* and the *New York Times* bestseller lists.

JOURNEYS TO IMPOSSIBLE PLACES

IN LIFE AND EVERY ADVENTURE

SIMON REEVE

HODDER

First published in Great Britain in 2021 by Hodder & Stoughton
An Hachette UK company

This paperback edition published in 2022

1

Copyright © Simon Reeve 2021

The right of Simon Reeve to be identified as the Author
of the Work has been asserted by him in accordance with
the Copyright, Designs and Patents Act 1988.

A CIP catalogue record for this title is available from the British Library

Paperback ISBN 9781529364057
eBook ISBN 9781529364033

Typeset in Bembo by Hewer Text UK Ltd, Edinburgh
Printed and bound in Great Britain by Clays Ltd, Elcograf S.p.A.

Hodder & Stoughton policy is to use papers that are natural, renewable
and recyclable products and made from wood grown in sustainable
forests. The logging and manufacturing processes are expected to
conform to the environmental regulations of the country of origin.

Hodder & Stoughton Ltd
Carmelite House
50 Victoria Embankment
London EC4Y 0DZ

www.hodder.co.uk

To Jake

Contents

Introduction

I am in an impossible place. A magical place. An ancient woodland of twisted and stunted old oak trees, giant granite boulders and thickets of moss. Inside the wood, greens are vivid, shapes are contorted, racked and ruckled. Every surface is carpeted in lichens, the weirdest dangling from branches in long tresses. This is Wistman's Wood, a wild and wonderful oasis of life sprouting on the side of a valley in the heart of Dartmoor National Park, and it feels otherworldly, like the forest of elves.

Among the many myths and ghostly tales that surround the wood, it is said the trees were a sacred grove planted by Druids. Wisdom and knowledge certainly seem to pulse through the oldest oaks. The older they grow the more the branches contort, and with the gnarled roots they work together with the rocky floor to keep out grazing animals. This is not an easy place even for humans to penetrate. Many have slipped, fallen, sprained. One of the few creatures said to prosper in Wistman's Wood is the venomous adder, which has plenty of crannies to slither inside. But that could be another myth, much like the red-eyed hellhounds of Dartmoor, huge black dogs that were once said to chase through the woods on the scent of blood.

I have my own big black dog, Obi, my companion on visits to this impossible place. It has long been one of our favourite walks, almost a pilgrimage, as we tramp and stamp and explore. When the pandemic hit, like everyone else my travels were restricted. But I am lucky enough to live on Dartmoor, a magical corner of England where my wife Anya and I moved years earlier, uprooting from London to plant ourselves in an area of endless natural beauty. More than the open moorland it's famous for, what I love about Dartmoor is that it brims with forests, lakes, waterfalls, cosy villages and pubs with open fires, all within the 368 square miles of the national park. And among the most alluring of all of these, at least for me, are its ancient woodlands, especially Wistman's.

During the start of the pandemic, the wood became a sanctuary that could staunch the negativity that started to swim through my head. Even at the best of times, and I have been blessed with many of those, I struggle with negative thoughts. I can be overwhelmed by them, almost overpowered. Even a happy experience can be contaminated by a lurking voice in my head that keeps up a constant chatter that something is not quite right, something is not quite good enough. These attacks are almost all aimed inwardly. I target fierce criticism at myself, sometimes even loathing. When such thoughts run wild, it can be a battle to bring them under control.

Walking to Wistman's is a chance to cleanse the mind. But I cannot say I love the bare hills that surround it. The absence of trees, and even the plastic geotextile fabric somebody thought would hold pathways together, which now spills out in infuriating tatters to pollute the ground and the experience, confront me as powerful negatives. Deforestation in the west of Dartmoor was probably started by hunter-gatherers thousands of years ago. But I push through barren land to the mystical world of Wistman's Wood beyond because the reward is so huge. As soon as I enter an ancient woodland it feeds my mind and enriches it with magic. I pause and reflect and breathe deeply and I find myself transported on to a different plain: to an impossible place.

Dartmoor is a national park in the south-west of England, open to all. It might not sound like an impossible place, particularly for someone who has been lucky enough to visit around 130 countries. But for me, an impossible place is somewhere – it can be anywhere – that is special, mystical, extreme, frighteningly dangerous, blessed with inspiring people, an Eden of wildlife or staggeringly beautiful. The key is that it is somewhere I was never meant to be, because exploring, travelling, and even living in any of these places was never my destiny.

I come from a very ordinary background. I wasn't born into wealth, privilege or a family of globetrotters. I grew up in Acton in west London, and initially my world was very small. Our brief holidays were on the south coast. I never flew abroad until I was an adult. In my last book *Step by Step* I explained how I had a chaotic youth: fragile head health, lost in teenage rebellion, avoiding school, hitting the pub, failing exams, vandalising, carrying knives, stealing and destroying. By my mid-teens my confidence and mental health were shot to pieces. I flunked out of school without any real qualifications, and spiralled down into darkness. I had no ambitions, no girlfriend and no job. Things were so bad that by the age of 17 I stood on the edge of a bridge and looked into the final abyss.

But I stepped back and I struggled on, despite profound feelings of helplessness and hopelessness that often left me bedridden and sozzled by drink. I went on the dole, then on a life-changing adventure in wild Scotland, and gradually, slowly, despite failure piling itself on failure, lifted myself off the floor. Eventually I got a proper job in the post room of a newspaper. Within weeks I was making myself useful. For the first time I sensed opportunity. In return I showed curiosity, and I volunteered. Being a blank canvas meant I didn't expect anything. I had no degree, no public-school education, no years of hard study, all of which might have burdened me with a sense of entitlement. I was grateful for everything. So I sorted the post, lugged mail sacks, shifted packages and photocopied cuttings. Then came small missions and more responsibility. I became a researcher, then a writer, working on investigations into arms dealers, organised crime and especially terrorism. By the age of 20 I was transformed. I started researching and writing my own book, *The New Jackals*, which took me five years of struggle, adventures, undercover operations, near-death experiences and bizarre encounters. It was published in 1998 and became the first in the world on Osama bin Laden and al-Qaeda, long before most people had heard the name. I wrote other books, mainly on terrorism, followed by my first forays into television, where I fronted travel programmes about countries that were little known and little understood.

I made it to an impossible place. Having grown up expecting nothing of myself, I still feel I don't deserve this life. I never expected to become an author, to find my Anya, let alone marry her, and to live in a beautiful corner of Devon. I was never supposed to become a TV presenter, circle the globe three times, or journey round the Indian Ocean, the Caribbean or the Mediterranean, travel the length of Russia or North America. I have always felt like a bit of a nobody. A lucky nobody.

I presumed others could see that reality. A couple of years ago I was approached out of the blue by a theatre promoter who suggested I share stories from my life and journeys on a live theatre speaking tour. It sounded like a new challenge, and a way to get the heart beating a little faster. I chewed through biros considering what to include and leafed through thousands of photos to put together the script and a show. I threw my all into it, trying to be honest and revealing about not just my journeys but also my early years. The audience was likely to consist of people who, through the licence fee, had helped shape my journeys and I didn't want to short-change them. I tried the script out on Anya a few times, then the promoter and tour manager hired Leicester Square Theatre on a Wednesday afternoon and we ran through the entire script and they gave me some pointers. And then I was into the first show.

I was stunned by how well it went. People clapped. People even cheered. What really took me aback was how warmly audiences responded to my personal story. There were gasps. People thought I had come from a completely different background. I sensed their understanding and empathy. Young men, old men, mothers, fathers, came up to me after the shows and clasped my arm and told me their troubles or those of someone they loved were similar to mine. So I talked more about my start in life. How hard it had been for me, and how hard it is for others who fall through the cracks and don't have the increasingly normal path in life that takes them from school to university, or school to a job. Not everyone fits a box. Not everyone has opportunities. Not everyone finds it easy. Life can be a struggle, and I opened up about mine. The tour became an emotional, draining, cathartic experience. It was extended four times and took me to a series of incredible venues culminating in a sold-out night at the London Palladium.

On my long list of impossible places, this was one of the ultimate. As a hopeless teenager I used to trek on foot week after week to a jobcentre less than 200 metres from the theatre, looking for work but, more than that, for a life. When I finally made it into the Palladium I struggled to hold my emotions together. Occupying my dressing room the previous night had been Madonna. Nothing could illustrate my transformation from troubled youngster to functioning adult more than the relative ease with which I embraced the challenge of walking on to the vast stage of one of the most famous theatres in the world to deliver my monologue to a live audience of more than 2,000. With Anya, my family and friends in the audience, I will never forget entering from the wings and telling tales for more than two hours. The evening was one of the greatest honours of my professional life.

That was mid-February 2020. Straight after the Palladium I began packing my bags and then headed to South America to begin filming a new TV series. The previous autumn the first half of my journey down through the entire Americas had been shown on the BBC, in which I travelled from the frozen north of Alaska through Canada, the US, Mexico and Central America to Costa Rica. I was due to spend much of 2020 filming the second series in South America, travelling from the top of the continent to the toe. The series of five programmes was mapped out like a view of faintly receding hills. As my small filming team and I set off to shoot the first episode of the journey, we knew what we might be able to do on the second. The third journey had a discernible outline, the fourth was an aspiration, and the fifth was based on nothing more than looking at the lower half of a large map of South America and realising we needed to get to the bottom. One thing I knew for certain: the whole adventure was going to be epic.

We started the new series in Venezuela, travelled through Guyana and French Guiana into Suriname and then into the depths of the Brazilian Amazon. Meanwhile in Europe, coronavirus was spreading apace. By late February there was an outbreak in Italy, and the first patients had died in France, the UK and the US. We were in perhaps the safest region of the planet, because at that point South America had zero confirmed infections. But while I was staying with a detachment of the French Foreign Legion in a remote jungle base, it became clear the pandemic was likely to be a disaster. Speaking to home on a satellite phone, standing in the dark noisy jungle, with bats and giant insects flitting around, I was told cases were rocketing and borders were beginning to close. We made it into Brazil, had a medical check-up to ensure we were free of any diseases, and journeyed deeper into the jungle to film with a remote indigenous community. We were the last people they allowed to visit. By the time we were on the plane back to the UK, it was clear the virus was a wildfire, burning unchecked. The optimistic among us thought that maybe the situation would improve in a month or two. Then we arrived home and pretty much the next day everything changed, with travel banned and mass gatherings cancelled, panic buying, shops and restaurants closed in France and a state of emergency declared in Spain.

It quickly became apparent that 'adventure traveller' is one of the least viable professions during a global pandemic. As the UK went into lockdown I had a dawning realisation, and horror, that I would not be walking into any more remote South American villages any time soon. With thousands losing loved ones, key workers risking their lives on the front line of the pandemic, and so many people enduring infinitely more painful lockdown restrictions than I was, it felt absurd to discover people out there were worried for me. Poor you, they would say to me remotely and virtually. Being stuck at home must be terrible.

Initially I thought I would be able to handle the confinement. It was a belief based on my long-held knowledge that at some point I would be forced to cease journeying. I sometimes say it as a joke, but I have always known somebody younger, wittier and better-looking, with even more photogenic hair, will inevitably knock me off the telly and my travels would end. I had always genuinely thought that whenever that happened, I would take it gracefully, put away my passport, stick closer to home and accept a less exhilarating life. The great disappointment, perhaps even a seismic shock, was the realisation I had been kidding myself. Deprived of the chance to travel, I was confronted with the truth that I missed it as a profound physical and emotional loss. I needed the thrill of travel. Going without it was like going cold turkey. My name is Simon, I had to confess, and I am a travel addict.

Before the pandemic it had become ever easier to reach distant countries in a matter of hours, and many had started to equate travel with a recreational luxury, lying by a pool for a week or a fortnight and topping up a tan. For me, true travel is far more fundamental. The desire for movement is encoded into our DNA. It's how we became who we are, and it is nothing less than a reason for existing. My journeys and adventures have brought light into my head. They have gifted me experiences from which I have learnt and grown. And humans have always needed to explore. Over the centuries our desire to travel has had profound consequences, including innovation, brutal conquest, trade, settlement and love. Travel has helped to create our culture, civilisation and forge the modern world. Our endless adventures are evidence of something fundamental: going on a journey is the essence of our species. Our desire to travel and explore helps to make us human.

Yet it wasn't the act of getting on a train or plane that I missed, nor the chance to mechanically tick off another nation

I had visited and further increase my country count. It wasn't even the opportunity to see spectacular landscapes or enjoy and endure the memorable food found abroad. The reason I travel is to meet us, ourselves, to connect with our brothers and sisters and cousins elsewhere on Planet Earth. The encounters I have with our fellow humans when I go on a journey tingle every atom of my being, fill me with a nourishing thrill that I'm alive, and are at the heart of every adventure I have and every programme I make. Which is why I missed travel so palpably, and so painfully.

Of course the one thing we were strictly forbidden from having in the lockdown was encounters with other people. So, stuck at home, Anya and I channelled our energy and emotion into looking after our lad, Jake. We read, wrestled, attempted home-schooling, played catch, Lego, dress-up, Nerf wars and endless games of football. In one three-hour match the score got to 46-46 and I thought my heart might pop. I would never want to give up those experiences and memories, even though I felt like my world was shrinking back to the size of the parochial life I knew when I was a teenager, and I feared returning to a state of mind before my world, and with it my eyes and my heart, had begun to open.

I didn't mind the uncertainty of living in a pandemic. That didn't trouble or frighten me. I'm used to that. When I'm travelling there is drama and madness every hour of every day. I even immersed myself in the drama of the pandemic, reading the news avidly and checking websites like every other amateur epidemiologist. But as someone without a real role in the crisis, what bothered me was the boredom.

On a journey there are so many different encounters, feelings, smells, tastes, that I experience a sensory overload. After a couple of days it feels like I have been away for a week, and after a week it can feel like a month. By contrast in the early weeks and months of the pandemic, life became a Groundhog Day experience. It had been decades since I found myself doing the same thing day after week after month, and I found it crushing. To see doors to travel being closed then barred, and sensing that something absolutely fundamental had been withdrawn, even abolished, stirred in me a sense of doom and dread. I felt it as a darkness.

So I fell back on some simple but profound advice I was given in a jobcentre as a teenager. Take things step by step. Everyone is different, but for me the single most important thing I do when life is challenging or I am coping with a moment of pain or heartbreak, is take a step. I go for a walk. In any direction. Whatever the weather, whatever the temperature. It doesn't matter if it's pouring outside or hailing. The act of walking was one of our few freedoms during the pandemic, and especially during the lockdowns. It was a powerful tonic for physical and especially mental health. And if we could do it somewhere green, all the better. Because, of course, Mother Nature always listens.

Taking things step by step is my personal mantra. Not everyone has the luck or luxury of a national park on their doorstep. Not everyone has mobility and relative fitness. Not everyone can take a physical step. But perhaps we can apply the idea to our mindset. Taking a step can be about opening up. We have been facing a mental health pandemic for years and it is vital we talk more about our troubles, to our friends, to our families, and to the dozens of wonderful charities now working on head health. Because not everyone has someone who can listen. When I was a teenager with terrible head health I had love around me, but needed professional counselling and the Samaritans. I would call their freephone number from a payphone by my local park. Listening is a skill. The Samaritans are really good at it. We should use them more.

During the first months of the pandemic, I was blessed not only with greenery to walk, a partner and family for talking, but as another source of mental support, I had a dog to exercise. Without Obi I may easily have sunk a little lower. But he became my companion as I taught myself to rediscover a love of the local and to live in the moment. It is hard to look into the wide-eyed happy expression of a loving dog and not see hope or not feel joy.

Obi was great for morale as Anya, Jake and I tramped around Dartmoor, exploring Wistman's Wood and dozens of other tors, moors, commons, glades and forests, whenever it was allowed, but he isn't a miracle worker, and I still struggled. Unfed addictions can produce withdrawal symptoms. As months ticked by without a travel fix, my symptoms took the form of four walls closing in, with a ceiling being very slowly wound down from above.

It was Jake who really gave me strength and salvation. The child helped the father. He has always been understandably uninterested in whatever I do on my long absences. But during lockdown, we began to talk about my journeys. He asked questions. I realised I had a chance, a window, to go back and explore my past adventures, not just to relish the experiences and memories, but to identify the lessons, understand them, and share them with Jake. I went back in my head and my heart, in my dreams, to the impossible places I have visited on my favourite journeys. I went back to seek guidance from what those journeys have shown me, gifted me, taught me; to remind myself also how they have shaped me, and to share that with my son as lessons for our future. My last book *Step by Step* traced the first decades of my life from depressed and unemployed teenager through to my early TV series *Meet the Stans* and *Places That Don't Exist*. They were thrilling experiences but low-budget projects, which restricted what we could do and how far off the beaten track we could stray. They were followed by my journey around the entire equator, my earliest major prime time television adventure, and from then onwards almost every journey blessed me with lifetime memories and profound experiences.

I concluded *Step by Step* after I travelled across Africa on the first leg of my *Equator* series, during which I contracted malaria and nearly died. Now I want to take you and Jake on the epic and thrilling adventures in the years that followed, in beautiful, tricky and downright dangerous corners of the world, as I travelled further through the Tropics, to remote paradise islands, jungles dripping with heat and life, and on nerve-wracking secret missions. I want to share with Jake, and with you, what my encounters gifted me, and the deeper lessons I draw from the joy and raw grief I have experienced in my personal life, from desperate struggles with my own fertility and head health, from wise friends, fatherhood, inspiring villagers, brave fighters, my beloved dogs, refugees, farmers, fishermen and a thoughtful Indian sadhu. Above all, I hope this book will help my son to walk his own path in life.

These are the journeys that taught me most about the land, the sea, humanity and existence, and they start with visiting a paradise island in Indonesia on the second leg of my equator adventure.

These are my journeys – to impossible places.

CHAPTER ONE

Borneo

I arrived in paradise on a small rickety boat, under a scorching sun and the brightest blue skies, paddling the final stretch through crashing waves towards a long strip of glorious golden beach fringed by tall tropical palms waving lazily in the breeze. Leaping down into shallow warm water I splashed on to the sand and checked my GPS for our location. We were bang on zero degrees, directly on the equator.

Breathless and wet, I dropped my bags and paused briefly to enjoy the feel of hot sand between my toes and to take in the scene. It was an impossibly beautiful place that looked like an island for a castaway or a luxury holiday brochure. Local villagers began to emerge from wooden huts and homes set just back inside the tree line and a crowd quickly gathered, welcoming my small filming team and me to one of the remotest communities I had ever visited. Elders shook my hand and children ran around. It was their first encounter with a foreigner and they went into a frenzy of excitement.

Following the equator around the world, the imaginary line that girdles the middle of our planet, I had arrived in the Batu Islands, 60 miles off the west coast of Sumatra, the most westerly of the large islands that make up Indonesia, an archipelago of 240 million people scattered across 17,000 islands who speak more than 300 local languages. My plan was to follow the equator east to Sumatra and then across the Java Sea to the huge islands of Borneo and Sulawesi. I was in my early thirties when this adventure started. I had written books and been in extreme situations, but I certainly was not a seasoned traveller, and I only had limited experience of impossible places. I still had so much to see, and so much to learn.

In the Batu Islands we had formal greetings with some of the elders in the community and I explained what we were doing. The equator is just an imaginary line, but it also marks the heart of the Tropics, the region of the world home to both the greatest concentration of wildlife on the planet and intense human poverty. I explained I was hoping to understand more about their lives.

Slightly wide-eyed with wonder, I was allowed to join men from the village as they went fishing in a shallow lagoon protected from the wilder sea by the island reef.

'Why are you only carrying those hefty sticks?' I asked one villager.

'We are going to fitabo,' came the faintly unhelpful reply.

We spread ourselves out in a full arc in the sea, the villagers looking eager and excited, and me feeling completely unsure about what to do or what was about to happen. Then an elder on the shore blew a huge conch, and the men began whacking the sea with their thick sticks, almost as though they were trying to beat the water to death, while shouting and singing at the top of their voices. It was complete chaos.

Fitabo, it transpired, was a stunningly simple method of fishing where the men would arrange themselves out in the water and then begin walking slowly back towards the shore, driving the fish ahead of them until they would either beach themselves in terror, or could be literally scooped out by hand. It took about ten minutes, and they caught enough fish to feed most of the village. Rarely have I seen the natural world instantly provide such plenty. Soaked, I was just starting to understand the whole experience when it ended. The villagers looked at me and laughed when I tried to continue. The job was done. They headed back to their hammocks for a rest, while I wandered into the jungle with some women from the village. They plucked fruit straight from the trees, from heavy branches that sagged with weight and colour. Rice was scooped from sacks traded from passing boats and ships.

It felt as if I'd arrived in a mythical paradise, a home to a remote and peaceful community living a subsistence lifestyle in a tropical idyll. I had the sense of being a backpacker in the 1960s or '70s, arriving on a gorgeous, unknown Thai island, where the mind could be free of the clutter of Western civilisation.

To a visitor from afar there were only minor obstacles and challenges to grapple with. Take, for example, the loo. The only toilet in the community was a ramshackle affair, the size of a small cupboard, made of old branches and palm leaves, and perched on a rock out over the sea. The questionable design meant the waves should wash away anyone's business. It looked like it might collapse if someone sneezed on it, let alone if a 14-stone Brit popped inside.

'I'm not mad keen on using that,' I said to Amalia, our local guide. 'Might be a bit safer to go into the jungle with a spade.'

'It's a short walk,' she said. 'But mind the snakes.'

Early on in my journeys I developed cast-iron insides, which held me in good stead when gulping down every type of strange, dodgy, undercooked delicacy and local food poisoning the planet can offer. But my guts let me down on the Batu Islands.

That afternoon I needed a toilet. Fast. There was no time to wander deep into the forest. I headed to the rickety latrine, quickly, and a group of laughing kids saw me and began calling to their friends, which did not bode well. I didn't want to use their toilet, but I had no choice.

I opened the door and clambered into the cupboard, which creaked and shook. There was a hole in the floor of the loo where business was transacted, and I swiftly realised there was something missing. The tide was out. There was no sea under the hole to wash everything away. That was bad enough. But I still had to go, and just as I was moving everything into position, and precisely because there was no sea, a huge pack of enormous ravenous pigs appeared under the toilet, waiting expectantly below the hole for whatever might appear. I held on to the sides of the toilet and silently prayed. But the pigs didn't stay down there. They were in a complete frenzy, and the snouts of two of them came up through the hole, their sharp teeth snapping away at my undercarriage, and I was forced to shift myself around in the toilet to avoid them like a demented disco dancer. The children outside were shrieking with hysterical laughter, and the whole toilet creaked and shook and moved perilously backwards off the boulder, and I thought the whole structure was going to collapse into a pile of poo and ravenous pigs. I threw myself out of the door, just in time to avoid one of the taller pigs forcing itself up through the hole, and scarpered through the village utterly mortified and trailed by loo roll and hysterical children eager to see what other humiliations I could offer for their enjoyment.

I kept a low profile for at least an hour, and then joined the fishermen on the porch of one of the huts. Only one of them had not heard the story of my toilet disaster, which the others quickly remedied. We all had a laugh, a chat, and then a guitar appeared and the men began to sing. I expected jolly tunes akin to sea shanties, but there was a mournful quality to their music. Most of their songs appeared to be about youngsters leaving the islands, and how nobody should ever forget their homeland. I struggled to see why anyone would want to leave. They seemed to have food and family in abundance.

That night I slept on a thin inflatable mattress on the floor of one of the huts, under a mosquito net that I spent a good half hour carefully erecting and arranging. After being endlessly bitten and contracting malaria on the first leg of the *Equator* series, and nearly losing my life, I was desperate to avoid being infected again.

The next morning I woke to tragedy. A young boy in the village had died overnight. Nobody was sure what had killed him. There was no medic or doctor in the village to check. I watched from afar as his coffin, covered with a purple cloth with a white crucifix, was carried out of the family home. What especially surprised me was how it was treated as a normal event. There was grief, but no indication, as there would be anywhere with better healthcare, that this could have been an avoidable tragedy.

'The health system doesn't work here,' said Amalia, my guide. The villagers had no idea what kind of sickness or fever the boy had suffered, she said, adding: 'They said maybe he got a curse.'

In the hot and humid tropical climate of the Batu Islands, the burial took place straightaway. The coffin was carried through the palm trees by a group of villagers to an idyllic spot near the beach, where it was lowered carefully into a deep hole. The young mother had lost her husband the previous year. She was distraught.

'Life can be tough here,' I said to Amalia. 'Life can be short here,' she replied.

The nearest professional medical help was a long boat trip away from the village. The islands looked like paradise to me, but it would have been dangerous and foolish to ignore their reality, and wrong to over-romanticise their poverty. Tens of millions of people in remote parts of the world would love to enjoy just some of the healthcare, education, lighting and electricity that many of us quite naturally take for granted. For me it was a reminder that if you've got a fever or toothache or a tumour and no access even to paracetamol, it can be a grinding, painful exist-ence living in paradise.

I left the Batu Islands on a chuggy little wooden cargo boat to make the overnight journey east across the sea to Sumatra. I was travelling with two much more experienced film-makers. The cameraman had endured just about every conflict zone on the planet and even had his blood group tattooed on his arm with an arrow pointing at his vein. We watched and filmed a glorious sunset together, then I slept rough on a bench and the next morning woke feeling stiff and achy. As the sun rose over the ocean, the boat crewmen were playing dominoes. I went over to watch and they motioned that I should join them and play. I stayed British for a moment, holding my hand up for a second to say, 'No thanks, I'll just watch.' Then I thought about the advice I give others about always saying yes. *Of course* I should play dominoes. I sat down, we shuffled the tiles and the game began. The language barrier was total, but the game broke it down. We played, and we laughed, and then about ten minutes later I noticed the guys had started filming me.

Bloody hell, I suddenly thought; this is a journey Michael Palin could have been on. I've gone from writing books on terrorism to fronting something resembling a Palin Journey. I froze for a second, a domino in my outstretched hand, feeling an extra weight of responsibility. I remembered watching Michael Palin in the TV series *Around the World in 80 Days*, as he travelled on a dhow from Dubai to Mumbai while reprising Phileas Fogg's journey. Michael was carrying an ancient device called a Walkman, which played songs on tapes. He put his headphones on to the ears of a sailor and gave him a blast of Bruce Springsteen, much to the man's delight, and mine watching as a youngster in Acton. His journey around the world was one of the few travel programmes I ever watched, largely because Michael was genuinely interested in the people he met and treated them with respect. Telly travellers before him often literally stood above the locals, peering down at them from under a Panama hat. They treated the funny foreigners as exactly that, with strange customs, eccentric religions and unacceptable food. Michael was different. He sat down next to people and rarely made jokes at their expense.

I never set out to become a C-list version of Michael Palin. Travel was more of a novelty when he was in his element. His shows were inspiring, fun and a glorious showcase for rarely visited corners of the world. I was travelling at a different time, on a genuine adventure but with issues and journalism as my focus, looking for people with real, serious, often dark stories. But in some ways I was guided by Michael's legacy. I have certainly always tried to treat the thousands of people I've met with total respect.

It felt as if everything was changing for me as I travelled around the equator. I was on a journey unlike anything I had undertaken before. My previous television adventures had been brief sorties into obscure parts of the world. Now I was trying to tell the story of the equatorial zone known as the Tropics. Defined by the Tropic of Cancer to the north and the Tropic of Capricorn to the south, the belt going around the middle of the planet measures more than 3,000 miles from north to south.

This trip across Indonesia was perhaps my first journey where impossible things happened day after day. We crossed Sumatra and travelled east to arrive in Borneo, the third largest island in the world – a place of magic and mystery. When I was growing up every syllable of the name 'Borneo' spoke of adventure, beauty and impenetrable jungle. As a name it was as evocative as Timbuktu and Zanzibar. But Borneo stands above all as a place of immense biodiversity. Just to give you one example, the UK has 34 native species of trees. Borneo has more than 5,000.

I started my journey across Borneo by learning more about the people who lived there. In recent years, some members of the main ethnic group, the fearsome Dayak tribe of former headhunters, had been attacking another ethnic group called the Madurese, who had been resettled in Borneo by the Indonesian government as part of a policy of moving people from over-crowded islands in the south of the country. Over several years the Dayaks were thought to have killed around 6,000 Madurese. Eyewitnesses said many were cannibalised after their deaths. We passed through one town where the Dayaks had been on the rampage. In Borneo I was with a guide called Jihan who had personally seen the bodies, even a headless corpse, lying in the streets.

She took me to visit a Dayak village to meet some of those involved in the fighting. The centrepiece of their village was a striking wooden stockade and a cluster of bright flags on poles. The villagers were in a celebratory mood, performing a Tiwah, a religious ceremony dedicated to the dead. We were welcomed as honoured guests and I was invited and nudged to take part in slow rhythmic dancing. To the resonant sound of gong music, I had a traditional Dayak sword with a beautifully carved bone hilt strapped around my waist and my face daubed in white powder.

This was all very lovely, and looked great on camera. But there was a real darkness about the community. I asked one of the elders, a short dapper man called Robert with slicked back silver hair, what had happened during the conflict.

'They attacked us first; they killed two people from our village,' he said. 'If you are good to us then we will be very good to you. If you treat us badly, then we will treat you worse.'

He poured us both large glasses of local firewater.

I looked down at the sword around my waist. It had a sharp blade and the feel of a ceremonial machete. The scabbard was carved from wood, painted red, bound with woven rattan and adorned with dyed pig bristle and tufts of human hair.

'Would this sword have been used in the fighting?' I asked.

'This is our traditional weapon which we've used for a long time,' said Robert. 'When we had our fight with the Madurese we used it. Many Madurese were beheaded with these swords. We chopped their heads off with this.' I was aghast, but I couldn't let it show.

Robert said he had not directly been involved in the fighting, but was giving out orders. 'My son fought,' he added. 'The Madurese killed his best friend. If they were Madurese, my son did not hesitate to kill them. Off with their heads. If they were Madurese, he had to kill them. It was payback. We destroyed everything, including their livestock.'

He poured us both another drink, and then another. The tempo of the dancing increased.

Robert was feeling very jolly. And generous. A show of Dayak hospitality went slightly further than I was expecting. We ate a group meal together with Robert's family and villagers, and then there was a flurry of quick conversation. Jihan listened, and paled.

'What's wrong?' I hissed to her.

'You won't believe this. He wants to adopt you,' she hissed back.

'Sorry, what?' I laughed. 'I thought you said *Adopt*.'

She nodded quickly: 'Just go along with it!'

Sitting cross-legged and barefoot among a large gathering of villagers, wearing a yellow bandana and with my face still covered with white powder, rice was placed on my head, representing power and food for the community. I was anointed with the blood of a sacrificed chicken.

'Normally they use human blood,' said Jihan. 'They're making allowances for you.'

'Good luck to you and long life, to the new member who will be adopted into our family,' intoned an elder, deadly serious. And with that I became Robert's 12th child. As a ceremonial gift they insisted I take the antique Dayak Mandau sword I had been wearing earlier. It remains one of my most treasured mementoes.

As I left the Dayaks I felt torn. They had been endlessly welcoming to me, but they were also openly admitting involvement in, and responsibility for, mass killing. It reinforced what I had found during the previous decade, when I had been investigating terrorism, arms smuggling and organised crime, which was that situations are rarely clear-cut, hardly ever black and white, and good people can do bad things, while bad people can definitely do good. Humans are just so damn complicated.

I asked Robert what my duties were as his newly adopted son. 'Your responsibility is to remember us,' he said. There is no danger of me forgetting the encounter, and I still have the sword, which now finds a home on my bookshelves, next to a book called, appropriately, the *Atlas of Improbable Places*.

Indonesia was full of shocks and surprises. It is a vast nation, one of the most biodiverse states in the world, and a priority for global conservation with more mammal species than any other nation, an incredible 515 species by most counts, including endangered orangutans and critically endangered Sumatran tigers and rhinos. With just 1 per cent of the land area of the planet, Indonesia's rainforests contain 10 per cent of our known plant species, and 17 per cent of all known bird species. It is a small world in one country.

A few years earlier I had travelled through Malaysian Borneo in the far north, canoed down the Kinabatangan River and came across ten species of primate including the orangutan, Bornean gibbon, long-tailed and southern pig-tailed macaques, three types of leaf monkey, the western tarsier, slow loris and the bizarre proboscis monkey. I love the proboscis, which endures a ridiculous nose and severe flatulence. The poor creature spends much of its time leaping and swimming across rivers trying to avoid crocodiles. There were eight different types of hornbill for me to admire, plus the dreaded crocodiles and a herd of pygmy elephants, although when you're canoeing close to a high bank and looking up, I can promise you a pygmy elephant looks like a giant. On the same adventure I visited the Gomantong Caves, a cathedral-sized home to hundreds of thousands of swifts and bats whose droppings form a hill at the base of the cave. It is one of the most astounding places on the planet. As I clambered up the hill in darkness I could hear a crunching sound with each step, and pointed a torch to the floor to see the dung alive with huge insects swarming silently over my boots. The stench was overwhelming. Another traveller near me watched as I panned my torch, then screamed the entire time as she ran from the cave.

My favourite plant on Borneo is the Rafflesia flower, which has no leaves and not much of a stem, but a huge five-petalled flower the width of a small dinner table. One type of Rafflesia is the largest flower on earth, and smells like rotting flesh. Its local name translates as 'corpse flower'. This all makes a wonderful spectacle for any traveller, but there is tragedy as well: Indonesia's teeming biodiversity is in mortal danger.

My main aim as I followed the equator across Indonesia was to get up close and personal with orangutans, Borneo's wildlife star, the largest arboreal mammal on earth and the only great ape found outside Africa. No species on the island is more clearly in danger. The orangutan population had collapsed by a catastrophic two-thirds since 1990. More than 2,000 orangutans a year were losing their lives due to the destruction of their rainforest habitat for logging, mining, ranching, dam building, road construction and agriculture, plus a fourfold increase in palm oil production in just over a decade. It's only one of more than 740 species, 140 of them mammal species, that are threatened with extinction in Indonesia. It was a story I was determined to explore on my trip round the equator, so I went to meet some surviving orangutans and, equally importantly, the people battling to save them.

In the south of Borneo I teamed up with Zacky, a zoologist from Orangutan Foundation International, an organisation dedicated to protecting the species from extinction. The patch of planet that Zacky was guarding is Tanjung Puting National Park, a rare protected area in a country that has lost three-quarters of its native woodland. We sped there on boats, along rivers cutting through dense forest. Young and earnest, Zacky had cool sunglasses, a man bun and a deep personal love of orangutans that he demonstrated as we moored inside the park and he escorted me towards dry land along a wooden walkway. A lone orangutan saw Zacky and came to greet him, shuffling along the boardwalk from the other direction.

'Don't worry,' said Zacky, 'I can handle him. You go on.'

With his arms outstretched, Zacky valiantly tried to shield me from the orangutan as he passed us by, but our assailant was too fast. He lunged and nabbed my bag of supplies, and I watched in awe as he sat down and examined the contents. He bit the end off a water bottle and took a long drink. Then he let out a satisfied burp, had a quick pick of his nose, and wandered off towards the river in search of more loot. I was literally mugged by a thirsty orangutan named Pan.

After watching Pan disappear towards the river, we walked to the research centre as the rainforest on either side squawked and screeched. The translation of orangutan is 'man of the forest', but in that area of Borneo there was less and less forest to go round. So there were 6,000 of them crammed inside Tanjung Puting.

'You're in luck,' said Zacky, 'the King is here!' The King, a huge dominant male orangutan called Kusasi, was sprawled on the grass, fiddling with his dark cheek pads and watching to see if workers would leave the kitchen door open long enough for him to grab a free lunch. As we slipped inside the kitchen hut for a welcome chat and a bowl of rice, Kusasi leapt towards the closing door, trapping us in the kitchen while his black leathery fingers curled through the mesh over the windows. But there was no sense of aggression. The King was just trying his luck. Inquisitive orangutans will pinch almost anything not nailed to the ground. One female called Princess even stole boats and paddled downriver to get to her favourite riverbank foods. When the conservation team submerged their canoes to discourage joyrides, Princess teamed up with other orangutans to tip the water out and right the boats.

Zacky's sanctuary had adopted 120 orphaned orangutans and the staff were feeding and training them to be rehabilitated into the wild, even though the foundation was running out of safe forest for releases. Most of the infants shared a similar horrific backstory, where deforestation meant their mothers were forced into the open to forage for food, leaving them vulnerable to hunters or loggers. Baby orangutans were kept and sold as pets, while adult orangutans who got in the way were usually trapped and clubbed, shot, stabbed or burnt to death.

So it was moving and humbling to help Zacky and his colleagues carry a group of young orangutans on a training trip. Without their parents, they can find the rainforest intimidating, and needed to be taught how to forage. Osbourne, a hefty young infant, grabbed me around the neck while his feet gripped me tightly around the waist. He seemed restless. Zacky advised me to stroke his head.

'He's pretty similar to a human baby,' he said. Osbourne grew calmer, and even started scratching my chin. Just as I was getting broody it was time for Osbourne to start practising a few essential life skills. I introduced him to a likely tree, and lifted him on to the lower branches. But the poor thing climbed back into my arms. I tried again, lifting him on to a branch, patting the tree, and making encouraging noises, as if I was taking the stabilisers off his bicycle. Osbourne looked up at the tree, looked back at me for reassurance, and began to climb. It was food for the soul.

Many times in the years that followed, I have encountered remarkable brave souls who have seen what is happening to the world's wildlife and have accepted the challenge of protecting it. But Zacky was one of the first. In the time I spent with him, I came to realise Zacky was on the front line of the great war of the 21st century – the struggle to protect our planet from irreversible apocalypse. It is a battle that should lure anyone wanting a just cause and moral purpose. Zacky was a battle-scarred hero who had taken on the impossible job of building a wildlife ark in the jungle and defending it from attack and incursions by poachers, farmers and loggers. The equator journey and my other early travels in the Tropics were the start of this practical education about the conservation battle for our natural world. It was through spending time in impossible places like Borneo, with the likes of Zacky, that I really started to learn and understand what was happening. The lessons came as a series of devastating revelations, and one of the first took place in Borneo.

The fate of Indonesia's orangutans is tied to climate change, the biggest issue facing our century, and overpopulation, part of its cause. Linking them both is deforestation. Zacky took me on a trek deep into the forest to follow the buzz of a chainsaw. Although the forest was protected, trees were still being felled by loggers and villagers, who could often respond violently to conservationists when caught. We found a small group of local men who were the first link in a supply chain that can end with your local hardware store or furniture shop. They had felled two trees that day, which they would sell to a local middleman, who would sell to a regional middleman, who would sell them to a merchant in a Borneo coastal town. Eventually those trunks would end up on a container ship bound for the wealthier world, to be turned into blinds or parquet flooring. Meanwhile much of the deforested land would be turned over to the production of palm oil, the super-crop that, staggeringly, ends up in close to

50 per cent of the packaged products in supermarkets and is bought by pretty much all of us. No one link in the chain is individually responsible, but collectively we all are.

This was where my environmental education really began. It was so shockingly clear the planet was in peril. In Borneo I saw the destruction of the rainforest with my own eyes for the first time. It had already been under way for many decades and has continued ever since. However this was my initiation to the disaster, where I learned one of the fundamental rules of our environmental apocalypse, which is how it often begins.

There is a domino effect. It often starts with the advance scouts of the fossil fuel giants, who scour the planet for oil, coal and gas. Their geologists study the maps, flying in helicopters to even the remotest of places, calculating where to investigate and explore. They will pinpoint locations, then send an advance party of construction workers and loggers to clear a small square area in the jungle to create a landing pad that is then used to fly in parts to start building a drilling rig to check what lies underneath the ground. For them it's a roll of the dice. Many times they will come up with nothing. Sometimes they will hit the jackpot. The first team who go in there have to carve an expensive rough road through the forest to carry in equipment and truck out core samples and that becomes a key element of deforestation. After they have upped sticks, having found no oil, or coal, or gold, the road is still there. So they are followed by the loggers, who will use the road to wipe out the forest for five or ten miles on either side. After them come the farmers, who will clear the land still further for cattle or crops. They will finish the job that began with the test drilling site.

Zacky took me to see a wasteland at the edge of the national park stripped bare but for a few denuded stick-like trunks, spindly silhouettes on the horizon. In front of me were bare mounds of earth surrounding a few blue tarpaulin huts. It was stark proof of the epic destruction of our natural world. To think this used to be the natural habitat of orangutans. It looked more like the Somme. And then astonishingly, in this emptied wilderness, punctuated by a few miserly stumps, I spotted a couple of orange dots. Two orangutans were trapped in the open among the destruction. Zacky sent his rangers to investigate. Without our help perhaps they would have been clubbed by poachers, or starved because of the loss of their habitat. The sight sickened me at first. But then it made me angry. This was once just about the closest our planet had to a Garden of Eden, and this destruction was happening on our watch.

In the years since my anger has turned to fury because of our collective failure to do anything about the assault on the natural world. We know what's going on. We are not just failing to stop it, we are not just complicit, but our society actively drives it with our consumption of everything from peanut butter, containing palm oil, to Venetian blinds, still so often made from trees from virgin forest. At the root is uncontrolled capitalism, a lack of control and regulation about where our stuff comes from, and the ghastly pursuit of profit and greed. It is left to heroes like Zacky and NGOs to risk their lives and investigate and expose the activities of Western and Chinese corporations, billionaire Indonesian timber barons and dodgy politicians. But even when names and proof of horrific environmental crimes are put in front of governments, nothing adequate has been done that even begins to match the scale of the challenge.

The environmental catastrophe inflicted on our natural world is closely linked to the issue of population. Nowadays I often hear people dodging the question about whether there are too many people on the planet. Let me be explicit. Yes, there definitely are. But it is easy to fall into the trap of thinking the problem of overpopulation is limited to poorer countries. They are not the greatest problem. The real issue is wealthy Westerners with their colossal appetites and enormous carbon footprints. Collectively we have not found a way of living sustainably. Perhaps we still will. But at the moment what I see is the most creative and brilliant creature that has ever existed soiling its nest and destroying life for everything else.

BRITISH AIRWAYS

oneworld

BARNETT/ALEXIS MISS

BA 166 18OCT
TEL AVIV YAFO > LONDON

GATE	BOARD AT	GATE CLOSE	SEAT
B6	**0610**		**2E**

GROUP1

CLUB WORLD

BAGS 1/21

CHAPTER TWO

The Dance of the Turtle and the Deer's Head

I was completely surrounded. Long, thin, furry torpedoes were circling me, watching me curiously and trying to decide if I was prey, predator or a game. Like a powered missile, these beguiling creatures could twist themselves backwards while moving at full pace forward, shifting and correcting their angle with a movement of their long front flippers.

I had landed on the Galapagos Islands and headed straight out on to the Pacific Ocean, plunging off the side of a small boat into clear, cool blue water and diving down in search of some of the remote archipelago's few native mammals. Within moments I was spotted and then mesmerised by six pivoting, pirouetting, darting dancers. The Galapagos sea lion, so clumsy and cumbersome on land, has an astonishing speed in the water. Seeing them in their natural element was an utter treat, and a breathtaking welcome to the place that changed the story of the human race.

It was a visit by a young Charles Darwin in 1835 that transformed our understanding of evolution and gave these islands a permanent place in history. As the equator line also passes through the Galapagos – the volcanic archipelago of 19 islands 600 miles to the west of the continental mainland – this was my next stop after Indonesia as I continued my journey around the middle of the world.

To finish the *Equator* TV series I would cross the Galapagos and then the width of the entire South American mainland. The equator passes through Ecuador, then some of the most dangerous parts of Colombia and along the Amazon River in Brazil. It was a journey I had been dreaming about for months, we had been planning for weeks, but I had never truly imagined I would really be able to undertake. It felt impossible. An adventure that promised to take me through our greatest rainforest, the lungs of the planet, and to some of the most precious natural habitats on earth.

I had a real excitement about visiting the Galapagos, a place of fable with its own cachet for any traveller. The Galapagos were everything I imagined they would be, and more. The landscape is a strange otherworldly place. At the water's edge of most islands, the rocks are battered by the ocean and spattered in huge white splodges of guano. Inland, low-lying slabs of umber rock are smothered in succulents and stunted cacti. Much of my time on the islands was spent among species that have been able to flourish away from mankind. Having erupted volcanically out of the sea millions of years ago, the islands and their inhabitants were free to evolve without being pestered by humans. On the ocean currents it takes a minimum of two weeks for any drifting animal to reach the islands, longer than any mammal can survive without fresh water, and blessedly beyond the reach of most seafarers until Spanish ships with large sails appeared in the 16th century.

Isolation and the absence of predators have also made the islands' wildlife almost ridiculously relaxed. Keeping to identified paths in nature reserves still meant I wandered rudely close to eagles and blue-footed booby birds, and could get incredibly close to huge leathery land iguanas. The boys were chasing the girls. They were busy and focused, and weren't remotely bothered by my presence. Like other reptiles and snakes, the iguanas have a hemipenis, a two-for-one arrangement that means if one is out of action, the male still has a back-up.

Almost all of the islands' reptiles are found only in the Galapagos, and many have flourished. One exception was Lonesome George, an 80-year-old giant saddleback Galapagos tortoise – the last of his kind. Kept in a compound, he was a magnificent old bruiser who seemed determined to resist all attempts to perpetuate his sub-species. For years he had ignored two females who'd been moved into his pen. A Swiss scientist had the unenviable job of trying to harvest his sperm.

As a living laboratory and uniquely precious habitat, a whopping 97 per cent of the Galapagos is in a national park. It does mean that a lot of it could feel controlled. On some of the islands, markers indicate where visitors are allowed to walk, so that it sometimes felt like being on a guided nature walk rather than a truly raw encounter with the flora and fauna that shaped Darwin's discoveries. I mentioned this to Paul, my guide in the Galapagos, a biologist and naturalist originally from the UK. His response stuck with me.

'There have to be real controls,' he said. 'They have to be enforced. Nature has to be given not just a chance, but proper protection. The Galapagos are still what nature can do if humans stay out of the way.'

Of course he was right. The very name 'the Galapagos' draws tourists in such numbers that the ecosystem requires extra protection. Visitor numbers to the Galapagos National Park had more than doubled over the previous decade, reaching 100,000 tourists a year. It was a tricky balance. The islands need visitor money to fund protection of the fragile environment their presence threatens.

To illustrate the point we headed to the capital island of Santa Cruz. It was a four-hour crossing on an angry sea. This was early in my television adventures, but I was already gaining a reputation as an unlucky charm on the water, a Jonah to whom bad things happened. I would step on to a boat in calm seas and the ocean would soon swell. It was almost bizarre. But I had good sea legs. On this occasion, as we thundered through the chop, I was reading a copy of *The Week* while colleagues were vomiting over the side. Eventually even two of the boat crew had their heads out at the back.

Santa Cruz was surprisingly built up and populated. Tourists were bringing in up to $200 million a year to the Galapagos, but not everyone was benefiting. I sat down for a game of cards with a bunch of fishermen who fleeced me of a few quid while explaining there was no work because of fishing quotas imposed by the government to protect fish stocks. The fishermen had gone so far as to besiege the Darwin Research Centre, wielding machetes and knives, and holding 30 scientists and animals effectively hostage for four days and refusing them food or supplies.

'All the problems started because in the park there are too many conservationists,' a fisherman called Jose told me.

This was one of the first times I came across a troubling fact that has since cropped up over and over again on my travels: protecting the natural world so often impedes on local people's ability to make a living. But increasing numbers of fishermen were actually coming from the mainland of Ecuador to the islands to work. They wanted to fish and they wanted fewer regulations. Humans will always demand more. I believed then, and believe now, that Paul was right, and there have to be controls.

We left the islands and flew 600 miles east to Ecuador on the South American mainland. The small country takes its name from the equator, and the population is a mix of indigenous tribes, descendants of African slaves, and descendants of Spanish colonisers. A full 70 per cent of the 14 million population live below the poverty line, many of them as farmers. Our initial idea was to follow the equator line as closely as we could, through the agricultural heart of the country, filming on farms and with people who worked the land.

We hired the services of brilliant drivers and their sturdy 4x4s and set off along zero degrees, but soon discovered that sticking to the equator might be a significant challenge. Driving along remote back-country tracks took us into some of the gloopiest, stickiest mud I've encountered anywhere in the world. Time and again we needed winches to extract us from the glue. At one point while I was driving, and after some team discussions, I promise, I decided the best way to skirt a small but particularly impassable mud lagoon was to gun the engine till it screamed, then race our old Toyota Land Cruiser along a steep slope to the side and jump it off the bank like Evel Knievel. The back wheels landed in the mud, but inertia propelled us forward.

It was all exceptionally good fun. And the car was equipped for stunt driving. The shock absorbers had been strengthened, and it even had an inclinometer for checking the angle of the vehicle on a crazy slope. I was impressed to discover that even though once or twice I managed to tip it beyond its supposed tolerance level, it still stayed the right way up.

The high point of our 4x4 adventure came at the end of a long day when we reached the outskirts of a village where we had been hoping to stay. There was a river running between us and our beds which, from our admittedly rudimentary map, we hadn't been expecting. There was no sign of a bridge, and it looked far too deep to drive across. The villagers who waded and swam across to greet us, however, were sober and sensible and somehow convinced us that we could actually float the cars across.

'We'll stand on either side in the water and hold you in place,' they said.

Even at the time this did not sound like a great idea. With hindsight it sounds slightly absurd. But we were fired up and enthusiastic. We went for it, in the dark, filming with night vision as a dozen villagers stood waist and chest deep in the water on either side of our cars. By halfway across, the water had reached the top of our doors and was lapping against the windows. Then the river deepened, my car started to float and the front began turning downriver. I had visions of impending disaster, with my car rolling over in the water and being washed away, but the locals braced themselves on each side and pushed and guided the car through till the wheels touched the bank on the other side. It was completely bloody brilliant.

'Beers for anyone who's wet!' I shouted ecstatically after we landed. That night we emptied the local shack shop to thank everyone for snatching a small victory from the watery jaws of defeat. Then over a meal of tinned sardines we recapped what we'd shot and an hour later reluctantly concluded that sticking too closely to the equator might take a little too long, and might not produce the variety of footage we were aiming to show. There were only so many muddy wheel spins we could get into a programme, even if the success of *Top Gear* suggests otherwise. But my idea had never been to stick religiously to the equator, just use the line as a way to tell tales about little-known or completely forgotten corners of the world. My passion was real stories, people, serious issues, all of which were hard to film and capture if we kept getting stuck in mud.

So I bade a fond farewell to the old Land Cruiser and we headed east to Ecuador's much bigger neighbour Colombia, synonymous at the time with death squads, assassinations, cocaine and murder, not to mention kidnappings of Westerners. The equator runs through the Putumayo region in the south of the country, which was incredibly dangerous. The civil war that had been ongoing since the 1960s between the government and left-wing guerrilla rebels from the Revolutionary Armed Forces of Colombia, aka FARC, was at its most intense.

I wanted to cross the border on the Putumayo River, right near the equator. But the Colombian authorities forced us to detour north, away from the equator, to a heavily guarded immigration point at Ipiales, after which we doubled back to Puerto Asis, a jungle town in the south that was then at the heart of the multi-billion pound cocaine industry, and I met up with Juan Pablo Morris, a brave, fresh-faced Colombian journalist who would be my guide. He warned us that government forces had militarised the town, almost invaded it, in an attempt to recapture the entire region from the FARC. First things first. I asked Juan Pablo if the town was safe.

'The town is a little bit difficult for everybody,' he said cagily. I sought clarification. What does that mean? 'Very, very dangerous,' he replied.

We wanted to travel as inconspicuously as possible, but the local army commander, a Lieutenant Colonel Quintero, insisted on personally escorting us further east, along with his armed bodyguards, in his pickup truck and a convoy of vehicles. We might as well have painted a massive target on our backs. We drove out of the town and into the badlands of the jungle beyond, and then the colonel revealed he had a bounty on his head. I was hitching a ride with one of the FARC's most wanted men.

'They can't stop me, it's my mission,' he said. 'We die the day we're meant to.'

The colonel seemed like a personable chap. He even brought along his well-groomed little terrier called Mixi Marie, which he had dressed in a cute red bandana collar. But it was clear we were in a situation where anything could happen. Dozens of soldiers had been killed in recent battles, and FARC were still launching major attacks. We could turn a corner, suddenly encounter a FARC roadblock, and we would be sitting ducks in crossfire between troops and rebels. It didn't make me any more relaxed to be told, several times, that it was almost impossible to tell the difference between the military and FARC, as they both wore the same camouflage outfits and carried the same weapons. The only difference, apparently, was that FARC fighters wore wellington boots.

Eventually we managed to shake off the colonel, hire a car and driver and continue on our own along dusty unmade roads east. We were racing along until we went round a bend and flashed past men with assault rifles hiding in bushes at the side of the road. Our driver braked hard, but it was too late for us to reverse away. More men leapt out just ahead of us to man a rudimentary checkpoint, their weapons trained on our tyres and windows. We rolled forwards, hands up, hearts beating, looking at their footwear. It was the regular army.

'FARC were seen here yesterday,' a soldier told us. 'They will say: "There are some gringos around; let's take them."'

Again they tried to accompany us, and again we had to forcefully insist we travel alone. I knew it was dangerous, but if we travelled with soldiers nobody would be willing to talk openly with us, and I was desperate to meet the local people trying to survive in this danger zone.

Later that day we pulled into what remained of a small, unnervingly quiet village. It had been attacked and captured multiple times by first one side and then the other. We paused on the outskirts, trying to assess the risk of entering. There were only a few people flitting through the shadows around ramshackle buildings surrounded by bushes. I wandered in among overgrown streets. It felt like a ghost town. Most of the inhabitants, we were told, had abandoned their homes to hide in the woods, in tents, caves or even holes in the ground.

Eventually one villager emerged from a field, the president of the community. He was a farmer in his mid-thirties, wiping muddy, sweaty hands on his tatty T-shirt. Wiry fit, he was nervous but determined and brave. He told us that men had come to the village and questioned people, then shot them in the head. I asked him who was responsible.

'It was the army,' he said.

This was hard to hear. Whether it was a rogue unit, or the real army, mattered little. Try as they might, the people of the town were simply not allowed to leave. The army wanted them there because it needed a population in that remote area to show the government was still in control, although they were not above randomly executing locals in raids if they suspected them of sympathising with the guerrillas. FARC needed them for support and as a human shield against aerial bombing raids by the military. Some of the men and women I spoke to in that area were among the most traumatised people I've come across anywhere in the world. They were like wraiths, civilian hostages forced to haunt a front line they were desperate to escape.

The region was ground zero for the cocaine industry. Lush, green and incredibly beautiful, it was ideal for growing the coca leaf. So the locals were also used and abused by drug cartels who wanted labour to grow and harvest Colombia's infamous crop. The depth of suffering I witnessed in the Putumayo area caused me to think a great deal more about the responsibility of Westerners whose consumption habits have a direct effect on communities such as this. Up to that point I'd been less critical of people using hard drugs. From then on I found it hard to avoid judging anyone using drugs produced and supplied on the back of unbelievable human misery.

What was so hard to compute was the fact that the village, and the whole region, failed to conform to any horror film archetype. It wasn't a parched desert or frozen wasteland. It looked like paradise. And yet still people were living in terror. Tens of thousands of Colombians had died during decades of fighting between the army, FARC and also right-wing paramilitary units. Millions had been displaced from their homes. In that region it was clear that many villagers were suffering, regardless of who was in charge. I was reminded of an African proverb: when two elephants fight, it is the grass that suffers.

There was another lesson to be learned the following night. We made it to the relative safety of a nearby town that had an army base. It seemed peaceful enough but while we were in a small bar eating dinner, a car bomb exploded nearby. After emerging from underneath tables, we discovered no one had been injured. Even if we wanted to we couldn't film anything because we hadn't brought a camera with us. I was already realising that almost everything on the journeys was filmable, but it was one of the problems too. We only had one hour of television to fill each time, and it was exhausting for the team to be constantly on duty. They needed to be able to down tools and have a break. Nowadays we compromise by taking a small camcorder out after hours, just in case something surprising or awful happens.

Putumayo wasn't just a danger zone. It was also one of the most biodiverse regions of the planet. We were on the far western edge of the wider Amazon ecoregion, which contains more than half of the planet's remaining rainforest and is just about the most critical natural treasure we have left. At least 10 per cent of the Amazon is actually inside Colombia, and the region is still largely covered by tropical rainforest, or jungle.

I met up with Carlos Enrique Zaens, a calm, gentle, bushy-bearded conservationist, and we pottered down the Putumayo River by boat towards the La Paya National Park, where he was the head ranger. The Putumayo meanders for hundreds of miles in a south-easterly direction and is an early sub-tributary of what eventually becomes the mighty Amazon River. The enfolding embrace of the tall trees on each bank and the stillness of the waters contributed to a lovely sense of peaceful intimacy as we gently cruised east into the park, a place of extraordinary natural bounty.

The steamy heat and the background noise of the jungle – the chirping, grunting, tweeting, snorting, leaf rustling and branch cracking – gradually increased with every mile that we travelled as if a volume dial was slowly being cranked all the way to maximum. Carlos talked almost poetically about the native species around us and his encounters with giant anteaters, jaguars, woolly monkeys, red howler monkeys, pygmy marmosets, tapirs, red brocket deer, manatees and two species of fresh-water river dolphins. There were hundreds of birds in the forest, including macaws, guans and toucans, but there were also a host of other creatures in the park that have barely been identified let alone studied by science.

I loved hearing Carlos talk with passion and wit about the world around, and I was also grateful for the change of scene, but this soon became another instructive moment for me as a relatively new adventure traveller. It started to pour down. Heavy rain turned into a tropical storm until it felt like we were being shot at by heavenly water cannons. I could really feel the impact of the water on my body, and realised I might have been a little slapdash in my kit preparations. I had no dry bags with me for equipment and my poncho started to leak. It wasn't one of those TV travel shows where I could cheat and casually leap across into a safety boat that was lurking just out of shot. We were in a proper storm, in a tricky region of the world. We had to prioritise survival. The boat was filling up alarmingly fast, and when I turned to Carlos to suggest we start baling I found he was already frantically emptying the boat. I converted a Tupperware box for our food bars into a bucket and chucked rainwater overboard for hours till we reached a safe patch of land where we could camp.

That night Carlos built a small fire and then said almost apologetically that we would need to smother the flames and slip back to our boat if we were attacked. I asked what he was talking about, thinking it was a mistranslation and the threat was surely four-legged. Very matter-of-factly, Carlos talked me through what was around us. Some of the inhabitants were perhaps best avoided, he said, among them caiman, venomous snakes and scorpions. But the real danger came not from wildlife but from humans. The national park was completely lawless, he admitted, and it was being fought over by the army, FARC, right-wing paramilitary death squads, drug cartels, poachers, wildlife trappers, hunters and illegal gold miners. My eyes widened.

'They are everywhere. They could be watching us now,' said Carlos, with a grimace that I mistook for a grin.

I thought he was teasing, and laughed loudly.

Carlos put his finger to his lips, suggesting I lower my noise.

'How on earth can you operate here?' I said after a moment. 'How can you protect the park and the wildlife?'

'It is very, very difficult,' he said slowly. 'But we must try.'

I felt huge admiration for Carlos. Conservationists are killed every year in Colombia and around the world trying to protect precious corners of the planet. Everything Carlos said and everything I saw reinforced what I had first learnt from Zacky in Borneo: these were front-line conservation heroes, unarmed warriors in a just war. Like so many fellow conservationists, Carlos and Zacky put their lives on the line to try and save wild natural places. Whatever risks I was experiencing with my film crew were negligible compared to his year-round ordeal.

We ate boiled rice with fish, then found a tarantula in our boat, a large black caiman bumped against the hull, and Carlos put the fear of God into us again by saying he thought he had seen someone watching us through the jungle. Looking back, the experience I'd most closely compare it to was filming inside an inmate-controlled prison in Honduras. La Paya National Park was an alien, confusing, dangerous environment where threats could come from any angle, and I simply had to have faith in my guide.

East from Putumayo we had been told stories about a remote Colombian indigenous community, right on the equator, that was largely cut off from the outside world. The only way to reach them was by a small plane. I sat next to the pilot as we took off from a jungle airstrip in a tiny plane with a single propeller and an engine that sounded like it would struggle to power a lawnmower, then flew high over the tree canopy, which seemed to stretch unbroken from horizon to horizon. There was still so much beauty out there to protect and preserve. An hour or so later we began to descend, but I couldn't see an actual airstrip and genuinely worried the pilot had fallen asleep at the controls. But we cleared a small ridge, he smiled at me and jabbed a stubby finger at a tiny gap between the trees in the distance.

'You must be bloody joking,' I said.

He laughed slightly manically, and down we went. The strip was more like a line, but the pilot didn't even pass overhead to check for grazing animals or recent landmine damage. Instead we just waddled down, pulled the nose up at the last minute, chopped up saplings in our path and came to a halt after 150 metres. It was the most astonishing jungle landing I think I've ever endured.

Our guide Juan Pablo had made tentative contact in advance with people from the Piedra Ni indigenous community via CB radio to check they would be happy for us to visit. As we unloaded our bags from the plane, people emerged hesitantly from nearby fields. We assumed it was a welcoming committee. But by the time we trekked through the jungle to their village, we realised they weren't expecting us at all. The village sat in a clearing by a river and consisted of wooden houses with simple grass thatches, and a vast meeting hall, an amazing construction, with two giant roofs sloping all the way to the ground and end walls made from an intricate lattice of reeds. The tribe all wore incongruous T-shirts and shorts, hand-me-down clothing now traded to the furthest reaches of the planet, but they lived 15 days by boat from the nearest small town, and we were the first foreigners the community had seen in more than 20 years. It was quite possibly the most isolated place I had ever visited.

I was suddenly aware of an overwhelming weight of responsibility. Here we were, breezing in with our flashy tech and survival meals of freeze-dried food. Unforeseen consequences could flow from our visit. We weren't just there to film them. They were filming us with their minds, internalising an encounter that might have a dramatic effect on the future of their youngsters.

We were ushered into the village hall. Children seemed delighted to see us and played and smiled for our camera. The more senior villagers were wary. The shaman, a bare-chested man with red criss-crossed markings on his cheeks, seemed unhappy, so we stopped filming while the villagers had a long and tense debate among themselves about whether we would be allowed to stay. To be sent away without any footage would have been an expensive disaster, but we had no choice other than to wait for their verdict. I sat in a corner, respectfully, until eventually an elder spoke to me directly. What would I and the TV crew be getting from our visit, he asked?

It was a tricky exchange as everything had to be translated back and forth between their language and Spanish, which a couple of villagers spoke fluently, and then via Juan Pablo into English (I've since had conversations filtered through four languages, which takes even longer and really makes you doubt the end accuracy). The whole process of interpretation does at least give more time to consider questions and answers. My first response didn't hit the spot. I explained we wanted to show our viewers what was going on in this part of Colombia and that might make it harder for the cartels, loggers and guerrillas to walk all over the community. The elder looked me square in the eyes. He wasn't convinced.

'No white man works for free,' he said pointedly, both to me and to the wider community. It was stinging, but wise. I said yes, we were working and being paid, but I promised him that we were not there to destroy, steal, damage or harm. We wanted to help tell their story to the outside world. Juan Pablo began translating. And then, keen to be transparent, I added another thought.

'I cannot claim what we film will make a huge difference to your lives,' I said. 'It is just a ripple on a lake.'

It was the first time I used a line that I have said repeatedly in the years since. I don't want people to think their lives are going to be transformed by our presence. It is rare that television makes a sudden, profound change, even though I do still believe it enlightens, even educates. But I have to be honest with them. I would never want to force anyone to film with us.

He thought for a moment. 'We know the people who take the trees are coming this way and we fear them. Will what you're doing help to protect us?'

'I hope so,' I said. He looked deep into my eyes and I felt like my soul was being examined. But I felt calm. They had to want us there. He nodded slightly, gave a wan smile, and pulled me gently by the arm towards a fire in the middle of the hut. We were allowed to stay.

That night we sat in the dark in the hall with the villagers and by the light of the fire they performed a ritual dance to the sound of panpipes. It was a beautiful, completely ethereal sight. The Dance of the Turtle and the Deer's Head was saved for special occasions relating to the weather. Linking arms and stamping bamboo poles into the earth, everyone joined in, both the oldest and the youngest, who, it was hoped, would learn its formal choreography and pass it on in turn to future generations. Short of visiting another planet, this was as far from my world as I had ever travelled. I felt an overwhelming sense of amazement and achievement. I sat watching in the dark and shed silent tears of awe and delight.

The next morning the team and I took a dip in the river and all the children laughed at our pasty white bodies, which loosened up the atmosphere nicely before we were taken to visit a monument the Piedra Ni people regard as the centre of the world. The river was lined with rocks and pools of water they considered sacred, but none was more sacrosanct than an imposing riverside rock with a painted white ogre-like figure sporting long, curled arms and a straight, dangling tail. Above the head sat a semicircle that represented the sun. It was the centre of their world, and it had a tangible power. The elders chided us for spending too long filming the monument, and told us that looking at it was just as dangerous as looking directly at the sun.

'You could lose your sight,' said one earnestly. That said, he was completely delighted modern science agreed the monument really was on the equator, and that it helped to mark the middle of the planet.

As we packed and prepared to say farewell to the village, one of our local guides suggested we should leave two gifts as a thank you to them for hosting us. I thought he was talking about small presents, but then he mentioned gifting a bottle of whisky for the chief and an engine for the village canoe. I was horrified.

I would never promise any gift or payment in advance of filming, because nobody should be talking to us because they think they are going to get something in return. That might encourage someone to chat on television for a small fee and put themselves in danger, perhaps from a gang or a rebel group. But if a village or a villager is hosting us, feeding us, taking time off from their work or farming to be with us, why shouldn't they receive a small gift when we leave? Usually we sense that people want nothing, and a code of hospitality prevails. But sometimes it becomes clear they are hoping for a gift, or for help. Give nothing, and we risk insulting them. Give too much and we might be accused of bribery. Give the wrong thing and we might change their whole world. What if they use a small sum of money to buy a cheap chainsaw? My natural instinct would be that could change their world for the worse. But then why shouldn't they own a chainsaw, or a boat engine, or a box of paracetamol, or a thousand other modern blessings? Yes, that might destroy, help, hinder, change, but perhaps that's their choice to make. We did. We chose to industrialise and have washing machines, fresh water, fridges. It is a hugely difficult issue I have struggled with endlessly over the years. I still have no ready answer, but my rules now are generally don't give anything to children, unless they are in need of medical help, don't give cigarettes or alcohol, don't give too much, try to give local food, and try to give to women, because in my experience they are more likely to spend it wisely on the family.

Those rules are neither cast-iron nor foolproof. And standing there in the Piedra Ni community back then I wasn't entirely sure what to do. There was no way we could afford to buy them a boat engine, so we took an easy way out and we gave a modest donation to one of the elders, in full view of the others so they could have a community discussion about how to spend it. As for the whisky, we had a bottle in a bag for minor emergencies. I gave it to the elders as we said goodbye and immediately regretted the decision as we headed east.

We crossed into Brazil near Iauareté, on the Uaupes River, just north of the equator. It was like entering a large house through an unlocked back door, so remote there was no border post to stamp passports or even check them. Eventually we found a small army base. An officer, initially highly suspicious, said no foreigners had crossed there for years and questioned whether we were agents of the CIA.

Luckily our two new Brazilian guides suddenly appeared, as if by magic. Augusto was an English-speaking Brazilian journalist from São Paulo, and Chicao, a Brazilian adventure guide. In this remote region, largely free of telephones, let alone mobile phones, they had both been summoned by the miracle of our chunky satellite phone. It wasn't the most reliable communication tool, being at the mercy of clouds, the orbiting patterns of satellites and tropical damp. But by pointing its supersize antenna at the heavens we were occasionally able to call our production office in London and they were able in turn to call ahead of us and send messages to our guides and anyone else we were meeting with a rough indication of our arrival time. Miraculously, using cars, planes, boats, horses and their own two feet, Augusto and Chicao had arrived in just the right place, at just the right time. They explained what we were doing and the Brazilian officer allowed us into the country.

Chicao was horrified we were relying on just one fragile satellite phone for communication. If that breaks when you are in trouble somewhere remote, he said, you are completely stuffed.

'In the Amazon, Simon,' he told me, 'two is one, and one is none.'

In other words, if you take a vital, mission-critical piece of kit somewhere remote or dangerous, whether a sat phone or your contact lens case, and you don't take a spare, you are not just failing to prepare, you are preparing to fail. It was a vital adventure tip that stayed with me and has since helped save my skin and also our shoots.

We piled ourselves and kit into boats and set off down the powerful Uaupes, a tributary of the Rio Negro – itself a tributary of the Amazon – with Chicao at the wheel. It can be hard to grasp the scale of the Amazon, but as water flows east the river widens ever further until it is more like a slow-moving sea. By the time it flows out into the Atlantic, a generous measurement of the mouth makes it wider than the entire length of the River Thames, wider even than the distance from London to Paris. It is unimaginably huge, supplying 20 per cent of all of the fresh water flowing into the oceans on earth.

The Uaupes still felt enormous, but at least we could still see the other bank. The rainforest on either side remained largely untouched thanks to its remoteness, but farmers and loggers were slowly encroaching from the south. We reached the equator again and Chicao suggested we stop for a celebratory dip. There was much talk of piranhas, alligators, anacondas and other monsters that might lurk in the water, but the creature I most feared was a tiny fish called a candiru, a frankly evil little blighter that detects a urine flow and, given half a chance, likes to crawl up a urethra, causing unbearable pain, or so it is said. I took the warnings with a pinch of salt as I leapt into the river, but on a just-in-case basis decided to wee off the side of the boat rather than into the water. I wish I'd also remembered to take my passport out of my pocket. When I got back to Europe a stroppy Danish border officer tried to stop me entering the country because he objected to the damage. Telling him it was a result of a dip in the Amazon did not help.

One of the first communities we came to as we travelled further downriver was a small indigenous village of huts that at first seemed to have been completely abandoned. Eventually a teenage girl in a bright turquoise shirt shyly opened a door. It was as if she had been left behind. She was 17 and had given birth to a baby son a week earlier. She had no idea how she was going to feed him and his father had disappeared downriver, like many of the men, to work in São Gabriel, a small jungle town, which we reached later that evening. It was immediately clear there was little work to be had there. Scores of men from indigenous communities were filling their time drinking in bars from first thing in the morning. In Brazil alcohol was banned by federal law along the Uaupes and Negro rivers, and throughout the indigenous communities, but seemed to have the town in its grip.

The closest I came to evidence of a robust indigenous community in the Amazon that was holding on to its culture, while using the best of the modern world, was the Waimiri-Atroari people. We crossed their path after embarking on an epic drive across hundreds of miles towards the Amazon basin. The Waimiri-Atroari originally faced near annihilation at the hands of the state when Brazil was still a dictatorship, especially after the Waimiri-Atroari violently resisted the building of a key road through their territory. Soldiers and construction workers were attacked by warriors with knives and poisoned darts. In response entire villages were destroyed.

Just before it looked as though the Waimiri-Atroari might be wiped out, the government declared its indigenous people a national treasure and began protecting and supporting them. On a practical level, by the time I was visiting they had taken control of the trans-Amazonian artery that was built through their territory and would close physical chain barriers to block access each night to protect wild animals and their hunters, who mainly operate at night. When we passed through their land, we were told very firmly not to stop and not to get out. If we weren't attacked by wild animals we might be shot at with blow darts by Waimiri-Atroari. After hours of driving, it was with some relief that we finally crossed out of their territory in one piece and I met a Waimiri-Atroari warrior who explained his people had kept their culture and their community, but now had access to healthcare, modern dentistry, the internet, and an education system they have been able to adapt to reflect their own extraordinary world. It was, he said, now on their terms, and their numbers were finally increasing again. In another nod to the realities of the modern world, he proudly showed me they even had an artisanal gift shop on their border, where I took the chance to buy a set of hand-crafted bow and arrows.

Travelling around the equator had shown and taught me so much about the natural world and the brave conservationists who were trying to protect it. Nature needs defenders, but so do the vulnerable, the poor, and the indigenous people who live in the Amazon basin and in some of the most beautiful and threatened areas of the world. I remain convinced the only answer, as Paul had said in the Galapagos, is real controls, real protection and real laws, properly enforced.

CHAPTER THREE

Wrecking Bar

On our final night following the equator, we had a few drinks. One of the team had a couple too many. He told me it had been bugging him that when I was talking to people on camera, the conversation would roll on, and that I would chat away with them rather than just milking them for a single, simple point. He thought it was because I wanted them to like me. He wagged his finger.

'You need to relax more,' he said. 'You care too much what people think about you.'

He wandered off. I suppose I proved his point by thinking about what he'd said for days and remembering it years later.

Yet I don't think these traits are a problem, or at least not my biggest. There are certainly worse. For someone who thinks of himself as an ordinary person, caring about what people think has been a superpower. It has helped me to adapt and change myself, like a blank canvas or a chameleon, to fit into places that I had no obvious right to be. But when I'm talking with people on camera, usually through an interpreter, I'm not trying to get them to like me, I'm trying to show that I'm listening and that I give a damn. Often they're telling me about an enormous or emotional moment in their lives. So I listen. Carefully. With a real focus.

Left to stew about comments like that or any mistake, I can sometimes work myself into deep self-criticism. Luckily I have a caring partner who soothes and provides a more positive perspective. But when she's not around, it's left to my head. I've got better at dealing with my internal voice over the years, but it's still a work in progress. I have come to accept that a negative nagging voice in my head is not something fundamentally 'wrong' with me that needs fixing, or even shutting up, but that it's just another aspect of having a complicated human mind. I try to treat myself as I would a friend, and if I wouldn't say to a friend what my voice is telling me, then it needs to stop. Using a nickname that people have for me, whether Si or Reevey, instantly softens the internal voice and turns it from harsh criticism to a warmer thought. Give it a try. And I like to remember Anya's simple advice: 'Don't be so hard on yourself. And try to give just a bit less of a toss about almost everything.'

I told some of the story of how I met Anya in *Step by Step*. I saw her at a party across the room. Even at a distance she looked clever and thoughtful. She was also half-Danish, tall, blonde and strikingly beautiful. I caught her eye and she held the smile for a moment longer than was necessary. We went for a boozy night out together when we could flirt but hardly talk, double-dating in a bar and chaperoned by friends, and then met alone for lunch. After a long list of previous dating disasters I had some strange rules about avoiding women who were Scandinavian, only children, or had cats. Anya ticked the first two boxes. But generously I still took her on a meal date under the glass roof of the Great Court in the British Museum, and then walked us out past the Rosetta Stone and told her a shortish story about its history and role in unlocking our understanding of Egyptian hieroglyphics. Anya humoured me, listened patiently, then looked at the stone and began reading out the section of it written in Ancient Greek. It was one of the most impressive things

I've ever seen, and knocked me for six. Anya had lived in Egypt, Denmark and Greece, and spoke fluent Greek, Danish and some Arabic. She worked as a camerawoman, model, producer, editor, and on TV documentaries. She made me laugh and made me think. I was quickly hooked.

I had given up on the idea of proper relationships when my previous girlfriend had walked out on me just after my father's funeral in 2001. I was badly burned by the experience. I thought I was never going to find love or even a long-term partner. Then in 2004 I met Anya and everything changed. When I was least expecting it, my future, the future of my entire life, took on a wonderful new shape. Suddenly I was no longer a lone ranger trotting around the globe on TV. I was one half of a couple. We met each other's friends, family and extended clans, and then began working together. It didn't take long before I had moved into her flat in north London.

The flat was just up the hill from where I'd lived with another girlfriend, in an earlier failed relationship, and it occupied the basement of Anya's family home. Her parents had been given the house by her dad's father Louis, who came from an impoverished Jewish immigrant family and studied hard the way arrivals often do and became a solicitor. So it was a house that came with connections, heritage and history, a 300-year-old house in a posh area of London that used to be home to artists and shrinks but was increasingly the domain of investment bankers, hedge fund managers and oligarchs. By every known metric apart from geography, it was a hell of a long way from Acton where I grew up.

One of the first signs things were getting properly serious with Anya was when she decided to extend her little flat into the garden and renovate it so that I could fit inside as well with my stuff. She started asking what I thought we should do to make it feel like my home and not just hers. I was stunned. There are people who struggle with even married partners changing décor or putting up pictures. Anya was granting her new boyfriend an equal status in renovating her family home. It was an incredibly generous act on her part. I had squatted, dossed and rented, but I had never bought or owned so much as a broom cupboard. Anya felt the flat should be big enough for the two of us, with an office for us to work in as partners and space for us to breathe and be together.

We bonded over the renovation and put all our savings into it. Working on creating a home is a very romantic thing to do in the 21st century. In my book it counts as proper commitment. Despite minor skirmishes we both agreed what we wanted. Anya went to work on the flat, the new extension and the new bedroom, installing 300kg sliding partition doors, a miraculous fold-down bed that was perfect for a small London flat, a huge glass roof, solar photovoltaic cells for hot water and a brilliant little second bathroom nestling under the stairs. We decided my talents were best employed digging out a tree stump in the garden.

The stump was enormous and had occupied a giant corner at the end of the garden for more than a decade. We thought we could put a little garden office there, so the stump had to go. The tree had originally grown on a Victorian rubble dump. Old bricks and chunks of rock were embedded in the roots. I got a guy to come in with a mobile stump grinder, but he went through three sets of diamond cutting teeth and gave up. There's only one thing for it, I thought: it's time to get out my wrecking bar. Everyone needs to own an axe for bushcraft and a wrecking bar for life. There are occasions when we all need to be able to take things out by the roots, perhaps to plant our own, and this was one of them for me.

My wrecking bar was one of three prized elemental gifts I have inherited in life. I was never given a trust fund or a house. After my father died I inherited a simple gold-plated watch he was awarded on his retirement after a lifetime of work, and the white plastic family sick bowl he used when enduring cancer, the same one I clutched as a child while nearly dying from meningitis and pneumonia. From the dusty back of my Grandma Lucy's shed I inherited an old wrecking bar taller than me, as heavy as Thor's hammer, and as thick as a scaffolding pole with a blunt chisel end. It looks like Godzilla's toothpick and is brilliant for turning a chore into a workout. I got a strange satisfaction from chipping and hacking and hammering away at that stump, and ended up in the best physical shape of my entire life. I would spend an hour or two on it every day, spread over weeks and weeks, but eventually, finally, I levered out the remaining part of the extracted stump and brandished it proudly like the carcass of a terrible man-eating beast. Anya broke off from running the entire renovations inside to pat me on the head. Thanks to my heroic feat, it's since become an accepted truth in our family that I'm a blunt tool best applied to hard laborious repeat work. If you need a stump removed, a long wall knocked down, a trench dug at speed or 100 saplings planted, I'm your man.

Having helped design an extension and extracted a stump, I was well embedded in Anya's home. By the time I returned after filming the *Equator* series I was starting to realise Anya was the person I wanted to be with in old age, the life partner I wanted to share sunrises and sunsets with from a hilltop. I loved every single experience on the road, even when they were shocking, frightening or upsetting, but there was a huge sense of loss that she was at home and I was away, and I couldn't share them with her. It created a void in my travel experiences that began to grow as our relationship blossomed.

Friends were hitching themselves together around that time, so along with parties and picnics we went to a series of amazing weddings. But even as we attended celebrations that were full of hope and joy, the negative side of my brain struggled with the idea of commitment. I had been so damaged by the sudden termination of my previous relationship I felt like I was suffering trauma. Friends and other guests would ask us if we were going to tie that knot. I would respond with a deeply unromantic, 'Ah, we'll see.' Anya stayed cool.

'He loves his travels,' she would say. 'I'm not sure he wants to be pinned down.'

She was right. And she was wrong. I had a nagging feeling Anya was out of my league, and that I didn't really deserve happiness. Two wise friends gave me solid advice. First I laid out my worries to James, my brother.

'Do you think this relationship is right for me?' I remember saying. 'Is Anya what I'm looking for? She's a year older than I am, and she's not very driven or ambitious.'

James was horrified. He was calm in response, but adamant.

'Are you completely mad?' he said to me slowly, holding my shoulder for added effect. 'She's far too good for you. You need to put any doubts out of your head right away and wake up and recognise how lucky you are.'

I asked my close pal Ben Arogundade, an author who is something of a relationship guru, and was with me at the party where I first met Anya, what he thought. He spent ten minutes pointing out it was a miracle she was even going out with me. 'Simon,' he added at the end, 'everyone should try to marry someone nicer than themselves.'

For my failings, I do tend to listen to the wisdom of others. There was no single moment when Anya and I broached marriage. It became a possibility that floated around our life and events, and then an agreed mutual desire.

'But you're not a white wedding type, are you?' I said.

'We can have a bit of tradition,' she said, 'but we'd have to mix it up.' One of her concerns was not being lumbered with a dodgy ring I'd selected. For me a ring was a ring, which probably explains why Anya decided she would choose the design. Her decision wasn't just a comment on my lack of taste. Her father David designs jewellery, so she had it in her blood. He has pieces in the V&A Museum, but perhaps his most famous creation is the skull ring he crafted for his friend, the musician Keith Richards, which has played its own key role in creating Keith's look and style.

Anya's parents were divorced. Her mother Lotte seemed willing to accept me. I went to the pub with David, a gentle and thoughtful arty soul. In an old-fashioned, almost Victorian way, I thought I should check he was OK with me marrying his daughter. I wasn't officially requesting his approval, just checking. As a survivor of the sixties, David was completely the wrong audience for this old-school approach. Keith Richards says the last time he ever saw Mick Jagger do something altruistic was when Mick helped carry my father-in-law out of a party after he'd passed out. David was direct.

'You're wasting time,' he said. 'She's not getting any younger, and nor are you. When is it going to happen?' I was quite taken aback. I said, 'Maybe the year after next?'

'No, no, that's too late,' he replied. 'It's got to be next year.'

Everyone seemed to be in agreement. It was time for me to get a move on.

Lotte and her partner Peter had an indirect influence. Anya had made it plain from the beginning that being with her would involve spending time in Denmark and at Lotte's family summer house on the Danish coast. Here again I'd had to wrestle with my stroppy, negative thoughts. The globetrotter in me was grumpy. I felt like I was being dragged there. 'Well, what if I don't *want* to go to Denmark all the time?'

Around one in four Danes owns a summer house, so almost every family has access to a simple country home. Lotte's is on the coast of Jutland nestled among tall grass, sharp bushes and low trees. A grassy bank slopes 150 metres down to a low clifftop and the Kattegat sea. On the other side is Sweden. The house is beautifully decorated with painted wooden panels in a natural, relaxed Scandi style. It was on holiday in this perfect cosy home from home that the verdict of James and Ben was painfully reconfirmed, and I realised I was an idiot.

In another life Anya could have come from a dark mining town in the Urals, which I'd be obliged to visit twice a year. Instead she had family in Denmark, perhaps the best-run country in the world and a welcome antidote to the benighted, poverty-stricken countries I was visiting for work. The Danes have built one of the most contented societies the planet has ever known, and regularly come out top on the global happiness index, although admittedly their triumph does appear to be aided by excessive consumption of antidepressants. They're also relatively tolerant and friendly. Theirs is one of the least corrupt countries in the world, with rates of violent crime that are among the lowest on the planet. The Danes are even head and shoulders above other Nordic nations. It didn't take me long to realise I'd been blessed, and I began relishing trips to Denmark.

It was while I was in Denmark, doing a bit of soul-searching, that I realised I had spent my early dating years looking for someone who was 100 per cent perfect, as if that ever exists. Then another chunk of years looking for someone who was perhaps 80 per cent perfect, which was still asking quite a lot. Finally I had reached a point of acceptance that it's not about the 100 per cent, and it's not about the 80 per cent, it's about that 20 per cent, or 10, 30, whatever it is, that's not quite right. Can we accept that gap? Can we recognise that compromise is always vital? And can we work as individuals and partners to accept what can never be perfect and grow together to change whatever can be improved?

I felt I had found my life partner, and we were getting hitched.

Anya designed a simple, elegant ring and I found a jeweller in Arundel who could make it with Fairtrade precious metal and diamonds sourced from mines outside conflict zones, where the miners earned a decent wage, and for which children hadn't died and wars hadn't been fought. It matters. I have seen the suffering and death of men and children who mine for those more fortunate. I wasn't going to put a blood diamond on my wife's finger.

A month later I went to collect the ethical ring. I hadn't actually proposed, but I had a plan.

We were going to Istanbul. I love the city for all the obvious reasons. For its extraordinary location as the meeting point of east and west, and for its spectacular beauty. There is such a sense of depth, energy and history in Istanbul. I cannot walk its streets and tap its stones without sensing the glory and drama of human civilisation. It has an aura. I have similar feelings about Jerusalem and Rome. But Istanbul is my favourite. Anya had never been, but my friend Shahida, whom I met and travelled with while making my first TV series *Meet the Stans*, was getting married in Istanbul. She's from Uzbekistan in Central Asia, and was marrying an American, so they settled on Istanbul as the ideal location because it's wonderful, and there were no visa restrictions for guests travelling from the former Soviet Union or the US. An invite to a wedding in Turkey, in a city I love, was an honour and a thrill, and we realised we could tag on a holiday in Greece afterwards. I packed the ring.

Shahida's wedding took place outdoors in the shadow of a bridge over the Bosphorus, which connects the land masses of Europe and Asia. It loomed over all of us as the newlyweds made their vows. If you are going to form a union with another person, I can think of no location in the world that lays on such a grand symbol of connection. For dinner and speeches we moved indoors to a stunning old building next door that was evocatively lit, lushly carpeted and full of lovely and beautiful people from across Planet Earth. The whole event was amazing.

Going to Istanbul is something of a pilgrimage for me, never more than with Anya, the woman I wanted to marry. We spent extra days sightseeing and went to two of my favourite spots, firstly the Basilica Cistern, built by the Emperor Justinian I in AD 532. It's one of hundreds of ancient cisterns beneath Istanbul. In my view it stands as one of the great treasures of our species. Created to store and filter more than 80,000 cubic metres of water, it is now largely drained and open to visitors. To wander around this magnificent subterranean cathedral, with its colonnades of beautifully illuminated pillars, is to be reminded of how the ancients applied the aesthetic to the functional. They put more effort into beautifying pillars that would be underwater

than many modern architects put into designing public buildings visible to all, although of course the ready availability of
slave labour doubtless helped. What I love above all is the presence of two Medusa heads. They were installed upside down,
apparently so they can't stare the onlooker in the eye and turn
them into stone. Though breathtaking in their beauty, they
would have been forgotten underwater and unseen by anyone at
all for the first thousand years. Indeed for hundreds of years the
residents of Istanbul forgot about the Basilica Cistern altogether.
Forgot! It seems unbelievable. Then a scholar spotted someone
fishing in the city down a hole, and the cistern was rediscovered
and partially drained, enabling James Bond to row through it
in the movie *From Russia with Love*.

One of the fundamental desires that drives me in life is to
clamber to the top of a hill with people I love and share an
astonishing view. I was sharing an impossible place that had
meaning for me intellectually and emotionally. I wanted Istanbul
to impress Anya. I needed the buildings to affect her.

Anya is far too cool and Scandi to get worked up the way I
do, which can be frustratingly exciting, but often just encourages me to try ever harder. She was certainly warm and enthusiastic about the Basilica Cistern. But I almost cried in there.
In a cistern. I had been before, but to be there again, with her,
in that remarkable structure, lit so perfectly and with every
stone screaming to me about human capability and the wonder
of our species, was just overwhelming. I was moved emotionally, and I felt wonder and a deep sense of fortune just being
there.

My highs are possibly too high, just as my lows are probably
too low. Yet I want to be affected by places and people and life
and grief. That's the privilege of experiences. I want to be

moved and touched and emotional. That's what makes me feel alive. That's why I adore adventures and *need* to travel.

We crossed the road to Hagia Sophia, arguably Istanbul's most glorious jewel and another creation of Justinian. It served as the greatest church in Christendom for a thousand years, before Mehmet the Conqueror took the city for Islam and converted Hagia Sophia into a mosque in 1453. Mustafa Kemal Atatürk, founder of modern, secular Turkey, turned the building into a museum, a memorial to past glory, and it remains one today. One of mankind's most successful attempts to secure immortality through construction, it's a building to match the pyramids in terms of scale and uniqueness. For a thousand years, and for hundreds of miles around, there was nothing remotely comparable. Entering it for the first time, you would need a soul made of stone to avoid feeling awed. I hustled Anya straight upstairs to the galleried first floor for the best view and we walked towards the ancient stone balustrade that runs round the first floor. The dome, more than 30 metres in diameter, and held aloft over 40 arched windows, appeared to float above us on a circle of bright light. Anya looked out into the vast interior of Hagia Sophia and the halo above us, and she gasped.

'My God. That. Is. Incredible,' she said, moving a hand to her chest. It was exactly what I wanted to hear. She was touched.

I walked her around the first floor to a spot rarely seen by most visitors. On the top of the balustrade is a small piece of graffiti that says simply in runes: 'Halfdan was here'. It was carved into the stone slab in the 900s by a Viking who had probably voyaged down rivers to the Black Sea in order to fight and work and earn. I love the fact he must have stood there at that point, looked out at the astonishing cathedral, as it then was, and been completely overwhelmed with wonder, like Anya and

I more than 1,000 years later, and marked the stone with his axe or knife with a runic inscription in Old Norse.

We took a sleeper train to Greece and caught an overnight ferry down to the island of Symi. I felt I knew Istanbul well, but Anya had a deeper connection to this small island off Rhodes, which is rightly famous for a spectacular neoclassical harbour, to my mind perhaps the finest in the entire eastern Mediterranean. She had been visiting Symi since she was 14, when she arrived there by accident with her parents and they all decided to stay for the rest of their holiday. She fell in love with the place, returned with her best friend Miriam at 16 and has been going back ever since, developing a healthy obsession with Greece and learning to speak and write the language fluently.

As with Denmark, Anya took a non-negotiable stance on visiting Symi. We would be doing a lot of it, ideally travelling there overland on trains and ferries. Initially, again, I had seen this as tying me down, until I actually went and was completely cured of my scepticism. Greece, for me, is one of the greatest countries on the planet.

The first time I went to Symi with Anya it felt like arriving with a celebrity. So many people would say hello to her. 'Anya!' The greeting would come from every other shop, bar or fishing boat. 'Anya! Anya!' What better place to cement my status as her partner?

I had it all planned. One day we went for a long, hot walk over stony hills to the remote Nimborio beach. When we got to our favourite viewpoint with a sumptuous view across the gleaming blue bay, I positioned my camera for a photo, discreetly set the video rolling and went down on bended knee. Despite the fact that we'd had grown-up 30-something conversations about this in advance, I'm delighted to say my unflappable other half was still genuinely shocked and surprised. She had a bit of an emotional moment. And thankfully she said yes.

Next we had to think about where to get married. This was trickier than it sounds, because although Anya wasn't interested in an expensive wedding dress or costly hen do, she was adamant we should extend the wedding over three days and make it into a weekend house party. I loved the idea, partly because when I'm hosting a party over one night I spend most of the time filling glasses and feeding people, and then by the early hours of the morning it's all over and I feel I haven't talked enough to anyone.

As a skinflint my extensive research suggested there was only one vaguely affordable large house you could hire for a weekend in the whole of southern England that could accommodate dozens of people. Huntsham Court in Devon was a big old rambling mid-Victorian pile with sweeping stairs, oak panelling, stag heads and swords on the walls, and dozens of bedrooms for a giant house party. The owners of Huntsham were planning to give it a major renovation and overhaul, which would no doubt put the prices up, but for us it was perfectly shabby chic, well before shabby chic was cool. The only slot available for the next few years was a cancellation the following September. We snapped it up.

Two weeks before our wedding I came back from Madagascar, where I had been filming a journey around the Tropic of Capricorn, the southern border of earth's tropical zone. As the follow-up series after *Equator*, that journey had taken me across southern Africa, through the centre of Australia and then across Chile, Argentina, Paraguay and Brazil. I had to fit my travels around our wedding preparations, and then managed to write an entire book about the journey, called, you guessed it, *Tropic of Capricorn*.

The weekend before the wedding was my stag do in Barcelona. You would think that someone who had travelled as often as I had would know it's a good idea to get to airports with room to spare. But I have always had a problem with timing. Many have suggested 'Sorry I'm late' should be written on my gravestone. I realised Anya really knew me when she pointed out just a few weeks into our relationship that if I did everything 20 minutes earlier I would never be late and I'd slash my stress. For my stag I was so late the minicab was still waiting outside the flat in north London as the lads were calling from Stansted to say, 'Where the hell are you?' My friend Cory saved the day by charming a guard at the airport, who was heading off on a break. She hustled me past the priority queue for security to a featureless wall, put her ID card into a flip-up key slot, a concealed door slid silently open, my bag was given a quick check, and I was through and made the flight. At no point in all my journeys have doors ever opened or waters parted the way they did to enable me to go partying in Barcelona.

Apart from leaving more time to get to airports, I learned another vitally important lesson on my stag do. If you are planning to get drunk and go paintballing with your mates, do it somewhere cold. That way you will be wearing more than just thin clothing when your friends are required to ritually shoot the proverbial out of you, and you won't be left with purple bruises that last weeks. Luckily I had a mask on my face, otherwise it would have looked like I'd been in a punch-up in our wedding photos.

My stag was a blast with a completely wonderful group of pals, partying, paintballing, drinking, singing and stumbling around in Barcelona, relatively responsibly. Anya chose to spend her hen night on a significantly cheaper trip to the Isle of Wight and breakdanced on the beach in the rain. But then she is a remarkably low-maintenance partner in almost every way, thank goodness, which meant that at least one of us kept a lid on our wedding budget. For her dress she went to a vintage second-hand shop in north London and found some incredible outfits. My favourite had most of her cleavage spilling out over the top. It was completely inappropriate, I reluctantly agreed. She eventually plumped for a vintage outfit which she adapted herself with needle and thread. It cost 60 quid. I'm ashamed to say I spent more on my shirt.

If we were doing the wedding again with more money we'd employ an army of dedicated helpers. Instead, to keep within our budget, we had to conscript friends. A good pal and my brother James were both roped in as photographers, which I feel slightly guilty about now because they had to spend so much time snapping rather than drinking and enjoying. A close friend of Anya's agreed to film the service. Various members of our families kindly decorated the venue with flowers we bought wholesale and ivy and pine branches we pinched or gathered from the garden. Anya again led the way on budget watching and chose to do her own hair and make-up, and most of our catering was provided by a huge supermarket shop, although we did stretch to getting professionals in to provide our wedding meal.

Not all the guests were warned of their role in advance. People started arriving at Huntsham Court on the Friday afternoon to find me wielding a clipboard and marshalling forces. There were a couple of bemused protests. 'What? We came for a party and you're giving us jobs!' If I'm honest a lot of it was quite last minute. The moment I thought we might have pushed it too far was with the seating plan. Some people really go to town on them, thinking up clever names for tables that are then inscribed on elaborate scrolls. But while most other brides might have been pampering and powdering, half an hour before the wedding was due to start Anya was still finalising where everyone would sit, and the tables were identified by colours on a giant A1 chart that we hurriedly handwrote and then coloured in so quickly it looked like the work of a five-year-old.

But of course nobody minded or noticed and it was a fantastically happy event. We had 90 guests, with 65 staying in Huntsham Court for the weekend. They made for a wonderful mix – friends we'd grown up with in London, worked with, travelled with, and family from Norfolk, London and a contingent of large Danes. I don't think anybody took it too seriously except perhaps the vicar officiating at the church in the grounds where, after a registry wedding in the house, we walked for a singalong and a blessing. Afterwards it was back to the big house for James to roast me with his best man wedding speech, and a Danish ceremony where Anya's burly Uncle Lasse, whom you could easily imagine commanding a shipload of Vikings, played a traditional Danish song while everybody had to dance around us in ever-decreasing circles until we were squashed in between them, holding hands. We were basically crushed with love. It was absolutely one of the best moments in my entire life.

That night we had a fantastic party, with music laid on by our friends Milla and Tim and their band Saloon Star. Milla can sing almost anything and Tim can play almost anything and, while they're modest about advertising their band, they've played at all sorts of royal events, about which they remain irritatingly discreet. Regardless, we had a top-level band who know how to lure almost anyone on to the dance floor, and it's testament to their brilliance they even had my creaky legs moving.

I don't remember going to bed that night, but thankfully Anya and I woke up together. I staggered downstairs to find my wonderful mother-in-law Lotte had done most of the washing-up for the entire wedding, which still stands out to me as an astonishing act of selflessness. Sunday was lovely and laid-back. We had a giant roast and a massive football match organised by my pal Maurice wearing his Liverpool strip. We all threw ourselves into it with absolute gusto despite being shockingly hungover. The enthusiasm level was brilliant, possibly excessive, and several players had to be sent off for their own medical safety.

I wandered around the garden after the game, exhausted, happy, and chatting with people and catching little moments of interactions. Around me, people were dancing, talking, eating and giggling, some meeting for the first time. I just felt such pride. Everyone was wonderful. I had to pinch myself. It had all gone so much better than I could have ever hoped, or ever deserved. Our friend Nick was standing by a giant chess set asking Anya's old friend David whether he fancied a game and whether he played.

'I still play a bit,' said David, the former captain of the English chess team and a grand master, truthfully.

I stifled a laugh. It was all perfect.

CHAPTER FOUR

Minefields

There was no time for a honeymoon after we married, but even before we tied the knot, Anya and I had begun travelling and working together as a team. At first we just plotted and planned journeys together on huge maps spread out across our dining table with markers and sticky notes identifying possible routes. But as a camerawoman and producer, and someone who had trekked, travelled and lived out of the back of her own Land Rover on shoots and adventures, it was perhaps fairly inevitable I would try to rope Anya into the journeys more directly. After the *Equator* series, for which we'd often been just a three-person team of cameraman, director and me, I had already said I thought we needed an assistant producer with us on the road in future as an extra pair of hands and eyes, but also to film on their own as a second unit and pitch in with logistics and planning. I was convinced Anya would be perfect. We sent her filming showreel to Karen O'Connor, the Head of Current Affairs at the BBC, promised she was sane and hardy, they chatted, and it was tentatively agreed. On the plus side, I said, at least the accommodation budget wouldn't increase.

'Just one large sleeping bag, eh?' said Karen with a smile.

Anya began working on my programmes and travelling on the journeys from *Tropic of Capricorn*. We were partners. In every sense. Who gets to do that with their other half? Thinking about it now gets me misty-eyed. It is hard to overstate the scale of the privilege and good fortune. We had such stunning adventures together. She also studied the journeys, researched them, came up with ideas and stories, and has worked with me including writing and editing everything in the years since.

We developed a system to help us make decisions when there's something one of us wants to do more than the other. To resolve the issue we ask each other, on a scale of one to ten, how badly we want it. One of us might say five, but the other eight. Enthusiasm trumps apathy, every time. It helps with life, planning a journey, and even when I'm talking with the production team as they look for the elements to make an adventure and a rounded television programme. What really makes us decide to follow up on a lead is if someone in the team is wildly enthusiastic about it, and gives it an eight, or even a nine.

Perhaps what's slightly different about my journeys is that we set out to combine adventures with issues, what I perhaps pretentiously call the light and the shade. We don't shy away from problems. I'm not travelling to film a holiday brochure, which is why I've found myself in war zones and drug dens. In truth what I'm trying to do is to get people to take an interest in our world. By turning my programmes into a glossy adventure we can show people a beautiful part of the planet, but also inform them about tricky issues. I want viewers to learn about our world, and love it more.

To make the programmes we often look for extremes. Not just places that are extremely dangerous but situations or stories that are extremely surprising, extremely beautiful, extremely inspiring or extremely shocking. I need my buttons tweaked. Viewers want their buttons tweaked. It's not a bad idea for all of us as travellers. There's no point in any of us going somewhere beige. Look for extremes, because we all need to take more risks in life.

By the end of the *Equator* series I was honing this filming style. On screen it was always me going in first and the camera following. There was no script. Nobody was whispering in my ear through an earpiece what to say or what to do. We don't have a recce, where a producer goes ahead and works out what I'm going to do or where we'll put the tripod. That's increasingly rare in TV. We do have a plan – we certainly don't just turn up in a country without an idea of the journey we want to take or whom we want to meet – but when we arrive somewhere we have to decide exactly what to do and what to film as we go along. It makes for a more authentic journey that way, and I hope it feels like a more genuine adventure to anyone watching.

We can be spontaneous on the road, but what there had to be in the title was what TV types call 'the promise of pleasure'. When viewers are hopping between channels, just a few words about the programme will pop up on the EPG, the electronic programme guide. They need to see something in the series title that sounds alluring. So the name of a project is critical.

After following the equator around the world, and then the Tropic of Capricorn, what I really wanted to do next was follow the route of Marco Polo's outbound journey to the Far East, on an epic adventure that would have taken me through Iraq, Iran, Afghanistan and Central Asia, into China and across the Taklamakan Desert, also known as the Desert of Death. I became obsessed with the idea and the journey, and Anya and I spent months of time and money working up a proposal. But we could never find a title that encapsulated the journey while still sounding exotically appealing. 'The Journey of Marco Polo' was too historical. Ditto 'Overland in the footsteps of Marco Polo'. It might sound appalling that a commission for an entire project can hinge on just a title, but that is the reality of television and publishing and a host of other industries that are desperate to catch the attention of your flitting eyeballs. Eventually, we created a 26-page PDF proposal with a bumper set of photographs and maps, and sent it in to the BBC. The title was 'East: The Greatest Journey on Earth', which still didn't quite cut it. I have never had any sort of long-term arrangement or contract with the BBC. Every single adventure could have been the last. Every single project has been something I have had to propose to the BBC or another TV channel, or they've proposed to me. Decisions about each and every new adventure are based on the success or failure of the last project. It has been a nerve-wracking way to live. Many of my ideas have been turned down, and I've turned down many of theirs. So the BBC were under no obligation to give 'East' a green light and send me a cheque to make the series. I was on holiday when the decision came through. It was surely the most media moment of my entire life. I was skiing, standing at the top of a black run, contemplating a crazy downhill race, when a commissioner at the BBC rang me to say they were turning down 'East' because the title didn't have the elusive − and vital − 'promise of pleasure' that any project needed. I was completely gutted. I skied down that mountain dangerously quickly, raging. But they were probably right about the title. Instead they suggested I travel around the Tropic of Cancer, the northern border of earth's tropical zone.

Initially I was reluctant. The last of my three trips around the Tropics was definitely not my idea. Then I looked much more closely at maps of the regions crossed by the line and I realised the Tropic of Cancer promised astonishing adventures. The route would take me into the biggest desert on the planet, through the very hottest places, and the country with one of the world's most repressive regimes. It looked impossible. The thought made me tingle with the thrill and excitement.

The more research and preparation we did, the more I started to think the Tropic of Cancer could become my greatest adventure. While the equator journey nourished my love of the natural world, and my understanding of the challenges it faces, travelling around the Tropic of Cancer would become the journey that nourished my love of humanity, my pride in our species. Even as it took me into some of the darkest and most troubled places on the planet, the journey would teach me that we ourselves are the first and best reason to travel.

When I travelled along the length of the equator I visited ten countries and was given three hour-long programmes in which to tell the story. The Tropic of Cancer was of a different order of magnitude, with much more land to explore, and 17 countries and territories along the line, including some of the oldest civilisations on earth, the most powerful nations, the most overpopulated and the emptiest. It was 23,000 miles, across deserts, rivers and mountains – a massive undertaking. To accommodate the gigantic scale of the journey, this time I was given a whopping six hours of primetime to fill. My journeys were getting bigger, and bolder.

I started filming *Tropic of Cancer* on the west coast of Mexico and crossed the Sea of Cortés to Culiacán, a city at war with itself thanks to an ongoing battle between the fearsome Sinaloa drug cartel and an overwhelmed paramilitary police. I needed a flak jacket to go out on a patrol and raid with a heavily armed Mexican police SWAT team, before we headed east to Cuba and then the Bahamas. It was a beautiful start to the series but the adventure really began when the Tropic of Cancer hit the coast of Africa.

My epic adventure across North Africa began on the water and nearly ended right there and then. We were off the coast of the disputed territory of Western Sahara, just below Morocco, and I was bouncing around on the Atlantic in a Moroccan naval vessel, trying to board a small octopus fishing boat. In my arms was a £30,000 camera belonging to Jonathan Young, a ludicrously experienced cameraman. He had a long list of credits, had travelled the world and filmed in most of the planet's war zones – he even possessed his own set of class four body armour, but was travelling with me on these journeys for the first time.

The weather was appalling, and waves were crashing against the navy boat so violently we thought it might be tipped over.

'Do you really want to do this? Do you think you can do this?' shouted the navy captain through spray and chaos to Jonathan, who was closest. We were being really chucked around. Jonathan made the call.

'No!' he shouted back. 'It's too dangerous.' And then he looked up and saw me leaping like a splayed frog through the spray into the tiny octopus boat, clutching his unbelievably expensive camera.

'Oh feck,' shouted Jonathan, and he threw himself over the rail around the boat and jumped in with me just as the swell pushed our boats apart.

The fishing trip was the start of my journey across North Africa. Also travelling with us were Anya and Dominic Ozanne, a calm, intuitive and inspired film-maker who had directed two of the *Tropic of Capricorn* journeys. It was our first time working together as a team, and the biggest journey Anya and I had tried together, perhaps even risked, because we were planning to travel east for weeks across the great Sahara Desert, over borders that had been closed for decades, and through areas of immense danger. Of all my travels it remains one of the greatest adventures.

When setting off on a journey of that scope and scale, I need to know I can trust the people I'm working with. I need to know they are not going to freak out at danger, or the first sight of a gun, or say something at a checkpoint or in a palace or a women's refuge that is going to get us into trouble. I need to know they're not going to get endlessly drunk, bring a prostitute to dinner, or forget their camera batteries. I was married to Anya, had already worked with Dominic, and instinctively felt I could trust Jonathan. Whether he initially felt the same about me is for him to say. But we have since worked together on dozens of journeys, travelling the planet and having enough experiences to fill several lifetimes. So hopefully I've passed any of his tests. The fact that I didn't drop the camera in the Atlantic, and we got the filming sequence we wanted, made for a good bonding experience. At its best the relationship between a presenter and a cameraman or camerawoman is intimate, and I like to think I had a meeting of minds with Jonathan. A thousand times in the years since I have felt deeply blessed to be travelling with him, not least because despite being fantastically experienced, he never loses his sense of excitement during an adventure. We've been on top of mountains and lost in a slum, and he will still turn to me with a big grin and say with genuine excitement: 'I can't believe we get to do this!'

He never loses sight of the fact that travel is a privilege, and being paid to go on a wild journey that opens your eyes and heart is almost excessive good fortune. He is physically big, strong, proudly Yorkshire, and just an inch taller than me, so when he's filming me from the front the camera is at the right level. But most importantly, Jonathan is also brilliant at operating under pressure in difficult situations. I cannot stress enough the physical challenge of capturing energetic images while walking backwards, being bothered by a militant or a monkey, all the time tinkering with the camera settings with the dexterity of a saxophonist, as often as not while sweating buckets. His task, on top of filming my encounters, is to make an endless series of rapid decisions about what to get in the frame in order to establish the character or a location. Whether we're in a city or an empty landscape, he brings back a fantastic gallery of extra shots, or cutaways as we call them, for our editors to play with and work into the final programmes. When I stop nattering into the camera, Jonathan will move quickly to hoover up a basket of shots, pirouetting like a hyper-alert ballet dancer, moving through 360 degrees as he films a bird taking wing or a flag fluttering, then drop to his knees to film a child playing in the sand or a soft-focus shot of a flower in a ravine. Sometimes I think he is endowed with supernatural powers.

The boat we had leapt into together was owned by Abdul Hak, an octopus fisherman wearing a big khaki sou'wester coat and a mucky baseball cap. He was a Moroccan who had settled in the disputed territory of Western Sahara, a Spanish colony until 1975. After Spain's withdrawal it was annexed by Morocco, triggering a bitter and bloody war with the indigenous Saharawi people who claimed it as their homeland. A ceasefire brokered by the United Nations in 1991 brought an uneasy peace but did nothing to resolve the question.

'The Sahara is Moroccan,' insisted Abdul as his boat bounced around in the ocean. 'This land does not belong to foreigners. It belongs to us. It is the homeland of our ancestors.' Like tens of thousands of other fishermen and settlers he had been drawn south by tax breaks and a fishing industry worth many millions in export earnings. Our smiling official guide took the same party line and was adamant we were in Morocco. The Moroccan state backs up this claim with a heavy-handed police presence. We felt this ourselves in the dusty coastal city of Dakhla. Everywhere we went we were followed by plain clothes officers from the Moroccan security services.

Tens of thousands of local Saharawi people fled into exile after the Moroccans took over. We heard stories that many of those who were left believed they've been sidelined in their own land, by what they view as an illegal occupation. A Human Rights Watch report had accused the Moroccan authorities of using arbitrary arrest, violence and harassment against activists. Saharawis were accusing the Moroccans of terrible abuses and torture, and many had been silenced. But using encrypted messaging services and local human rights workers, we managed to make contact with Saharawi activists who were keen to see us and we arranged to meet them at night. First the team and I had to shake off our guide and two guys from the secret police, who were drinking endless cups of coffee in the reception area of our hotel.

Anya, who understands Arabic, slapped on some make-up and a dress and went downstairs to monitor the spies while having her own coffee and reading a guidebook like any other tourist. She watched and listened as the secret police began quizzing hotel staff about what we were up to. They seemed satisfied, and when they left she went to hire a car for us and parked it nearby.

Later that night I slipped out through the back with Jonathan and Dominic and I drove us to the side of a petrol station where we'd arranged to meet an activist, Rachid, who campaigns for the human rights of the Saharawi people.

We waited in the shadows until a vehicle pulled up in front of us and flashed three times, as planned, then the driver sped off. I tried to follow through traffic while Jonathan and Dominic ducked down in their seats in case we were spotted. It was dark, many of the vehicles on the roads were the same, and most had no rear lights to make their number plates less visible. Another car cut in between us, then the car I was following turned and drove down a warren of back streets until he pulled up at a semi-derelict apartment block in a poor part of town. The driver just sat in his car, so we sat in ours. I flashed him once. He got out and looked at us, so I stepped out, by now wearing a shemagh headscarf around my head. Then Jonathan's big frame emerged from the back seat. The guy looked at us, panicked and jumped back into his car. Clearly I had been following the wrong vehicle. Maybe he thought we were a CIA rendition squad.

We got back into our car slowly and calmly, then pulled away with a smile and wave at the guy. The last thing we needed was him calling the police on us. Back on the main street we found Rachid's car waiting patiently, signalled to him, and followed him down more dark back streets. He drove around the block a couple of times to make sure we weren't being followed, then stopped by another shuttered apartment block and came over to our car to say the briefest of hellos.

'I'll go over to the block and turn the lights out in the hallway,' he said, pointing across the road. 'Each time I open the door, one of you needs to run over and go up the stairs.'

It didn't feel remotely safe. Westerners were being kidnapped by militants in North Africa, plus that area of town felt sketchy. If the secret police wanted to nab us, this was where it would happen. I went first. I raced across the road, inside and up an unlit staircase, with my heart pounding. I had a flashback to more than a decade earlier when I was researching the rise of Islamic terrorism on my own, and over and over again I found myself walking into strange, dark buildings with people who might have never let me leave.

Jonathan and Dominic each came next, and we climbed the stairs and emerged into a small lit room where four campaigners wearing robes were sitting on floor cushions waiting for us, and finally we could talk openly with Rachid, the spokesman of the group, a handsome and quiet man in his thirties. It was a Saharawi safe house. Rachid told me the Moroccans had come to their land and occupied it. 'We are still asking for independence, no more no less,' he said. 'There's oppression here, and the secret police are everywhere. There is no freedom of speech. We can't ask for independence openly. We can't even raise the Saharawi flag or talk about what has happened to the Saharawi people.'

Rachid also said he had been picked up by the police just a few weeks earlier and beaten for attending a human rights convention. Each of the activists in the room had tales of terrible brutality inflicted on them and people they knew by the Moroccan security services. Another campaigner even showed me photographs of beatings and bruising he had received on his back and down the back of his legs.

I was deeply moved by the encounter. Despite knowing that there could be more such punishment, they were prepared to talk to us in the hope the outside world would learn more about their situation and story. It was humbling and sobering to know they would take such a risk, and it was a bravery I saw several times along the Tropic of Cancer, and became a standout feature of the entire journey. It is depressing, of course, that such bravery is necessary, but it's also inspiring, and a reminder to all of us, especially for me, of the value of freedom, of the rights we take so readily for granted, and of the incredible good fortune of those of us who live in countries where the secret police or gunmen are unlikely to come knocking on our door.

Following the Tropic of Cancer across Mexico, I had already met a wonderful character called Javier Valdez Cárdenas, a solid and modest figure in his middle years wearing tinted glasses and a goatee beard, who was an investigative journalist specialising in the cartels and the ferocious Mexican drug war. Just before I met Javier, a hand grenade blew up his office. He received international awards for his writings on organised crime and he was someone I could trust as a guide in the dangerous city of Culiacán. Javier had taken me to a crime scene where five policemen had been brazenly executed in front of an actual police station. Not content with killing, the cartel gangs resorted to brutally intimidating tactics, mutilating and even beheading their victims. A few years later I was deeply saddened to hear that Javier, who reported on the drug cartels with such bravery, became one of their victims. He was gunned down in the street.

Scores of other brave men and women have risked a great deal to share their stories with me over the years, to speak their truth through the camera to you watching at home. Their bravery is humbling.

In Western Sahara I felt a deep sense of foreboding as I left the Saharawi activists later in the evening.

'Viva la liberté!' they said.

Rachid and his friends were fully aware of the risks they ran by meeting me. In the final programme we blurred the faces of the other men in the room. But Rachid wanted to be identified. He wanted to be seen speaking openly on camera to highlight the mistreatment of the Saharawi people. Sure enough, a few weeks after we left, Rachid said he was detained by the Moroccan secret police, questioned specifically about what he had told me on camera, and severely beaten. He sent us photographs showing the injuries to his face and his buttocks. I still have them in my office as a constant reminder of the risks involved with my journeys, and the price people are willing to pay to get their voice heard.

'The imprisonment of Rachid ... and the others appears intended not only to punish them for their beliefs, but also to send a signal to others that the Moroccan authorities will not tolerate even peaceful criticism of their stance on Western Sahara,' Malcolm Smart, the director of Amnesty's Middle East and North Africa Programme, said at the time.

The Tropic of Cancer, curiosity and a genuine desire to learn more about what the hell is going on in the world had all taken me to the heart of one of the world's forgotten conflicts. I wanted to travel further east along the line to where more than 100,000 Saharawis were living in exile in camps in the desert. But to defend its section of Western Sahara, Morocco had built a vast fortified wall known as a berm stretching north to south for a staggering 1,700 miles. Manned by an army of 120,000, it is the most land-mined strip of earth on the planet. On the eastern side of the berm was the land controlled by the Polisario Front, who are considered by the United Nations to be the legitimate representatives of the Saharawi people. There was no way across the berm. To reach the Polisario Front camps we would need to take an enormous detour travelling hundreds of miles south along the coast into neighbouring Mauritania, and then come back up on the other side of the berm. Time, distance and landmines were all in our way.

We set off south through golden but often featureless dusty desert, and after hours of driving arrived at the border with Mauritania and met Hamdi El Hassan, who would be my guide for the days ahead. He was instantly brilliant and hilarious, a standout character with a warm and near-constant smile. But between the final Moroccan border post and Mauritania, we had to cross three miles of heavily mined desert no-man's land through a graveyard of cars, many of which had been blown up when they strayed from a series of indistinct desert tracks. Hamdi was in charge, but he didn't really seem to know the way. After a few minutes of crawling along, it became clear the driver didn't really know the way either. They had a little bicker about whether to turn left or right. There was palpable tension in the car. We crawled a bit further, took another turn, then came to a stop. We were lost. In one of the world's biggest minefields.

'Don't worry!' said Hamdi. 'Everything will be OK!'

Jonathan began chortling. I giggled. It was like a release valve. We both began laughing hysterically. It was just so farcical.

'We're lost!' said Jonathan, looking at me.

'In a minefield!' I said back, laughing at the madness.

Hamdi looked at us like we were bonkers. As well he might. Then we all pulled ourselves together. I was worried about Anya and Dominic, who were in the car behind. They had stopped further back and were waiting to hear what route we would take. We radioed to them and said we needed a moment to check the route. Then our driver said he thought we should be turning left. I said it looked like the most regularly used track was supposed to take us to the right.

'No, that's not correct,' said Hamdi calmly.

I opened my mouth to debate and argue with him, and then I looked over at him and realised that, actually, in that moment

I trusted his judgement significantly more than my own. I said nothing. Hamdi politely told us we were both wrong, and instead he told the driver to reverse, very, very slowly, past the burned-out shell of a truck. We rejoined another track.

'This is the way,' said Hamdi, sounding confident. We followed unbroken tyre tracks over a low bank and suddenly, with an enormous sense of relief, saw a stone archway that welcomed us to the border of Mauritania.

It was a great little lesson for life. If you're in a minefield. Emotionally. Professionally. Or even, heaven forbid, *Actually*. Don't panic. Follow the advice of the person you trust most. It might be you. But it might be Hamdi.

After an experience like that within an hour of meeting Hamdi, inevitably there was an instant bond. I really liked our new lifesaver. He proved to be a wonderfully eccentric travelling companion, always joking and joshing but also clever, wise, thoughtful and never anything less than frank and open with us.

He took us into the city of Nouadhibou, which sits on a peninsula jutting into the Atlantic, and to a bustling market to get some fuel and food for our journey. Hamdi explained that Mauritania is the divide, or the bridge, between Black Africa to the south and Arabs from the north. Shoppers were wearing long robes, with turbans for the men, both in purples, reds, blues and greens. It was a whirl of colour and cultures, and a lot to take in. As we filmed Hamdi buying a new robe, a woman, spotting our camera, seemed keen to inform us that Mauritania was doing fine, thank you.

'We have lots of wealth!' she hollered at us assertively. 'We have camels, we have goats, we have cattle, we eat day and night! We are very fat! I have a big belly because I am eating well, so no problem here in Mauritania!' After she'd wandered off, Hamdi explained that in Mauritanian culture, big is beautiful.

'I like a fat woman,' he added, wearing a po-faced expression behind his glasses. 'When you are touching bones you are as if touching rocks and stones. Smoother flesh is something a little bit exciting.' Size often equals status and attraction in Mauritania, and women's weight is a huge issue in the country, where there remains a troubling local tradition of force-feeding young girls to improve their marriage prospects.

We stopped by the coast to say farewell to the sea before heading deep into the Sahara and came across further evidence it's not always easy being female in Mauritania. On a shore littered with the rusting carcasses of old fishing vessels, we found local women doing a job that, for me, set a new benchmark for unpleasantness as they chopped and processed rotting fish in huge boiling vats. The stench was so powerful, so overwhelming, that years later I can still conjure it in my mind.

To travel deep into the desert and reach the Polisario-controlled areas of the Sahara, Hamdi had booked us on to a train for the long journey. But not just any train. It was one of the longest trains in the world. A staggering two miles from nose to tail, it consisted of 200 wagons transporting iron ore from the interior, accounting for an incredible 40 per cent of the country's exports, with a tiny, rudimentary passenger section at the very end. We loaded our bags on board, with Hamdi jokingly complaining about our 'many baggages', and then Jonathan and I went to film outside along the length of the train when it suddenly began to move.

'Shiiiit!' shouted Jonathan.

We dashed back to the passenger car and were pulled and lifted on board. Luckily the train wasn't in any great hurry and needed to perform a huge loop to turn round and head back east. It was an extraordinary sight to watch the front end head back on itself towards us while, two miles away at the rear, we were still chugging west at the other end of the arc. Then, for the next 18 long, slow hours, the train trudged across the desert, which we could only see through small porthole windows. It felt like we were in a filthy old spaceship crossing another planet, but I was itching to be outside, and to be in the desert. Luckily Hamdi, a charming nutter, kept us entertained with his sweet brand of naughty talk. He found the word 'tuna' particularly hilarious, saying in Mauritania it meant something very, very rude, while outside the desert passed in the night.

The train ride of 400 miles was a mere foretaste of what awaited us when we reached the end of the line at the desert outpost of Zouérat – an epic off-road journey across more than 600 miles to the Polisario Front camps in the desert, or as one of our team put it: 'From London to Aberdeen, without any roads.'

We loaded up a convoy of three rugged Land Cruisers and headed off on the biggest adventure of them all, into the Sahara Desert.

CHAPTER FIVE

The Sahara

Some of my impossible places are difficult because they are blighted by war, criminality or human suffering. Some are home to huge refugee populations or criss-crossed by desperate migrants. Some are unbelievably hot or astonishingly cold. Some are just bloody hard to get to. Almost uniquely, the Sahara ticks every box. I knew we were in for an epic experience.

We all have the same picture of the world's poster desert. Sahara – the very word conjures up an image of sand dunes rolling across the vast expanse of North Africa in wave after wave for many hundreds of miles while the sun beats down remorselessly from above. In reality the undulating dunes are only part of the picture. A lot of it is actually a stony wilderness.

As we raced along, I was desperately hoping we might encounter the Tuareg people, the nomadic 'Blue Men of the Desert' as they're sometimes known because of the traditional robes they wear dyed with indigo. For hundreds of years they have occupied the vast desert of Algeria, Mali, Libya and Niger, often controlling camel caravans of trade and living according to their own clan rules. They are also known as the 'Lords of the Sahara'.

Few travellers enter that lawless wilderness, and especially not foreigners. Break down in your vehicle and you're on your own, way beyond the reach of rescue. But take the risk and the reward is to travel hundreds of miles through astonishing landscapes such as I've never seen anywhere else. Initially it was utterly flat. There was nothing to see but white sky and dusty earth, plus an occasional lost camel. Then the odd feature began to punctuate the horizon. First a few patches of tufty, hardy grass, then brazen trees, and even hills weathered by the lashing desert winds into towering rocks that jutted up like lonely sentries. It felt like driving across Mars. Every so often we'd come across skeletons of camels and the husks of old vehicles that had been driven to their deaths and then abandoned to slowly crumble. For vast distances there was nothing. No roads, no signs, not even any planes passing high in the sky above. It felt like we had fallen off a map of the world. The sense of emptiness was profound.

At some point we crossed from northern Mauritania into the Polisario-controlled area of Western Sahara. There were no formal lines marking the border. But we were told we were the first Westerners to travel in the area for years. We stopped to pitch camp among some acacia trees providing protection from the wind. To imagine where we were, put a rough image of North Africa into your head. We were in the middle of the western end of the Sahara, 250 miles inland from the Atlantic coast and maybe 900 miles from the Mediterranean coast to the north.

After the sun went down and the heat of the day had left our bones, we were all sitting huddled around our fire when a Tuareg nomad appeared out of the black night, as if from nowhere. Wrapping his billowing blue robes tightly around his body, and without saying a word, he squatted on the desert sand next to our fire and warmed his hands against the night chill. Glancing over at me, he nodded a greeting, unperturbed and seemingly unimpressed by the sight of a small group of foreigners in this remote region of northern Mauritania. My jaw, by contrast, was hanging open. For several hours before we paused to pitch camp, we had not seen another living creature, let alone a wandering nomad.

He chatted with one of our local guides, who asked him where he had come from.

'Over there,' he said, gesturing in front of us at nowhere in the darkness.

'Where are you going?'

'Over there,' came the translation, as he pointed behind us.

There are strict rules about hospitality in the desert. Food, water and heat must be shared. We cooked bread and meat in the embers of our fire, and the Tuareg ate a full meal with us before he rose, bowed, and then disappeared back into the darkness with just a cheery wave. It was magical.

'Did that really just happen?' Anya said to me with a smile.

'This is mind-blowing,' said Jonathan.

I spent the next ten minutes shaking my head in disbelief and wonder.

The temperature was dropping rapidly, and we all layered more clothes to keep warm. We all understood, at least theoretically, that even in the desert it gets chilly at night. But the cold creeps up on you. The Almighty doesn't flick a switch so it suddenly goes from oven to freezer. Thanks to the heat you've endured all day, your brain cannot quite compute that at some point in the middle of the night you might be at risk of frostbite. So you get into your sleeping bag, thinking you're prepared for the worst, but the mercury just keeps on plummeting and you have to get up to apply yet another layer of warmth, adding long johns, then a jumper. Eventually we were all warm and ready for sleep. We had lined up next to each other, sweetly cocooned in our sleeping bags, all of us on our backs, looking up at the universe and the brightest display of stars.

In the morning we packed early and flogged ourselves hard across the Sahara for the rest of the day, and the next, in a race against the clock. We had to travel north to a military camp in the middle of the desert to film a Western Sahara independence day celebration, but a puncture, blinding dust, deep sand and wandering camels delayed us. Eventually we found ourselves travelling through an area bordered by low rocky hills and arrived, finally, at a structure, an old, semi-abandoned chicken farm. A middle-aged man came out to greet us wearing long, dusty robes and opened his arms wide.

'We are so pleased to see you,' he said in perfect English.

It turned out he was the Polisario Front's ambassador to the United Nations and their most senior international diplomat. We all had dinner together at a small table in a huge hall that used to be part of the chicken farm, and in these bizarre surroundings, in this forgotten corner of the planet, he gave us a breakdown on why President Obama would never be able to transform America.

'It's like this,' he said. 'In America, the president only has, say, 20 per cent of the power. Then Congress has another 10 per cent, the Senate has 10 per cent, the corporations have 20 per cent, the Supreme Court has 10 per cent, God has 10 per cent and then I suspect Rupert Murdoch has the rest.' We all laughed.

Anya and I were billeted together in a mouldy old room empty of furniture with a flickering single bulb hanging from a curiously long cord. I was spreading out our sleeping bags on the floor when I heard a chuckle from the adjoining washroom.

'Take a look at this,' said Anya.

In the corner of the tiled room, which had a bucket, a piece of hose attached to a tap, and a hole in the concrete floor for all manner of wash and waste to drop down, was a scorpion. It was huge, an almost translucent greeny-yellow, and had its back to the wall.

'Do you think the Moroccans put this here to get us?' Anya said with a smile.

We watched it for a moment as it tested the walls and air around it, then remembered we should film it, and then after we had exhausted every angle and shot, I scooped it into our empty plastic food box, very, very carefully, closed the lid and we took it for a walk outside. The ambassador took a peek and yelped. He said in English it was called a deathstalker, of all things, and that it was one of the most dangerous desert scorpions.

'It might not kill you,' he said. 'But the pain is so terrible you might wish it had.'

We wanted to release it a healthy distance from the farm so it didn't decide to return, so we climbed a low, rocky hill, set it free into the dark night, moved a sensible distance away, and then finally had a moment to ourselves in the desert to enjoy the magical life of the universe above.

We missed the independence day parade by a full day but the Polisario Front generously restaged it for us, with hundreds of young soldiers wearing camouflage and dark blue berets and brandishing semi-automatics lining up in formation in front of a long line of tanks. The Polisario, which had been formed from local tribes to resist what they saw as a Moroccan invasion, claimed they still had a standing army of more than 20,000. Officially they don't have officers, but we met a charming and modest man called Fadli Larossi who was the equivalent of a colonel and seemed to be in command. He explained he had been at university in Madrid when the war started, but abandoned his studies to sign up and had been in the military ever since. Under his thick moustache he had the warmest of smiles.

Fadli invited us to his tented home in a Saharawi refugee camp over the border in Algeria, which required another sweaty and spectacular drive across a couple of hundred miles of the Sahara. Our route took us near enough to the northern end of Morocco's sand berm barrier to see soldiers patrolling along it, but not close enough to set off the vast fields of landmines that, with the berm, also divide Western Sahara in two. The tragedy of the berm, and part of why it is such a scandal, is that it still splits relatives stuck on opposite sides after the war.

'It's dividing families,' said Fadli in a sad, lost voice. 'You will find some son there, some daughter here, some father there, mother here.'

Tindouf, where Fadli lived, was home to more than 100,000 refugees, all living in a vast network of single-storey houses and tents that fanned out across the desert. They had all been invited by the Moroccan state to return to their native land, but the offer of limited autonomy was not enough for the Polisario, which insists on full independence for Western Sahara. So instead they stayed put in the desert.

I asked Fadli what it meant to live on the independent side of the huge sand barrier. He explained he did not see his father or other members of his family for 30 years until the UN arranged a special visit in 2005. He expected that would be their last sight of each other. The vast refugee camp was one of the saddest yet also happiest places I've ever been to. The people were welcoming, charming and inspiring, but there was no getting around the fact they had been marooned there since 1975. Children in the camp had known no other life.

Fadli hoped that one day his youngsters could meet their

relatives on the other side of the divide, but it was difficult to imagine how or when that might come to pass. Even Fadli struggled to imagine the situation changing.

'This is our destiny,' Fadli told me.

Fadli had invited us to eat and film in his smart tented home,
with his wife and young sons and daughters. They all fell on
Anya. It was beautiful to observe how rapidly and intimately
women embraced her and took her in, chatting about their lives
and doing her nails and giving us a window into lives that are
sometimes hidden in traditional North African communities. As
a woman she opened doors into families in a way that would be
closed if we were just a group of guys. It was in the desert that
Anya had really come into her own. The hotter it was, the more
she seemed to thrive. She proved she was rough, tough and easily
as hardy as the rest of us at enduring the privations, heat and
difficulty. But the appreciation of her went a bit too far when
we travelled further across southern Algeria, to an ancient trading post on the edge of the desert where a guide took us to a
camel market.

'Nomads know wealth is not about owning banks or aero-
planes,' a breeder and trader in a huge turban and wealthy robes
explained to me. 'It's about having camels.'

He was a rich man, with several hundred beasts. Speaking
French through an interpreter, he earnestly said he was prepared
to offer me 20 camels in return for my wife. I politely declined.

Algeria was just emerging nervously from a ten-year nightmare,
a civil war sparked when the military-backed government
cancelled an election that the Islamist Salvation Front seemed
destined to win. The conflict had claimed at least 150,000 lives.
In many ways the country was still cut off from the outside

world, with visitors and foreign media effectively banned. But we had a secret weapon in the form of our London-based producer Elena Cosentino. One of the most spirited and persuasive people I've ever met, Elena never takes no for an answer, and she moved mountains to get us Algerian visas and secure permission for us to travel across the country.

An Algerian government minder shadowed us everywhere, and, at times, heavily armed secret police were guarding us. We had absurd situations where we were even followed around guest houses and hotels by agents pretending to be workers or guests. In one huge, dusty and completely empty hotel in the south of Algeria that had not received visitors for years, we were the only guests eating breakfast together in a vast empty dining hall containing perhaps forty other bare tables when a man wearing a football tracksuit came and sat down at the very next table, then completely blanked us when we tried to say good morning. We found the surveillance almost amusing, so all picked up our plates and cutlery and moved another five tables over. He did the same. Giggling, we kept asking him to at least tell us his name, but he never cracked. He simply had to keep a close eye on us, and we simply had to accept the monitoring.

In return for permission to film where we wanted in the far south of the country close to the Tropic of Cancer, we had informally agreed with the Algerian culture ministry that we wanted to film the culture of the Tuareg people, which, to the ministry's credit, they were trying to promote. I was keen, but then I discovered they wanted us to drive for two hours back into the desert, in the wrong direction, to witness a recital by a local, ancient Tuareg musician.

Algeria, now the largest country in Africa, is nearly 1 million square miles in size. To give you a sense of scale, if we transplanted Algeria over the top of Europe, it would stretch at its widest points north to south from Liverpool to Gibraltar, and east to west from Dublin to Warsaw. It is vast, and the last thing we wanted to be doing was head the wrong way. But we had little choice. Two hours then became three, then four, until finally we arrived at a sheltered camp on the far side of low rock hills. It was a glimpse back into the medieval Sahara. Tuareg tribesmen were perfectly attired, all in blue and white, sitting in a line on carpets in the sand in front of a veteran, elderly musician playing an imzad, a famous one-stringed fiddle, while sitting on another carpet on the ground under an awning of animal skins and surrounded by a low woven windbreak. Tuareg women rarely cover their faces, but the Tuareg men were all wearing traditional turbans that concealed everything but their eyes.

The entire scene looked like, felt like, and *was* a completely airbrushed government-sponsored heritage promotion. There were some haunting sounds, but nobody could confirm what music the veteran performer was playing, which meant nobody could sign a 'performers' release form' which we have to carry with us, and without which we cannot broadcast music for fear of opening the BBC to a massive claim by someone who owns the rights. Boring, but that's copyright.

'I think we might need to use the strawberry filter for this JY,' I said to Jonathan, which is a telly code for when you press the buttons on a camera but don't, shall we say, put too much effort into filming.

However we showed willing, and were allowed to continue our journey back, again, across the desert of southern Algeria to the oasis town of Tamanrasset, guided by an energetic chap called Said Chitour, who was fluent in English and a fountain of knowledge about every square inch of the country. He had been a tour guide until 1992, when the war began and the tourists stopped coming, and he then turned to journalism and became a facilitator for visiting film crews from all over the world, what we call a fixer. He was frank and forthright about the hell his country had lived through.

'You can't imagine how the Algerian people suffered from terror,' he said as we drank tea together. 'Nobody knows how our people suffered here – men and women, innocent people killed, slaughtered, kidnapped, raped; it was awful. I wish that one day the peace comes back totally in my country, and then the people will live normally as anybody around the world.'

Flanked by barren red crags, Tamanrasset is an ancient cross-roads in the desert, and as such it was on the route for migrants from sub-Saharan Africa heading for the Mediterranean and Europe beyond. Up to 30,000 were said to be in the town at any one time. For the previous few days they had started to become a familiar feature on our journey across the Sahara. We would see figures in the heat haze whose outlines, the closer we got to them, would solidify into small groups of gritty young Black men trekking along stony tracks at awesome speed. Often they'd be in flip-flops. There were very few places in the Sahara in which to seek shade, even fewer to find water and certainly none for food. They seemed to be running on empty. We were a few hours outside Tamanrasset and heading towards the border with Libya when we started encountering small groups who looked parched under the blazing sun. I wanted to stop and give them a lift.

'We absolutely cannot,' our guide Said said softly. 'If we do they might swarm our vehicle.'

'Swarm?' I said.

'They are not dangerous,' he went on, 'but desperate people will do desperate things.' He talked of migrants climbing on to vehicles and refusing to get off, and then more migrants doing the same until the vehicles collapse on their axles. Plus, he said, if the authorities caught us helping the illegal migrants they might kick us out and arrest the young men.

There were dozens, then scores, of young guys on the move. Clearly we couldn't take all of them. Still I found it very difficult to drive past. We talked on our walkie-talkies with Dominic and Anya, who were in the other car, and at their suggestion we started leaving water bottles a quarter of a mile ahead of each group.

Many times they would start running towards us hoping we would offer them a ride. We would wait until they could see we were leaving them water and our food and then we had to leave. It was awful. I hate being unable to help. I find it one of the hardest aspects of the journeys. But you have to understand we were not in Surrey. We were not an American TV network with helicopters as back-up. We were on our own and really quite exposed in an uncontrolled and dangerous environment. So we had to drive past and drive on. And my goodness there were hundreds of them. West Africans were coming from Senegal, Nigeria, Cameroon, searching for a better life, so many seduced by the filtered reality of satellite TV, or lured north by a relative or friend who had made it to Europe only to discover the only work was illegal semi-slavery on a farm in Spain, but who feared losing face back home and had sent them a selfie next to a flash car outside a supermarket or in Marbella. Riches shimmered like a mirage on the other side of the Mediterranean if they could only make it across the Sahara.

I can completely understand why so many desperate and

hopeful souls go on the long journey of migration. Humans have always gone on the move in search of a better life. I've seen poverty and struggle across Africa, visiting something like 24 countries on the continent, and heard intimate stories of migration from people at every stage of the journey, including from those who have made it across the water to places like Greece, Spain and Italy. I've reluctantly come to the conclusion that the migration of many young African men is often a disaster. Not always, but often.

I explained more about my feelings regarding migration and immigration in *Step by Step*, so it would be wrong to repeat them all again. But essentially I think it's often a tragedy and even a racket that deprives poorer countries of their brightest and best.

To pay the way of young men, families and even entire villages in West Africa will regularly borrow money in the belief that the lad could get a decent job in Europe. But the odds are not on their side. My impossible journeys could never, ever, remotely match theirs. Only the strongest and the smartest can survive the forbidding obstacle course of the Sahara, people smugglers, human sharks, corrupt officials and the sheer physical privations. So we end up with some of Africa's cleverest and most ambitious young men selling illegal CDs to tourists on the Costas. It seems one of the great wastes of human potential to me. Years later in Spain I talked to a clever young migrant who was working in the plastic greenhouse farms from which northern Europe gets its winter vegetables. I asked him how many of his friends had made a success out of migration. He could think of only one, and that was a guy who had literally won the state lottery.

'Everyone in Africa thinks that you'll find money easily in Europe,' he told me. 'That's a total lie.'

In south-eastern Algeria we drove through the Tassili N'Ajjer

National Park, a stunning patch of desert that offered us a parade of wind-carved rock formations, crenellated cairns and piles of boulders that were almost arranged architecturally. At sunrise the shifting sands were the colour of burnt orange, changing to gold by mid-morning, and then to bleached white by the middle of the day. It was utterly breathtaking. After a few hours we arrived at the border. Our goal was to cross into Libya through a post that, thanks to tense relations between the two countries, had been shut to Algerians for years and to foreigners for decades. It ought to have been absolutely impossible to enter Libya here.

But we had Elena on our side. Our producer had flown to see officials in the capital of Algeria and almost banged tables there and at the Libyan embassy to make sure her TV crew could cross the border. Eventually she got her way. We arrived at the dustiest, sleepiest, remotest, most flyblown outpost of Algeria's Border Agency. Desert grass was growing on the track that led through to Libya. Two young conscripts were on duty. One was asleep. An official had travelled the last leg with us to make sure we were able to cross.

'You will tell Miss Elena that we brought you here, won't you?' he said to us, just slightly nervously. Elena is now the Director of the International News Safety Institute (INSI). Next I'd like to see if she could sort out problems in the Middle East, resolve old conflicts, maybe run the UN. There could be nobody better.

As paperwork was completed it was time to bid farewell to Said Chitour. When we say goodbye to a guide or fixer, some-times it's the last contact we will have. They might be working with another TV crew the next week, and we'll be just one of dozens of teams they see come and go. But in trickier countries that don't allow much filming, we might be the only outsiders they see for a year. I was in occasional contact with Said after we left, and was horrified when, years later, he was arrested by the Algerian authorities and charged with espionage. Travellers and journalists who had worked with him collectively decided it could be dangerous for us to make a fuss about him internationally, as that would likely reinforce a suggestion he was too cosy with foreigners, but I talked about him on stage on my theatre tour and tried to impress on people the risks that guides and fixers like him take to be involved in the programmes. Fortunately Said was released after 16 months in prison.

We crossed out of Algeria to be greeted by a group of Libyan officials who had been required to travel all the way from Tripoli, the coastal capital, to stamp our passports and shadow and guard us into the country. Our guides come in all shapes and guises, and are often much closer to spies than enablers. Sometimes they defy any attempt to pigeonhole them. Having crossed into Libya we were met in the border town of Ghat by a very short and thoroughly shady-looking government minder in a red baseball cap called Ahmed Tareq. With his crown of black ringlets he bore an uncanny resemblance to the dictator Colonel Gaddafi. Ahmed would often wander off with me for a chat. He didn't speak brilliant English but told me several times he did indeed share a common ancestor with Gaddafi and that they were related. By the end of the first evening he also had us in stitches with a perfect Charlie Chaplin impression.

Ahmed was definitely quirky, but I owe him a major debt for taking us to visit one of the most spectacular sites along the entire Tropic of Cancer. Southern Libya has some of the most beautiful desert in the entire Sahara. After crossing the border we headed off-road, our route through the Sahara taking us over towering golden sand dunes for hours. We raced up the side of perhaps the biggest dune of all, our engine screaming, Jonathan and I both willing it on, and then we stopped at the top and looked out, speechless. The sun was baking, the sky was a perfect deep blue, and we were staring at a huge lake in the desert fringed by wetland grasses and date palms, nestling underneath vast dunes. It looked impossible, it looked too extreme – it looked like it had been created by CGI.

Despite being a bone-dry ocean of sand, there are vast reserves of water deep beneath some parts of the Sahara. In that area the water table reached the surface to form an oasis called the Ubari Lakes. The water, surprisingly cool, was as salty as the Dead Sea, so when Ahmed and I dived in we bobbed around like corks.

Water has always been one of the biggest issues for the countries of North Africa that straddle the Sahara. I had become a little obsessed with the story of the Garamantians, a Black African civilisation that traded with ancient Rome and developed complex irrigation systems to channel and control water in the desert so they could become proficient farmers. Sadly there was little of their civilisation left to film, and after travelling across Libya we were due to pause my journey along the Tropic of Cancer to head home for a few weeks to plan the future legs of the series. But Anya and I spent a few extra days up on the Mediterranean coast of Libya and went to visit the Roman site of Leptis Magna. Once home to 80,000 and a vital port for shipping grain from Rome's African colonies, Leptis Magna is one of the finest preserved Roman cities on the planet. Among the archaeological treasures to emerge from excavations that began during the Italian occupation of the 1930s were theatres, streets, a market, aqueducts and a basilica. It is a stunning place, full of giant rock walls and soaring columns, and fantastically romantic for us to wander around when illuminated at night.

In the years that followed, Libya suffered two terrible civil wars. In the first, pro-Gaddafi forces used Leptis Magna to cover and shelter military vehicles during the conflict that resulted in the dictator's death. Then in 2016, the site suffered an even graver threat as parts of the country fell to the Islamic State extremists. As Leptis Magna became vulnerable to capture by the forces of darkness, a small group of courageous local men, young and old, mustered there to defend it.

Just after Islamic State had been pushed away from the ancient site, but were still gathered in the desert just a short drive to the south, I travelled to Leptis Magna to meet some of the local Libyan heroes who had defended their heritage. They spoke eloquently about how they would have died to protect the planet's culture from the barbarians at the gate.

'We didn't have any training,' one of them told me, 'and the weapons were our own. But it was our duty. If we don't protect this heritage it will be destroyed.'

'We will protect this site,' said another. 'From one generation to the next.'

The encounter brought a lump to my throat. Their lesson was clear: our lives are nothing without our past, without our history, without our culture, without our civilisation and old stones. It all matters, because it gives meaning.

CHAPTER SIX

The Headmistress

I have always wanted to have children. Ever since I was young I knew I wanted to have a large brood of littlers, with all the squabbles and exhaustion and love that brings, and for years the thought of having a family seemed the most possible journey of all. Almost everybody does it, after all. There were times when I idly considered the optimum number. Perhaps four, I thought. That should do it. When Anya and I started dating we knew we were both too old to waste time on a relationship where the other wanted a completely different life. So we talked early on about the important stuff: whether it's best to earn money or enjoy life; urban or rural; action movies vs arty; kids or fancy-free. I took a deep breath and told her I could happily compromise on anything and everything else, but I *needed* to have children. Ideally several. She raised an eyebrow, humoured me, but made clear her absolute maximum was two because there were already too many humans on the planet. Secretly I thought she'd love the first couple so much she'd be happy to churn out more. Then after we started talking about getting married, she sat me down and laid out her cards.

'Look,' she said, well before we were engaged, 'I don't want to put pressure on you, and I'm not saying I have to have children, but biology means it's going to get harder for me. I don't want to end up on the other side of 40 and you say, "Let's have kids," and then I can't get pregnant and we end up splitting up because of it.'

I didn't take it in. At that point we were travelling the world, going once, then twice around the planet, and we had other ideas for journeys and books popping into our heads all of the time. We were travelling for up to six months out of a year, filming and writing. We were crossing oceans and continents and notching up decades of memories and experiences. I always thought the babies would come, but at an appropriate moment. They would be slotted into a schedule. Our schedule. Nature would play ball and fall in with our plans.

I was also a commitment-phobe, reluctant to agree to anything that tied me down. I wanted to carry on travelling and enjoying life, as I saw it. Anya and I were endlessly on filming trips but also holidays, exploring the Brecon Beacons, Scotland, hiking and skiing in the Alps, or taking the train further afield, to Denmark, Spain, Italy, even Greece and Albania. I loved every experience. I took my longest train ride with my brother, when we went from London all the way across Europe to Istanbul, with a pit stop in Vienna.

I was so in love with the experiences that I was blind to the passage of time and the potential joy of responsibility. Although already in my late thirties, in my head I was much younger, and infected by the delusion that obligations and relationships might stop me doing what I wanted, and prevent me having great experiences.

I was so wrapped up in my early journeys that I even said no when a close friend asked me to be a godfather to his daughter. Looking back now I feel ashamed that I wriggled out of the honour. And I am baffled as to what I was thinking. I don't recognise that person. I came up with reasons why I thought it wouldn't be a good idea. I wasn't the right person. I wasn't worthy of the responsibility. I was never at home. And I said I'd just recovered from malaria, I was travelling to danger zones and taking risks in life, and in truth perhaps I felt I might not be around for ever.

Marriage changed me. As it should. I signed myself up for a partnership. And the sky didn't fall on me. I was still able to have extraordinary experiences. Yet I wasn't even thinking about children.

It didn't take long for me to be on the receiving end of an almighty, life-changing jolt. Anya and I were married. We had just finished filming the *Tropic of Capricorn* series. It was a glorious August and we were staying at Anya's family summer house on the coast of Denmark, seeing friends and family, reading long books, playing slow chess, plotting future adventures, pottering on the beach and taking endless bike rides, when my brother came to visit.

With hindsight I should have realised James had something major to share. He came on his own, without his partner Elsa, and Anya could see he was glowing with excitement and joy. But I was too wrapped up in myself to see the train hurtling down the track. We walked down to the end of the garden and, as we looked out across the Baltic Sea, he turned and said he had something to tell me. I looked at him blankly. I honestly had no idea what was coming. My brain didn't even start running through options.

'Elsa's pregnant!' he said.

Now I look back on it I can think of only one other time when my brain has moved at such staggering speed as I tried to register and react to new information. I was in Australia with a bunch of burly firefighters in their workshop. I was in the middle of talking to camera, marvelling at their armoury of chainsaws, wrecking bars, hydrants and hoses. I picked up a large axe by the head and was in the middle of a sentence when I idly ran my thumb along the cutting edge. My axes at home are far from dull, but they won't cut anything other than timber. This axe was razor-sharp like a Samurai sword and my thumb split instantly. In that fraction of a second, even as words came out of my mouth, my brain fired off a rat-a-tat series of instructions. 'Don't stop talking. Don't tell them what's happened. They will definitely use it in the programme. You will look like a total muppet.' So I clenched my thumb into my hand and squeezed tight. I didn't break stride in my sentence. I watched it back afterwards, and there was just a flicker across my face. I carried on talking, moved across the room, talked to a firefighter, rested my arm and clenched fist on a bench vice, felt thick warm blood dripping from my hand, ambled around again and then we stopped filming.

'Erm, is that blood on the floor?' said one of the firefighters.

'Oh hell!' I said with surprise, opening my hand and letting the blood gush free. 'How did that happen!?'

This was like that. In the instant my brother announced that he was to have a child, my brain went from zero to 100 in a fraction of a second. Even now I remember the moment with astonishing clarity – the light, the sea, the weather, even the gentle wind rustling his hair, for goodness' sake. It was a moment of joy. My brother was having a baby!

Genuine delight was still spreading across my face and just starting to emerge in the form of an exultant roar. I was ecstatic for James and Elsa. My arms began raising to clasp his shoulders, when a series of electrical impulses fired around my brain like heavy machine-gun fire. It was a eureka moment for me. By the time my hands were resting on his shoulders, and even as my heart swelled with genuine champagne-popping joy, my head felt like I was being slapped hard on the forehead. You idiot, my inner voice was telling me. You total idiot.

My brain was whirring. James was having a baby. He is two years younger than me. My brother was taking the greatest life step before me. I was nearly 40. My wife was nearly 40. I desperately wanted children. But we had not even been trying. What on earth had we been waiting for? Anya's clock was ticking. *My* clock was ticking. I was nearly the age my dad was when he had me. I had always thought of him as an old dad and that, unlike him, I would have children when I was younger. Being an old dad was now to be my unavoidable fate too. In that second – in that fraction of a second – all of this rocketed around my head, and I realised I had made the greatest mistake of my life.

Perhaps the most painful aspect of the thunderbolt was my instant realisation we were now far too old to achieve my dream of filling our lives with children. We were too old to have three children, let alone the four that I still secretly hoped for despite Anya's warning years earlier. I would be lucky to get the two she had insisted was her limit.

I had done something I endlessly castigate and encourage others to avoid doing. I had waited. I had put something off. I had thought I had more time. I had missed what really mattered to me. I had been too focused on my journeys and adventures. I had missed getting on with what I wanted most in life: children.

Luckily, just as when I sliced my thumb on the axe, none of this showed on my face. I have thought back to it a thousand times. Perhaps it was self-obsession to let that moment of such joy be contaminated by my own regret. I have beaten myself up again and again for not focusing entirely on James's wonderful news. But we are complicated creatures. Life can be joy, revelation and sorrow in the same moment. The only thing I truly regret is my failure to realise the blindingly biologically obvious until that split second.

I still can't understand why I hadn't seen it before. Why was I putting it off? For years I had relished the prospect of one day having a family, of having children I could love and who would need me. The responsibility of providing for them would be my focus. Indeed, I'd go so far as to say that vision of my future, as a parent with children, helped to keep me stable and sane as I rushed around the planet. But parenting was a can that I kept kicking a little further down the road. Children were something that we would do at the best time for us. They would be scheduled in around one trip or another – because of course it could never be difficult to have children, could it? Almost everyone seems to bang them out.

Not that we actually had a house to fill with kids. We had Anya's little basement flat, recently extended. City dwellers living in small rooms often feel, consciously or not, that they aren't ready for children, and that the time isn't right. Perhaps that was another factor that caused us to delay. I had never owned a home, which still made me feel like I was a rootless 20-something. Nor did I feel financially secure. I was living from project to project. Looking back, I guess I was waiting for that mythical 'right time'.

I also blame Anya. She had lulled me into a false sense of security by looking years younger than her late thirties. There was no visual signal her years of fertility might be finite. I'd also heard lots of reassuring stories about women having kids in their forties, and if our family and friends had been wagging their fingers at us telling us to get a move on, well, I hadn't been listening.

Anya and I talked, late into the night.

'What have we done?' I said, wracked with regret.

'Well,' she said, rather more calmly. 'I think you felt the journeys were just too much of an issue.' Without wishing to invite you too far inside the bedroom door, let's just say we cracked on there and then. Out went the protection we'd unthinkingly been using up till then – it was almost ceremonially tossed out of the window – and we began trying for a child that very night.

I realise this is intimate. I wasn't sure whether to include it in this book. Especially because I want my son to read it. And then I thought what the hell. I have no choice. This book is about my journeys to impossible places. All my journeys. And as such it's about my experiences, my salvation, my successes, but it's definitely also about rocky roads and colossal failures. The details that follow might seem a little grubby, but they are a huge part of my story, Anya's, and that of thousands of other hopeful parents on the same emotional roller coaster. This is really just Life. And I want to be honest about what we went through. Because maybe it could even help someone else. When I was growing up, so much advertising and advice screamed at me and my generation that we had to be shockingly careful near the opposite sex. I had the fear of God put into me. If we even so much as whipped out our bits near them we might get AIDS, or end up with a teen pregnancy. Turns out it isn't always so easy for everyone. If you want to have children with a future partner, a sensible number, not too many, don't imagine that Mother Nature will be happy to twiddle her thumbs and, when you decide the time is right, dance to your tune.

We spent months trying for a child, and nothing happened. We started planning out the Tropic of Cancer journey. And nothing happened. We went to see an expensive fertility specialist, who gave us lots of tips on how to get pregnant. Some might seem obvious – when to have sex, how often, and in what positions. But everyone had a different opinion. We had acupuncture, hypnotherapy. The zaniest recommendation was that we should have sex upside down. Still nothing happened.

By the time of the first Tropic of Cancer journey, we had started to take a more sophisticated and scientific approach to conception, attempting to time it right according to Anya's body temperature. Which meant whenever, and wherever, we were. On a Mexican ferry, in an abandoned film set, up a mountain. It wasn't easy when we were on the road. But it was a damn sight more viable than if we were in different continents.

By the time of our adventure across the Sahara we were getting pretty professional about it. Everywhere, endlessly. It was wonderful, but also exhausting, and frustration was gradually giving way to fear. Because still, nothing was happening. The night after we encountered the mysterious Tuareg in the desert, my brother and sister-in-law became parents. Little Alice Reeve entered the world. We found out the news via satellite phone. I danced in the desert and cracked open an illicit small bottle of whisky I'd been smuggling around with us precisely for that moment. I could not possibly have been happier, and I derived a huge sense of reassurance from the idea that at least I was an uncle.

But nothing was happening for us. I had a looming awareness of what it would mean to miss out on having children. I told Anya that unless I could have children I was very likely to go mad. I didn't think I would be able to cope with life if I couldn't become a father. She felt much calmer, and counselled me it was very much in the lap of the gods. I simply couldn't face accepting blind fate. My attitude was more defiant. We work and work and work and we make things happen. We do whatever we have to do.

We had to pass through Algiers, the capital of Algeria, while filming in the country. Our fixer Said and a small squad of armed undercover Algerian secret police ('Just for your protection, Mr Reeve, nothing to worry about') took us on a tour of the famous Casbah, the old citadel of the city and traditional quarter, a warren of markets, tightly packed houses and tiny streets, where *The Battle of Algiers*, one of my favourite movies, was filmed.

We went down twisting alleyways to the Mausoleum of Sidi Abderrahmane Et-Thaalibi, the patron saint of the city, in an ancient part of the lower Casbah. It was a shrine, but also a place of learning and worship. People threw open their arms to welcome us in. A group of women gathered around Anya. They didn't get many foreign visitors. Within about two minutes they were asking about her children. When she said she didn't have any but we were trying, the women, immediately concerned and excited, hustled her away.

A short woman called Hania, wearing jeans, bright red glasses and a long red puffer jacket, pulled her along into an inner sanctum room, lit by candelabras, vaulted to a high ceiling and lined with turquoise tiles, and over towards an enormous wooden chest of drawers in a corner. Hania opened one of the bottom drawers and reverently removed a heavy cotton orange hooded cloak, embroidered and trimmed with gold brocade.

'Please, you must wear this,' she said, already starting to lift it on to Anya's shoulders. 'It is for baby-making,' she laughed, 'an ancient fertility cloak.'

Anya emerged back out of the room, looking flushed and self-conscious, for all of us to see, and whispered to me what was going on.

'Well I think we'll take all the help we can get, don't you think?' I said, as we both stifled a smile.

The women, who all seemed to be about a foot smaller than Anya, gathered around her, fussing and tweaking and arranging the cloak. And then they prayed for her. For us. For our future. It was sweet and poignant and done in a beautiful and sisterly way, and it brought home to us more than ever how badly we had miscalculated.

During our brief period at home in London we went back to see yet more pricey fertility specialists. By then we had been trying to conceive for many months and nothing had happened. They suggested that Anya should have some tests. The default perception always seems to be that there must be something wrong with the woman's reproductive equipment. They began checking her hormone levels, then her tubes, and everything seemed fine. So attention turned to me. The baby-making guru we were seeing suggested I should see an expert in male fertility at a different private clinic.

I filled in forms, questionnaires and long documents detailing my lifestyle and my nutritional intake, or the lack thereof. Then I entered the world of sperm tests. It was a demoralising and unsettling experience. First of all I had to produce a sample, which was sent off for analysis. Then Anya and I went together back to the clinic to learn the results. For a natural pessimist, I felt surprisingly chirpy. We were shown up to a small attic room that had a cold, medical feel about it.

'Feels like we're being sent for detention,' I said quietly to Anya, as the fertility specialist bustled in and sat down with my notes. She had a cool manner, like a headmistress, but perhaps she was just unwilling to comfort me with inappropriate warmth.

'I've got your test results,' she said, 'and I think you should prepare yourself for some bad news.'

I was still smiling wanly, feeling a little bemused and remote from the whole situation.

'I won't make any bones about it,' she tapped the papers. 'I'm very sorry to have to tell you, but you are basically infertile.'

You will not be able to conceive.

You will not be able to have children.

It was the starkest of messages.

I could hardly take it in. She started breaking it down in detail. I had loads of sperm, but their morphology was terrible. We'd never heard of the term, but she explained it relates to their shape and structure.

'Your sperm are deformed,' said the headmistress, looking over her glasses at me. 'They will never be able to break into Anya's eggs.' She started listing different figures from my sperm test.

I had 0 per cent normal sperm. Zero. Nothing.

They had also checked sperm motility. My sperm were swimming around in circles, or moving energetically without going anywhere. They were bloody useless.

'But surely,' Anya said, 'there's something we could do? He works all hours, eats fairly badly, doesn't get enough sleep. He could have earlier nights, live more healthily.'

The headmistress shook her head.

'I'm sorry, but no,' she said. 'I don't want to give you unrealistic levels of hope.' She was adamant that morphology is one of the hardest things possible to improve. As the specialist talked on, Anya listened. I was quickly lost to my thoughts, fears and raw emotion. I was completely reeling. I felt utterly sickened. I remember swaying in my seat. It didn't feel like reality.

There seemed to be no way around the specialist's verdict. Natural conception was impossible. I was told there was no chance that I could have my own baby. My sperm were not viable. I was on an impossible journey to an impossible place – siring my own child.

It was a long walk back, in every sense, to our flat in north London. I was in a daze, as if I'd been drugged. I was so disconnected I couldn't mentally associate myself with my body, which I now felt was badly letting me down. The sunny park looked like a film set with tons of people pushing prams. You never notice them more than when you're desperately trying for a child. I could hear the sound of every laughing child and crying baby. A DJ I knew from Radio 1 said hello, then a couple of people who recognised me from the TV. Anya says I looked straight through them. I was in a complete brain-fog daze. To my shame – because this was her loss too – she had to console me the entire way as I struggled with the dismal thought that I had no biological destiny. It was such a profound shock. I felt I had been deprived at a stroke of my very reason for being.

We tried to book another follow-up appointment at the original clinic to hear what they thought. We couldn't get one for two weeks, a very long 14 days in which I bounced along at rock bottom trying to grapple with a new reality. For the first time in decades, I was being told that I couldn't make something happen through sheer willpower or hard work. I had lost control of a situation where, more than any other, I wanted to be in charge. I was being told there was nothing I could do to change it. This was nature, biology and destiny. It was immovable, unalterable. My sperm were incapable of going on their own biological journey. Ironically enough, they were not good travellers.

I really started to beat myself up. The headmistress had mentioned how sperm are affected by heat. Sperm are sensitive and are particularly badly affected by environmental factors such as heat, pollution and chemicals. She told Anya that many men who spend their days sitting at computers, or drive taxis or lorries, are effectively cooking their sperm. Had I done the same with my trips to the Tropics? Over and over again I kept thinking of the time I had walked into a nuclear waste dump in Kyrgyzstan in Central Asia, wearing a full face respirator and a nuclear, biological and chemical warfare suit that was only a little thicker than a shower curtain. The sun had roasted me inside the suit to the point where I thought I was going to collapse. I had to sit down, on top of the radioactive nuclear waste dump. Even at the time I thought the physical proximity of my testicles – my reproductive organs – to the ground was A Bad Idea. Then there were all those journeys where I'd squashed and squeezed myself into tiny vehicles and small planes in tropical corners of the world. I just couldn't stop thinking that I had boiled or irradiated my own testicles.

Anya was also deeply upset, of course. But we were different. Where I thought of children as a mental imperative as well as a biological need, Anya had never felt the same requirement to derive a purpose in life from parenthood. She's one of the lucky few who is happy existing rather than seeking meaning. Perhaps in our case, the opposites really do attract. Where she is happy simply to be, I liked to do. I *needed* to do.

She was a lot calmer than me during those dark days, and took the practical position that all was not lost. She was sceptical about the sheer finality of the verdict, having heard from a good friend who had been through a similar experience, albeit with not quite so catastrophic a verdict, that sperm morphology could be improved by dramatically changing a diet.

'We are not giving up, change is always possible,' she would say, as I risked sinking into a miasma of depression.

With dark thoughts occupying my head, we finally got to see the original specialist. She was sympathetic and calming. My sperm test results were definitely not good, she agreed. But she did offer a little light. The headmistress, she said, had perhaps been a little black and white with her devastating conclusion. Although we would not be able to conceive normally, or even with IVF, there were other options. Had we thought about a sperm donor? Adoption? Fostering? Or it might be possible to inject my sperm directly into Anya's eggs in a more complicated form of IVF called ICSI. But before any of that, she thought we should both see a nutritionist – in another oak-panelled room in another expensive private medical practice in the centre of London.

Kathy the nutritionist was much more positive and hopeful, and gave me long lists of instructions about what I needed to cut out, and what I needed to include. The lifestyle reboot that ensued included some obvious changes. Smoking cannabis and drinking too much may have impaired my sperm. So they had to go. I had to dramatically reduce caffeine, chocolate, wine, sugar, salt and a lot else that made life tasty. The nutritionist prescribed berries for antioxidants and a healthy new diet. I started necking zinc tablets and other pill-sized treats and later started taking Wellman fertility tablets.

But I now know what I didn't then: something more funda-mentally worrying is happening between our thighs. Male fertility is in a downward spiral. Some experts believe the sperm counts of Western men have fallen by more than 50 per cent over recent decades. It appears male and female reproductive development are under attack by our modern world. Some have even labelled it 'Spermageddon'.

The sperm count is falling, and the number of defective sperm seems to be growing. Like me, men are producing more deformed sperm, sperm with two heads, and sperm that are static and listless rather than chasing energetically after a female egg. In women, many researchers believe there is evidence of an increasing number of miscarriages among women of all ages, declining egg quality – not just because of lifestyle or people having babies later – and more girls experiencing early puberty.

One of the most significant problems affecting fertility is endocrine-disrupting chemicals (EDCs), which can mimic and interfere with the hormones that regulate and run our bodies, blocking some hormones or tricking our exquisitely fine-tuned systems into over- or under-responding in different ways. EDCs are used in plastic and thousands of products to help make our stuff, including cosmetics, plastics, toys, clothes, soft furnishings and pesticides. They're even used in the linings of many tinned foods to stop them corroding. Usually they're not even listed on labels. Yet study after study has shown for decades they are very likely to be risky, dangerous or even catastrophically fatal. As far back as the year 2000, a Royal Society report pointed out: 'It is prudent to minimise exposure of humans, especially pregnant women, to endocrine-disrupting chemicals.'

In 2015 a series of reports by 18 of the world's foremost experts on endocrine science said the health costs of EDCs were up to nearly £200 billion a year in Europe alone, driving lower IQs, adult obesity and some autism cases. Yet still EDCs proliferate, and we use millions and millions of tons of these chemicals every year.

EDCs can make their way into the womb and the foetus, passing the problem down to the next generation. Some chemical companies seem to have actively discouraged safety testing of EDCs, so we still know far too little about what the hell they might be doing to us. The crisis is getting worse, with more women and men, in particular, discovering they are infertile. In terms of the potential impact on the future of humanity, this threat is possibly not far off our climate emergency for importance. And yet it's hardly discussed. Perhaps that will change as it is felt by an ever-expanding number of people who discover they are unable to have children. One senior epidemiologist has even suggested the reproductive crisis could mean that by 2045 most couples will need assisted conception. Some see this as nothing less than threatening the future of the human race.

On the flip side, of course, there will be those who say this might be better for the planet: 'Thank God for fewer humans.' But it ignores the emotional and mental suffering involved with infertility. We need fewer humans, but as a choice, encouraged by governments and through sensible birth control, not as a punishment inflicted upon us. Besides, human infertility is just direct personal evidence of the wider catastrophic damage we are doing to our world, Mother Nature and the environment. It's not just about humans. A range of species are displaying serious genital anomalies, including otters, mink and alligators. Fish, frogs and turtles are appearing with both male and female sexual organs. In one area of the US an astonishing 60 to 100 per cent of the male smallmouth bass studied had female egg cells growing in their testes.

So what should we do to improve our health and our fertility? Clearly the chemical industry needs to be forced to stop producing the harmful chemicals that end up in everyday products. Given the possible consequences, surely our approach to the use of artificial chemicals should be that they are guilty until proven innocent. Governments need to act. Quickly.

Having studied this because of my own problems, my advice, for anyone hoping, wanting or trying to have children is, for goodness' sake, take it seriously. Look it up yourself. But perhaps do what I did. The experts say we should keep food in glass rather than plastic, don't microwave things in plastic containers – switch them to an alternative. Don't get endless takeaways in plastic boxes, buy organic, eat unprocessed food, avoid scented household products and even avoid vinyl shower curtains. Swap your plastic food containers for steel, your plastic kettle for metal, and Stop Using Plastic Water Bottles. Basically live a healthier life, in a healthier place and eat healthier food. Easier said than done, especially if you live a stressed life and are juggling three jobs to make ends meet. And not possible for everyone, of course.

I was a prime candidate for infertility all along. I had consumed, breathed in and been infected by pathogens, viruses, chemicals and God only knows what else all around the planet. On my travels I had eaten food that tasted like plastic. Who knows, perhaps it actually was plastic. It was desperately painful for me to accept that my journeys might have been part of the reason I was going to be unable to have a family.

But Anya's positivity gave me hope. I had my lifestyle overhaul, cutting out so much that was fun. We saw more acupuncturists and alternative lifestyle gurus and assorted health geniuses. Some of their expertise we treated as gospel and some we took with a pinch of salt. We started doing British Military Fitness, intense outdoor group fitness classes run in parks by army instructors, and loved it. Or I loved it. Anya had to be dragged to it saying she wasn't going to be bossed around by a man in camo, but as soon as they made us do a few tests to get a measure of our fitness levels, she gave it her all. She did so many sit-ups to impress them that she had to spend the following day in bed unable to move.

Remembering this now, I am struck that it was Anya who also talked with our friends and asked around among other couples about their experiences with fertility. Like a stereotypical bloke, I pretty much clammed up. I didn't talk to mates about my infertility, or discuss it with anyone who was already a father. I've changed. I now know brooding in silence is the wrong way. We men don't talk about male fertility enough. We don't talk about anything relating to the intimacies of our bodies or our head health nearly enough. At that time my wife did it for me, and she kept me afloat by reminding me change was actually possible, whatever the sperm headmistress had said.

I made other changes designed to tilt the odds in my favour. Most of these were practical solutions aimed at giving my testicles a chance to do their thing. I bought new underwear that let everything hang loose, and traded my way-too-tight jeans for roomier combat trousers. At one point I tried out a rubber ring to sit on that was supposed to allow my undercarriage to hang loose. Seriously. I wanted to have a child and was happy to do anything. There's a whole world of desperation out there. I was instructed to always sit with my legs apart to keep everything that mattered from overheating. So the next time you see a photo in the tabloids shaming a man-spreader on a train, his legs akimbo and knees invading the space of his neighbours, just think, he might be working on his morphology.

CHAPTER SEVEN

India

We thought hard about travelling after my diagnosis. Journeys can be exhausting and there are always risks on the road. I asked the specialists whether I should give up the adventures, even though they weren't just my life, they had become my living. If it would seriously improve our chances of having a child, I was ready to stop travelling. But they pointed out that leaving home behind was also a chance for Anya and I to put our troubles and emotions to one side, to clear our minds of stress. Because we could travel together, we decided to continue.

'Lots of people go somewhere exotic when they're trying to conceive,' said one of our fertility specialists with a cheeky smile.

We restarted the Tropic of Cancer journey in southern Egypt, at the spectacular ancient ruins of Abu Simbel, built to honour Nefertari by her husband King Ramses II, a lucky blighter who managed to have more than 100 children. With my new healthier regime, encouraged and enforced by Anya, I was going to bed earlier, drinking less, eating better and exercising more. I have no idea if it helped, but while travelling I was doing three sets of 50 press-ups on my knuckles each morning, followed by three sets of 40 squats. I was an early adopter of resistance loop bands, essentially giant, thick, tough rubber bands that fit in a pocket but help to provide a workout almost anywhere, even, like a complete nutter, while sitting in a car – as a passenger.

We drove east through Egypt to the Red Sea and snorkelled on pristine coral reef, then across Saudi Arabia to Dubai, absorbing some of the glamour of that surreal and spectacular megacity in the sand, but also meeting a group of workers from India and Bangladesh. They were just some of the hundreds of thousands of migrants who travel to the Gulf in search of decent employment, and they told me horrifying stories of hardship and exploitation. Crossing the border we arrived in Oman, which could not be more different from its brash neighbour. In the ancient city of Nizwa, goats were still being traded in the livestock market. Rather than spending money on mega building projects, the government of Oman was keen to protect and promote its wildlife, and at the most easterly point in the Arabian Peninsula, we found rare giant green turtles laying eggs on a beach. Anya and I filmed and watched as their babies hatched and headed into the surf on their own epic journey.

It was India that I was most excited about visiting. I had never been, so was completely thrilled the Tropic of Cancer crossed the full northern width of the country. I owned at least three coffee-table books about India, and had grown up at a time when Merchant Ivory films were on the TV on a Saturday evening, and tie-dyed backpackers still returned from long, cheap holidays there, wreathed in blissed-out smiles. I thought of India as sprawling, soulful, spiritual, of course, but also booming and thrusting ahead.

We travelled by train to the far north-west of the country with our guide Amit Vachharajani, a bespectacled, easy-going chap with a near-permanent beatific smile nestling under his moustache. Jonathan Young was filming the journey again and Dominic directing. They had both been to India many times before, but I was travelling with fresh, wide eyes. Everything was new, everything was surprising, and everything about the country seemed impossible to me. I couldn't believe I was due to travel 1,500 miles across rarely visited areas of India. I couldn't even believe I was travelling on an Indian train. Like everything in the country, the national rail network was a little crowded. After all, each year it was carrying more than 6 billion passengers, roughly equivalent, at the time, to the population of the entire world.

Our starting point was the Rann of Kutch, a salty clay desert covering 10,000 square miles, which was also a threatened wilderness. We met up with Prince Dhanraj Malik, a passionate conservationist and head of what was once the local royal family – who rather incongruously still had an old stuffed tiger in a glass case in his dining room – and headed out on open-top local jeeps in search of one of the rarest animals in the world.

The monsoon rains were due any day, which would turn the Rann of Kutch into an endless swamp, but until then, under the bright tropical sun, the salty crystals in the earth each seemed to act like a mini magnifying glass. The light was refracted and focused to become the sharpest I've seen anywhere in the world. We drove past a small herd of nilgai, the largest Asian antelope, which to me looked like a strange cross between a horse, a deer and a cow, and then suddenly Dhanraj pulled us up.

'There they are!' said Dhanraj, pointing into the distance. I couldn't even see what he was pointing at, let alone what they were, but as we drew slowly closer, the shapes began to form into a group. The khur, or Indian wild ass, is an elegant beast slightly bigger than a donkey, sturdier and naturally well groomed. Shy creatures, their shiny tan hides were camouflaging them well in parched salt marsh. We crept slowly closer, until they allowed us to stop just 20 or so metres away while they ate and watched us carefully.

'They don't look it, but they're incredibly fast,' said Dhanraj. 'Perhaps the fastest creatures in India.' They also have astonishing stamina, capable of reaching a top speed of more than 40 miles an hour, and then throttling back to run at 15 miles an hour for up to two hours. Sadly that hadn't helped their numbers. They were a gravely endangered animal, threatened by commercial salt farms, pollution and poachers, all partly consequences of India's enormous and rapidly growing population. We went to meet men who worked for hours every day in the salt farms out on the marshes, barefoot and up to their knees in the water. Their lower legs had been ravaged. They told me that lifelong exposure to the salt so infects their limbs that on their final funeral pyre their legs do not burn.

It was that India, the country of impossible stories, suffering and stoicism, that I was hoping to explore along the Tropic of Cancer. The India I would not be visiting was the so-called tourist 'Golden Triangle' connecting Delhi with Rajasthan and the Taj Mahal. A lot of British travel programmes had been along that well-worn path a little too often. Thanks to the gift of the *Tropic of Cancer*, I was able to travel through states that had rarely been seen on British telly.

We hired vehicles to travel east out of the Rann and towards the city of Ahmedabad. Jonathan tried to warn me that Indian roads could be problematic, but I thought I was used to the worst the world could throw at me. I was wrong.

The scales started to fall from my eyes the moment we got into our hire car and turned on to a highway, and I realised these were quite possibly the most dangerous roads I had encountered anywhere on the planet. Within about two minutes we had dodged packed coaches, bullock carts, small cars, giant smoke-belching trucks, ramshackle tractors and cows. Nobody was obeying anything resembling a code. Everyone was driving wherever the hell they wanted, on whatever side of the road they fancied, sometimes driving three abreast straight towards us along roads possibly designed at most for two. Motorcycles would undertake us and overtake us, zooming around. And everywhere there was livestock. Sometimes just standing in the middle of the tarmac, chewing. It was like being stuck in the Frogger arcade game, where you've got to avoid being splatted on the road. It was madness.

I was sitting in the front seat next to our driver, with Amit in the back and Jonathan filming beside him. Within half an hour my knuckles were white from gripping the seat rests. Roads are my weak point. I am happy to go anywhere on the planet, and do just about anything, but I want to be able to wear a seat belt on the asphalt. Wherever I am, even in a war zone, the biggest danger is likely to come from a traffic accident rather than a bullet. It is almost my superstitious belief, as if I've decided that as long as I've clunked and clicked, nothing else can go wrong. Fingers crossed.

Two hours later it was dusk, and I suddenly realised we didn't have our headlights on. After a five-minute conversation we established that our driver believed putting the headlights on used up petrol.

'Don't forget that he also believes in reincarnation and might like to come back as something more interesting,' said Amit with a chuckle. I decided we needed to ditch the vehicles and take the train, or we might not survive.

The terrors of the road were perfectly illustrated during our first stop in Ahmedabad. I was crossing a bridge with Amit and asking him about the country's vast gap between rich and poor, illustrated right in front of us by a fancy high-rise hotel towering over a sea of slum dwellings. Despite images of 'booming India', it was clear that hundreds of millions were still living in abject poverty. Then the heavens opened and all of a sudden I heard a squeal of tyres, then the thud and grind of metal, and I turned and watched open-mouthed as scooter after scooter skidded on newly wet tarmac and bodies tumbled on to the road. Jonathan swung his camera towards the pile-up while I ran into the road and stopped a distracted truck driver crushing a young woman in a now dirty white sari. She picked herself up and thanked me as if I'd just passed her a dropped newspaper. And still more scooters and bodies tumbled.

Fortunately no one seemed to be seriously hurt. What was most remarkable was there was no sign of anger or rage. Nobody shouted angrily at anyone else. I wonder if perhaps a peaceable acceptance of chaos has actually become part of India's mentality. At one huge intersection I stopped and watched a camel-drawn cart weave its way through a dense throng of cars, scooters, bicycles and green-and-yellow tuk-tuk taxis. There was no sign of police, rules, lights or lines on the road or rights of way. Somehow, though, there was calm. Even in the business centres of the busy cities there were innumerable deep potholes, road-works that had been started but seemed destined never to finish, and plenty of street-walking sacred cows. In almost any other country, such anarchy and disruption would lead to road rage. Here there was relative composure and acceptance. Still, we had judged it wise, wherever possible, to stay off the roads and stick to the trains.

However, that wasn't always possible. While staying in a remote national park east of Ahmedabad, we received an urgent message that one of our team had to return to the UK due to a family emergency. Using our satellite phone we were able to find them a flight leaving in the morning from a city four hours away, but to get there we had to leave immediately and drive through the night. It was possibly the most frightening drive I've ever endured. Twice I had to grab the wheel during the night as the driver began to nod off, and there were a dozen times when we narrowly avoided colliding with trees or trucks. It was completely astonishing how many Indians were still moving at night. Eventually, after I could see the driver nodding off for a third time, Jonathan and I decided enough was enough and we stuck him in the back and shared the driving between us.

Two hours further along the Tropic – by train – we came to the city of Bhopal, which will be forever associated with just one terrible event. In December 1984 a cloud of poisonous gas leaked from a pesticide factory there, blanketing the city, and killing between four and ten thousand people. The American owners of the factory, a company called Union Carbide, since bought by US firm Dow Chemicals, were blamed for the disaster. Indian courts ordered the firm to pay compensation, but it was a fraction of what they'd have paid if the victims had been Americans.

I was trying to live a healthier life, and wandering around the site of one of the world's worst industrial accidents might not have sounded like the finest idea. But I could vividly remember hearing the dreadful news about Bhopal as a child. It was an almost unimaginable catastrophe in a faraway place. At the local Methodist church, which my parents dragged me to, we had talks about what had happened, and began raising money for the victims. Hundreds of thousands of people had been injured by the leak. I delivered donation envelopes to every flat and house in one small area of Acton, and read the leaflets that went along with the appeal detailing the tragedy of those who had died, and the suffering of those who had survived. I could still feel my horror. I had to go.

It felt surreal, and emotional, to then drive into the hulking ruins of the factory. An accusation of corporate failure was stencilled on to a perimeter wall: 'POISONED SOIL WASTE-DUMP DOW.' But what I found truly shocking was that the factory had never been properly cleaned up and remained horrendously contaminated.

A former worker showed me around. He was campaigning for the victims of the disaster. Even before the cataclysm of the gas leak, he said the factory owners had been poisoning the surrounding area by dumping toxic waste in the grounds of the factory.

We walked across eerie, overgrown scrubland, grazed by goats despite the fact I could smell a powerful chemical stench leaching out of the rocky earth. Under the field was the water supply for the nearby slum. When the rains came, the shallow pools all around would overflow and flood toxic liquid into the water system. Soil tests conducted by Greenpeace showed mercury levels in the groundwater to be 20,000 to 6 million times higher than normal levels.

I walked to the edge of the factory site, along a well-worn path, and was stunned by how close people were living to the contaminated area. Families with nowhere else to go, who could afford nothing more, were surviving in a slum that had grown up around the edge of the disaster zone.

A water sample taken from a hand pump near the plant, and tested in the UK, was found to contain 1,000 times the World

Health Organization's recommended maximum amount of a carcinogenic toxin called carbon tetrachloride. Another chemical, known to impair foetal development, was measured at 50 times the safe levels set out by the US Environmental Protection Agency. People living near the site – even the milk of breast-feeding mothers – were being poisoned.

More than a quarter of a century after the Bhopal gas leak, it was still a disaster area, with a whole new generation of victims.

I met up with a remarkable young woman from the slum called Sarita Malviya. At 16 she was already a leading campaigner for the new victims of Bhopal. Beautifully dressed and wearing lovely ornamental jewellery, her hands bore the imprint of striking henna markings. She told me her family had moved to the area only eight years earlier and had no idea that the water was polluted.

'Within a year we realised that people here had all sorts of illnesses – headaches and nausea, irritation of the skin and eyes,' she told me as we sat on a rug in her home. 'And there were children being born with all sorts of deformities – with their fingers stuck together, with hare lips and completely bald. So I wondered why all this was happening here and not where we used to live.'

I was appalled by what I saw in Bhopal. A quarter of a century after the disaster, neither the Indian government nor the chemical companies had cleaned up the site to protect future generations. It is completely obscene, reveals the colossal failings of corporations, and the Indian state, and shows just why chemical firms need to be carefully regulated.

We crossed the state of Jharkhand towards neighbouring West Bengal, through a dangerous area of India known as the Red

Corridor because of a major Maoist insurgency by left-wing groups. Tens of thousands of armed rebels were effectively mounting a rural rebellion, or people's war, against the government. It started in 1967, and in the decades since, thousands and thousands of civilians, soldiers, police and rebels have been killed. The conflict was hardly known in the outside world, but there had been a recent upsurge in violence as Maoist guerrillas fought to capture control of the area. Targeting the police and armed forces, they claimed to be fighting corruption on behalf of the rural poor. In response, the government was sending in thousands of soldiers to try to retake control. The *Tropic of Cancer* was taking me right through the middle of it.

I needed someone who really knew the territory to take me through the conflict area, so I met up with Abhra Bhattacharya, a guide who specialises in covering eastern India, at a guest house just outside the town of Lalgarh in West Bengal. He has a ready smile and an easy laugh, even under stress, and over the next few years I got to know him well as he became a regular fixture on my travels to the country. For now, having shaken hands, he took me straight into the middle of a civil war.

We went to meet up with troops who had just moved into the area to retake it for the government, but the conflict lines were blurred. As we crossed a river bridge, Abhra explained we were leaving behind an area of government control and crossing into a Maoist area. Eventually we found a small Indian army base, where we were given flak jackets and allowed to go out on patrol in the countryside and through remote villages with a detachment of soldiers armed with assault rifles, and even a mortar. The Indian soldiers were edgy and ready for war. They had to sweep the ground with metal detectors in case of roadside bombs.

None of it was the sort of thing you expect to see in TV documentaries about India, but the root cause became apparent when we visited Madhapur, a nearby village caught in the middle of the conflict. We had to walk to the village because the road simply turned into sand about a mile away and our car could go no further.

As we walked into Madhapur I had an almighty shock. A man was making a wooden plough, by hand. I looked around, and I could see nothing of the modern world. No electricity cables, no phone lines, no water pipes. In Madhapur there was no running water, no education and the nearest health centre was about five miles away and had no doctors. I asked a village elder what the government did for them, and where their children went to school.

'We're not getting anything from the government,' he said. 'There's no public water supply in our village – only private wells. The road is only half built and not by the government. The village council raised the money and the villagers had to do all the work themselves.'

Villagers said the only time they seemed to hear from the government was when the police and army mounted aggressive operations to search the area for possible rebels, sometimes breaking down their doors at four in the morning, creating huge local resentment. Though police brutality isn't something I would have associated with India, human rights groups had criticised the government reaction to the insurgency and identified numerous cases where the police had beaten and even killed suspects.

It was at this point that my vision of progressive, modern India took a massive dent. I had already witnessed the reality of urban poverty, but more than 600 million Indians were still enduring poverty in forgotten rural communities like Madhapur. It wasn't just that they had been left behind by India's economic boom, it was that the boom was something of an illusion. Vast numbers of Indians were still living like they did hundreds of years before. It was mind-boggling that people could be so far removed from basic state provision in a country with a space programme. Suddenly, I could understand why the Maoists still attracted so much support. The villagers had learned the hard way that when you're far from the centre of power you are insignificant, your voice is ignored and you get nothing.

In the years since, I have met countless middle-class Indians who, shockingly, seem proud their country is destined to over-take China as the most populous on the planet. To me it feels like a hollow achievement to brag about when so many Indians live such stunted, stifled lives. The reality is that the poverty I've encountered in India is endemic and widespread, easily comparable to the pockets of extreme poverty that I've seen in Africa. Many middle-class Indians hate it when I bring this up, but perhaps they need a wake-up call. The country is still leaving far too many behind.

For the last part of our journey we drove across the country to the city of Kolkata. But at least we were on India's biggest and newest road, the rather grandly named Golden Quadrilateral highway, where I naively assumed that road safety standards might have risen from 'suicidal' to merely 'risky'.

It was the first really impressive bit of government-provided infrastructure I'd seen in the country. But it turned out that even modernised India could not insulate us from chaos. Travelling along the motorway we found ourselves slaloming past ox-drawn carts, goats and cattle grazing on the central reservation, cyclists carrying and balancing sacks of grain and rice, and overloaded buses with passengers travelling on the roof.

'I think people are still getting used to these new, bigger roads,' said Abhra.

The highways were terrible, but this corner of India – West Bengal and its capital – was to become my favourite part of the country. I instantly warmed to the Bengalis I met, who had a feistiness about them; an attractive kind of bolshiness. They have a tendency to elect communists, and if they don't like something they go out on strike.

I came to the end of my exhausting first visit to India feeling confused about the place. Few other countries feel quite so weighed down with problems – the caste system and the grinding poverty, the mushrooming population and the absence of infrastructure. At that point I felt annoyed that so many other visitors seemed to ignore those aspects of the country. To me, occasionally, it seemed irredeemably broken.

But it is India that I was finding challenging, not Indians. I felt full of warmth and admiration for its people, who were endlessly good-natured and tolerant. There is such ability and talent in India, if only it could get a lucky break. I heard so many stories of redemption from people, of how they had triumphed over appalling circumstances. One horrifying but inspiring story came from a young man working with one of my guides. As a child he had become separated from his family when they all went on a trip from their village to a city festival. The child had nothing on him indicating where he was from, or who his parents were, but he was taken in by a street gang of other kids who lived in a railway station. Eventually he became their leader, and got them all to sleep on the top of the ramshackle kiosks in the station to avoid the attentions of rats and people traffickers.

One day my guide was doing some filming in the station, paid the kids for some help and recognised the boy's potential. He took him on as an assistant. By the time I met him he had become a guide who owned a car and was dating a local Bollywood actress. From a tragically unpromising start in life, he had made it.

The only thing I found hard to stomach about north-east India was the tendency of almost everyone I met to disparage Bangladesh, where I was heading. Many would sneer at the mere mention of their neighbour. Eventually I stopped mentioning where the Tropic of Cancer was taking me next.

We began our journey in western Bangladesh near the Indian border by joining a lovely old wooden riverboat, roughly painted blue and white, with two main levels, simple cabins for our TV crew, and a little galley for a chef to whip up some food. Our plan was to cruise for almost a week down the mighty Padma River towards the capital Dhaka, filming whatever we encountered. The waterway, known in India as the Ganges, is a vast carotid artery pumping through a water world criss-crossed by 700 rivers. The trip was spectacular as we drifted past lush banks that bloomed green and teemed with life.

Up to 60 per cent of Bangladesh floods every year, and its population of 160 million, the seventh largest on the planet, are crammed on to all available patches of dry land in an area smaller than England and Wales. But it overwhelmed me with its spectacularly colourful countryside and some of the friendliest and most welcoming people on the planet. Whenever we stopped to film, huge and fascinated crowds would gather to watch us. This was before smartphones became cheap and ubiquitous, so we were the entertainment.

Much of what I loved about the Bangladeshi people was embodied in our guide Tanjilur Rahman, who boarded the boat with us. A small, wiry man with wild hair and a stringy beard, Tanjil looked a little bit like a religious leader. Though humble and quiet, he has an intensely charismatic air. If he ever decides to found a cult, I'd follow him.

We pottered down a side river to search for traditional fish hunters. You hear them long before you see them. Sharp screeching penetrates the air by the riverbank, on the edge of a village in the Narail district, where ranks of canoes held large bamboo cages and pairs of furry otters, which are world champion fish catchers. Villagers in the area harness the otters for a fishing partnership that dates back thousands of years, and one that was used in Britain until the late 1800s. At dusk, when I set out on a small narrow boat with Tanjil and Robin, a local fisherman, the otters were barking noisily at each other, excited by the prospect of another night hunting, pulling in a catch on which they also feed. We drifted lazily downriver in the still darkness, oil lamps and candles throwing deep shadows on to the lush banks, until we reached a quiet fishing spot on a bend in the river where trees draped their heavy branches into the water, and our torches caught flashes of silver from fish hiding among the submerged leaves.

Robin opened the bamboo cage and released his two harnessed otters into the water, carefully adjusting their rope leads so one swam around at the front of the boat and the other at the back. Then he lowered a large net into the water and shuffled it under the dangling tree branches. A swift tug on the ropes attached to his otters, and the pair were chasing fish into the net, which Robin then lifted back into the boat, dumping the catch at our feet. It was an amazing sight, and a side of this country

Westerners rarely see. We tend to associate Bangladesh just with disasters, flooding and tragedy, but it is also a lush, beautiful country.

Tanjil took us back upriver to rejoin the main Padma the next day. Nowhere feels like it's more on the front line of our climate emergency than Bangladesh. Eighty per cent is floodplain. Most of the country is pancake-flat, only a metre or less above the rising sea level, so the boundary between water and land felt incredibly blurry. Picture Holland, without dykes or wealth, and you're a quarter of the way there. Riverbanks just consisted of mud, without any rocks to hold their structure in place, meaning they were vulnerable to erosion, which was accelerating as the snow melt in the Himalayas way upriver increased.

As it rained hard early in the afternoon, we happened to chug past a bank that looked ready to collapse. Then suddenly a little further along the river I spotted long rows of white sandbags that gangs of men were hurling into the water to shore up the bank.

I shouted to Anya, who was filming in the wheelhouse, asking if we could stop and take a dinghy in for a closer look. It wasn't planned – it was a proper case of 'What's happening over there?' We were able to moor up and step ashore just as huge chunks of bank crumbled away and toppled into the water, despite the frenzied efforts of a group of villagers. Scary great fissures gaped in the earth at the water's edge. More ballast was delivered by boat. I was told that in the previous fortnight the river had eaten 500 yards into the village, while in the previous four years it had claimed 2,000 homes in this community alone.

'I have lost everything. My cows, my goats, my trees, everything. I have just got my home left,' said one wiry man with a greying beard. He sheltered under a basic umbrella and laid out for me what climate change meant for him personally. 'It's been happening for a long time, but now it's getting faster and it's coming closer. When we want to sleep we can't because we're scared by the noise of the land falling into the river. It sounds like shooting: "Boom boom!"' He pointed to his corrugated iron house only yards away from water. No wonder he looked frightened and angry.

This was climate change unfolding right in front of my eyes. Increased erosion now makes tens of thousands of people homeless every year, turning them into environmental refugees. It felt like the beginning of a climate catastrophe on a biblical scale, because even a small rise in sea levels would devastate millions in Bangladesh.

We sailed on towards Dhaka, thinking about what we'd seen. Eventually our boat approached Sadarghat, Bangladesh's busiest port. It was an amazing spectacle, like something out of a painting by Turner. Countless other vessels, from crowded ferries to tiny local commuter boats, all fought for space on the river. Nowhere was competition hotter than at the dock, where hulking boats gunned their engines and then wedged past one another to unload their passengers, jostling for space. Ours could only stop for a few minutes and we disembarked by clambering off our boat on to another, crossing that and finally setting foot in the most chaotic megacity I've ever had the shock and pleasure to visit.

Dhaka was both stunning and squalid. Its population of 13 million was swollen by hundreds of thousands of new arrivals each year from the impoverished countryside. It was evocative and atmospheric, with beautifully decorated rickshaws and children leaping off every riverbank. But there's no hiding the filth and appalling poverty that scar many lives in the city. As we walked along we attracted, like the Pied Piper, a small group of shoeless, sometimes shirtless, urchins who spend their days collecting fragments of plastic or glass bottles for recycling. There were a quarter of a million such children living on the streets of Dhaka and some of them were extraordinarily young – four and five years old.

But that wasn't the worst of it. There was a hidden army of young labourers scratching a living behind closed doors. Tanjil took us to a factory where some of them worked, reachable through a brightly coloured child-sized entrance. It was a glass recycling plant where they made bottles for export to South Korea. It looked like something straight out of Dickens. One of the workers I met was Jahangir, a lovely boy with a beaming smile, who worked for the equivalent of 30p a day – enough to buy his family a small bag of rice. Factory owners liked to employ children because they're cheap, they have nimble fingers – and they complain less than adults. There was plenty for them to be upset about. It was more than 40 degrees Celsius outside, and the heat standing by the furnace was almost unbearable. So were the choking fumes. Another boy, even smaller than Jahangir, had a weeping burn on his forearm where it had been singed by a hot pipe.

After his shift, Jahangir led me out of the factory to show me where he slept. It was little more than a platform on stilts up a rickety ladder. Under it was a huge pile of discarded glass, which his little sister walked past in bare feet. 'If I had a home then I wouldn't have need to work,' he said. 'I could have gone to school and my mum would have worked.' I asked him why they had come to live here. 'Because of hunger.' That answer, so simple and yet so honest and profound, summed up and laid bare all the despair and misery I had witnessed as I journeyed along the Tropic of Cancer while crossing the Indian subcontinent.

It seemed obvious to me that the factory was fundamentally wrong and should be closed down overnight, and the children stopped from working. But the older labourers, who had all started at a similar age, wanted me to understand what can happen when foreign intervention prevented them from earning a living. 'If we throw them out of work, what will they live on?' one said. 'If they don't work they will die of hunger, so they go out begging or stealing. For hunger they do anything. They do many things if they are hungry.'

It was an eye-opening conversation. Child labour was almost a necessary evil for some children. Nearly 5 million children in the country were earning vital income for their families or themselves.

The future wasn't totally bleak for Jahangir. His boss had been persuaded to give him a few hours off each day to visit a special centre for working children run by the United Nations Children's Fund UNICEF. There, working boys like him were given a free lunch, a shower and space to learn and have fun. By giving the kids a basic education, UNICEF hoped to break the cycle that can trap generation after generation in abject poverty. But it also gave them the chance simply to be children. As they played and relaxed and socialised, I saw something that was rare elsewhere in Dhaka: smiles on the faces of children. Yet even there I heard an acknowledgement that child labour was a problem that would take a long time to fix.

'The reality is that many of the families are really dependent on the earnings of the children,' said Farzana Ahmad, one of the women running the UNICEF centre. 'If they can have a safer working environment, and if they have scope of going to school and some free time for recreation, then they are having the chance to have a different kind of life.' That was the dual goal:

trying to improve working conditions for the children, and teaching them skills that might help to give them and their kids a better future.

Filming with Jahangir had a real impact on all of us and we wanted to do something for him. We thought of buying him shoes, but none of the children would wear them – they were too used to walking in bare feet. He said he wanted a bike. So we left some money and Tanjil later sent us photos of Jahangir taking possession of a green mountain bike. He definitely deserved a bit of a childhood.

While he lived on in my memory, I had no idea if Jahangir would even survive into adulthood. But years later, during the pandemic, when we were putting together a compilation series called *Incredible Journeys*, UNICEF managed to track him down. At the age of twenty he was his own boss, driving a battery-powered rickshaw taxi, and was married with a young son whom he wanted to educate properly. The UNICEF team in Bangladesh showed him the film we'd made with him all those years before, and he cried at the sight of his mum, his younger self and his friends. Watching it back at home in Devon, I cried too. So did Jonathan, who'd filmed in Bangladesh, and filmed me in my lounge. It was deeply moving to see that Jahangir had made it out of his perilous childhood. Perhaps it was even grounds for cautious optimism. Change is definitely possible.

The Tropic of Cancer doesn't loiter for long in Bangladesh, but my first visit to the country left a deep emotional impression. We left the streets of Dhaka and drove east to a beach by the river to watch some young men taking part in kabaddi, the national sport. Players have to go into the other team's half and keep holding their breath while they try to tag someone out – without being wrestled to the ground. To prove they're not breathing in they repeat the word 'kabaddi'. Needless to say, Tanjil and I had to get involved, after Tanjil politely asked everyone not to break our limbs. The plea must have got lost in translation, because I was really thrown around by those guys. I might have been twice the size of everyone else, but I didn't spend my days working physically in a brick factory. Some of them were pure gristle and sinew.

I try to have a couple of simple rules for such situations. Don't fake it, and be respectful. Everyone taking part and watching seemed to love the fact I played the game properly, even if I did end up battered and bruised. I didn't get much support from my colleagues. When I was slammed to the ground I'd look over at them filming from the safety of the side, but there were no concerned or sympathetic looks. Not even from Anya. I remember saying, 'Surely you've got enough shots?' And they'd go, 'We didn't quite get that bit. Could you just do a bit more?' It felt like being put on the rack and left there.

We headed for the border. Bangladesh is almost completely surrounded by India, and I was due to head through two remote Indian states, Tripura and Mizoram, both bang on the Tropic of Cancer, towards India's long jungle border with Burma. After hearing so many condescending remarks about India's smaller neighbour, I hugely enjoyed the irony that the border post in a remote corner of Bangladesh was clean, well lit and orderly, with a computer and uniformed officials. The Indian border post, by contrast, was a hut without electricity or an official. Eventually we found somebody. I had to light and hold a stub of a candle so he could write down our details. The wax poured down over my hand as he inscribed our names in an ancient rotting ledger. This was the India with a space programme. No foreigner had crossed there in months.

My last act leaving Bangladesh was to bid an emotional good-bye to Tanjil. Of my many farewells with guides all over the world, this was one of the most painful as he had become a friend over the course of my visit to the country. 'I'll see you again,' I said hopefully.

We waved farewell. Bangladesh is packed and it's poor. It's also one of my favourite places in the world. Because for me the best thing about travel is the people you meet. They're what's most beautiful about our planet, and why going on a journey is such a delight.

CHAPTER EIGHT

Risk

Looking back now, I wonder whether part of the reason I so readily embraced the whole idea of this journey was because it was a counterbalance to the uncertainty of infertility and the process of attempting to have a child. The journey was a quest, a challenge, and one that I felt I could endure and complete, with maps and planning and schedules, even when following the line began to take me towards serious danger.

When I first traced the Tropic of Cancer line around the world on a globe, I could see that it cut right across Burma. Myanmar, as its military dictatorship called it, had a terrible reputation for human rights abuses. Burma was a place where rebel armies were fighting government soldiers in seemingly endless conflicts, human rights activists disappeared, terrible suffering was inflicted on ethnic minority groups like the Shan, Chin and the Karen, and much of the population lived in fear.

It was not the easiest place to film even at the best of times, and the ruling generals had recently banned many foreign film crews from entering. Tourists were still allowed to visit Burma, but the line went through remote parts of the country that were not on any visitor route and hadn't really been seen by foreign TV cameras for years, if at all. I found that intriguing, almost exciting. What was life like in those remote areas of Burma?

What was going on off the tourist trail? The desire to follow the line into unknown parts of the world had been the main reason I wanted to make the series after my Marco Polo project was rejected.

We had one of our first meetings to discuss the situation in Burma in the Frankie Howerd Room at New Broadcasting House at the BBC. We pored over detailed maps we'd bought from Stanfords in Covent Garden, the famous travel bookshop, then talked about the armies fighting in Burma, which included the Arakan Liberation Army, Chin National Army, United Wa State Army, Ta'ang National Liberation Army, Shan State Army-North, Karen National Liberation Army and the Kachin Independence Army. Then we were booted out after an hour because someone else at the BBC had booked a high-level meeting about a cookery show.

One possible way inside Burma, though still not safe, was to try to go in undercover as tourists, perhaps via one of the main cities, and try to do some covert filming. But when we investigated further we were told the Burmese secret police had a small team of officers at the main airports who special-ised in finding hidden camera equipment. Apparently they were remarkably efficient. When discussing situations like that I always want to know specifics. Being told 'there is a risk' isn't quite clear enough. Is it a small risk or a major risk? I usually ask for a percentage chance. I need to know the likely situation we are dealing with or projecting ourselves into.

We thought there was a 60 to 80 per cent chance that if we were caught in Burma pretending to be tourists we would be arrested. We would probably be deported fairly swiftly, but perhaps we would have been held for a few days or longer.

I was strongly in favour of going into the forgotten areas of Burma, even if that was more dangerous, and staying faithful to the original concept of following the Tropic line. Andrew Carter, the lovely and committed director who would be travelling with Anya and me for that leg of the journey, spent weeks investigating all the options. Along with other members of the team he talked to campaigning groups, NGOs and charity workers operating in Burma, international journalists and undercover camera specialists about what was possible, and what was not. Everything was considered.

We studied all the options and gamed out the likely consequences, and eventually decided our best chance of actually getting into the country, filming, and getting out with the footage, was to try and sneak across the border from a remote region of India into an area of Burma populated by the Chin ethnic group, one of several populations in Burma that had suffered horrific abuses. The highly respected campaigning organisation Human Rights Watch had recently reported that Burmese soldiers were using torture, arbitrary arrest and killings as part of a campaign to suppress the more than 1.5 million largely Christian Chin people.

We could talk to people in advance as much as we liked, but one thing we couldn't do was completely guarantee safety. If we were going to attempt to travel through tricky parts of the world and film an adventure like this, we all had to accept risk and a degree of fear.

We don't get anywhere without confronting fear. The richest rewards in life come from a bit of risk-taking, from pushing ourselves out of our comfort zones. When we take chances, we get the best memories and experiences.

We confront fear by testing ourselves, by exercising our confidence like a muscle, and by building it up. Start with experiences that resemble small weights: 1kg, then 2kg, then 5, 10, 20, 30, and your tolerance of new situations, and even danger, increases. Start with simple encounters, as if you are an arachnophobe trying to overcome a horror of spiders. They wouldn't start by stroking a tarantula, they would build up to it. First they would look at a cartoon picture of a spider, then a real photo of a spider, then a kids' toy spider, then a realistic spider, then a small real spider, and so on and so on until, yes, maybe one day they could be stroking a tarantula. Exercise your confidence muscle enough, and eventually you can run towards your own demons.

Once we tackle and defeat the issues or experiences that frighten us the most, our minds readjust and reset on to a more adventurous plane. We develop and we evolve.

Personally, I didn't leap out of a box ready to walk into Burma, go to danger zones or track terrorists. I was a depressed, terrified, suicidal teenager. I spent years changing myself from a frightened kid to a more confident adult. I did it step by step. I started small, with experiences that I could cope with. After I began working as a post boy on a newspaper, sorting the mail, I started running errands for people, getting them a sandwich, doing their photocopying. Then I volunteered to be sent out on errands to talk to people, then questioning people, going to demonstrations, riots, bombings, investigating crimes. Initially I was terrified. But taking things step by step was the key. Soon I was working as an investigative journalist, sometimes undercover, sometimes in disguise, tracking arms dealers and terrorists. I built up my tolerance for fear and my understanding of risk, until I felt comfortable going to really tricky parts of the world and travelling to war zones.

Of course it's possible to take that tolerance too far. A few years ago I was in San Pedro Sula, Honduras, then the most dangerous city in the world outside of an active war zone. We had been filming in areas of the city riddled with gang violence, where there were daily shoot-outs and murders, when we had a phone call warning us that two police officers had just been assassinated by gunmen on a motorcycle.

I was with the brilliant cameraman Craig Hastings, and we grabbed our flak jackets and helmets and raced off to the scene of the murders with our guide. We managed to link up with a police car and tailgated them at speed through heavy traffic on a motorway until the road became completely blocked and we were stuck. After a moment of swearing, one of our guides then jokingly suggested we cross the grassy mound that was the Honduran equivalent of a central reservation, and drive the wrong way down the motorway. I thought he was serious, and turned to Craig in the back and asked if it was OK with him. He nodded and said it was fine. Our driver bumped the cars in front and behind us to make space, then we crossed on to the other side in our big 4x4 and started driving the wrong way up the motorway, dodging cars coming at us. I thought back to it afterwards and decided it had felt worryingly normal. I realised I'd been munching on a flapjack and Craig had been texting. I wondered if we were becoming just slightly too immune to risk.

When deciding whether I was prepared to enter Burma, perhaps the most vital element for me was the team. I had to trust the people I would be travelling with. There are times when we might need to run together towards gunfire, or a bombing. But I also needed to believe in the wider group working on the journeys, including Sam Bagnall, the executive producer, and

Simon Frost, the production co-ordinator, who was organising equipment, coordinating accommodation, permits, visas, travel and schedules. On a journey like this, Frostie's job could be a logistical nightmare.

Sam and I had worked together on a couple of journeys by this point, and I trusted him completely. After the exec for the *Equator* series had left the BBC, it was suggested to me that Sam might be a good fit moving forward. Most of the TV people I had met seemed to have been called Sam. Generally they had gone to a good school and then Oxbridge. I wasn't sure which of the various 'Sams' he actually was, so I was quite wary at our first meeting – which was a bit of a blind date – in a fancy Chinese restaurant in Soho in central London. When I walked downstairs he was already there and he looked up, gave me a big beaming smile and, even before he'd said a word, I felt immense relief and a certainty we would click. I was right. We've worked together regularly in the years since, and he's been a partner, foil and friend.

Sam already had a reputation as a tough film-maker, largely picked up from when he worked undercover on a TV series about football hooligans. His fundamental rule about storytelling on TV is that you've got to see it. Show not tell. No commentary, or PTC from me (a piece to camera) can ever substitute for putting the story on the screen. In the edit suite, Sam is magnificent at cutting to the chase and sensing the best way of structuring a tale from scores of different clips. But most importantly for me, Sam has always been committed to making programmes like mine, often shot in dark corners of the world and incorporating stories and issues that usually only get seen on Channel 4 by people who all read the international news section of the *Guardian*. Sam and I really believe it's important that we get as many people as possible to take an interest in what's happening on the wider planet, and we package and structure programmes in ways that entice families to sit and watch them together.

In due course Sam was given a more senior job and a grander title at the BBC. I take all the credit. I told him he was wearing the wrong sort of spectacles. They were too old school for working in television. He looked like he was still hoping to infiltrate the Chelsea Headhunters. I said he had to go and get some pretentious and wanky glasses, the sort 'media people' wear. He went to an expensive opticians in London's West End and told them exactly what I'd said.

'Sir,' came the response, 'you've come to just the right place.'

But Sam wasn't just a producer behind a desk. Early on I got to know him in the field. For a programme about Argentina he flew out with Jonathan Young and me to form a three-man team. As an undercover expert on football hooligans, he was giddy with excitement as we went to film an iconic grudge match between Boca Juniors and River Plate in Buenos Aires at the legendary Bombonera stadium. We arrived just as the game was about to start. It felt as if we were walking into the Colosseum in ancient Rome. The atmosphere was more intense and electrifying than any game I'd ever experienced. The passion of the supporters was fanatical, like an energy force field. There were fireworks, smoke grenades, toilet rolls hurling through the air. Then the Boca fans set up a mortar to launch a home-made firework at the River Plate fans. In response they pulled out live chickens from under their jackets, ripped the heads off them and threw the bloodied bodies at the Boca fans. I looked at Sam expecting him to be a little stunned, but he looked at me and, above the din of explosions, he shouted, 'It's just like Arsenal!'

Later on that trip we were in a town in the foothills of the Argentinian Andes. Sam speaks fluent Spanish, and he woke up early and walked a short distance to collect our hire car through falling snow, marvelling slightly at the number of people who seemed to be packing cars and trucks outside their homes. The manager of the hire firm was closing up.

'What's going on?' said Sam.

'Everybody's leaving town because of this,' said the guy, gesturing quickly outside the window. Sam was a bit bleary-eyed.

'Because it's snowing?' queried Sam in disbelief.

'That's not snow!' said the manager. 'That's ash! The volcano has erupted.'

The manager threw the keys to a hire truck at Sam, who jumped in, raced back to our guest house, and banged on our doors. It was all over the news. A huge volcano had erupted on the other side of the Andes and was busy smothering the lower half of South America. The ash was now like talcum powder in the air.

'I don't think we can film,' said Jonathan, looking gutted. 'The dust will kill the camera.'

We tried some shots outside with a basic tape camera but it died within a few minutes. Then we stood in a coughing huddle in our hotel foyer, and, in a rapid way that colleagues can do when they're also friends, made a swift assessment of the situation. Although we had several filming days remaining, the coverage area of the volcano was vast. We realised that if we didn't leave immediately we could get stuck. The conversation took no more than a minute. Then we began reminding each other what we needed to grab to have with us. Jonathan said we needed both satellite phones. Sam asked if we had swimming goggles. I remembered the trauma kit and some scarves. We ran back to our rooms, chucked the rest of our belongings into our Peli hard cases and were on the road within ten minutes.

The goggles were for keeping the ash from our eyes, the scarves to keep it out of our mouths and noses. The satellite phones were for ringing contacts to find out how bad the ash cloud was and how we could escape. As we hightailed it east out of town, there was a haunting sight. Sun was piercing through clouds of ash to create a luminous morning glow. In a field the ash was piling up on the backs of cattle who were all wheezing, struggling to breathe and slowly suffocating. It was like the apocalypse. The ash seemed to drift in clouds, sometimes thickening so dramatically we could see only 20 metres ahead, then only 10. We drove with our lights on full, hazards flashing, and pressed our faces up against the window while we shone powerful torches through cracks in the windows to check we were still actually on the road. Vehicles would suddenly loom up out of the ash, either ahead of us or a few times coming in from the side as if to ram us. Somehow, with the help of our GPS and pure luck, three hours later we made it to the far edge of the ash cloud without sustaining even a scratch. All the while we were checking how we could get further out of the area. We were told the ash would reach the Atlantic coast by the end of the day. Our team managed to book us the final three seats on the final plane leaving the south of the continent. Driving non-stop all the way from the Andes, we made the flight. Back at Heathrow I theatrically shook my hair and left a little deposit of Andean volcanic dust on the desk at customs.

Just like the rest of us on the filming team, Sam had personal experience of adventures, danger and how to deal with situations when everything is going wrong.

Many years ago I spent a little too much time with American spies and special forces guys while investigating al-Qaeda for my first major book. I was drinking in a bar in Virginia with one of them when he said something that really stuck with me. He had been on operations alongside his British counterparts and said that although American special forces teams had access to more resources, such as equipment, planes and satellites, the British were especially good because they endlessly ran through war-game scenarios. They practised, over and over. They prepared.

'Then when it all goes south,' said the American admiringly, 'they really know what to do.'

Thinking through scenarios in advance became something of a guiding principle for me whenever I was heading into a dangerous situation while researching my books. It also became really useful on my TV journeys, where we don't have a producer going on a recce beforehand and setting up loads of pre-scripted encounters, and instead we sometimes walk into extremely tricky places and I have to react. We don't wait for things to go wrong; we talk things through beforehand, over and over, and work out what we're going to do if disaster hits so we know all our options in the moment. There are times when we absolutely cannot wing it.

This is where my negativity can be especially useful. Although we are now often surrounded by a cult of positivity, with endless books, lifestyle coaches and corporations encouraging us to think we are all winners who can simply visualise and then manifest our own success, being relentlessly positive can simply mean we fail to prepare for complications. A bout of negative thinking can actually be healthy, especially when you are planning to do something difficult or dangerous. Imagining the worst-case scenario with a bit of 'negative visualisation', which in my case probably just flows naturally from my cynical grumpiness, helps me to prepare, mentally and practically. Why is a plan not likely to work? What does my negativity suggest might go wrong? If we've got a long trek through the jungle and a clamber up a rock face, we don't want everyone on the team to be convinced everything will go smoothly. Someone needs to be the negative voice that suggests one of us could sprain or break an ankle. Making sure we take a light splint and an ultralight fabric stretcher the size of an apple could then make the difference between a manageable crisis and a full catastrophe.

Practising a bit of negative visualisation as a more regular mental health exercise is a technique recommended from the time of the stoic philosophers. By thinking briefly and calmly about disaster, about how we would cope if we lost something or someone we love, or if we were to fail at a race, business or project, we can be reminded about what we actually already have to be thankful for, and simultaneously build our resilience and personal ability to cope with disappointment or worse.

In the weeks before we headed towards Burma we gamed out our plans, talking through what could go wrong and what we would do. Never, before or since, have I spent more time preparing for an adventure or mission. But we knew we had to minimise any risk that was within our control, because there was plenty more that would be far beyond our power to influence.

For a journey or an expedition, but also any new project, business, and in so much of life, preparation is the key to success. You've got to be aware of how hard it's going to be. You've got to be flexible and realise that no plan survives first contact with the enemy, as army types say. You need to be working with a good team, and you have to trust and use them.

But then if things go wrong, or *when* things go wrong, what are you going to do? Whether I'm in a war zone, up a mountain or dealing with an issue at home or in life, the first thing I ask myself is whether it's worth it. Do I want to be where I am? Do I want to resolve the problem enough to use my time or risk my life? Do I *need* to do it?

If the answer's yes, then I start to work through the problem, thinking about my next action, my very next step. Whether it is turn the gas off at a fire, trek for miles or call someone. What can I control? It's critical that we focus our minds on what we have the power to shape, rather than what is uncontrollable.

Then I start thinking about my overall plan. What do I need to achieve by fixing a problem? Where do I need to get to? And then how am I going to get there? One of my favourite quotes is from American General Douglas MacArthur, who said: 'Have a good plan, execute it violently, and do it today.'

There are times when many of us feel we can't get out of bed because the challenges are too great. Personally I try to avoid perceiving any specific problem or task as the mountain it might actually be. I choose to see it as separate smaller elements. There's always the journey to a mountain, the approach, the foothills, and an easy stretch at the bottom. Breaking it down makes it less overwhelming. Then I start to tackle the challenge step by step, using that same piece of utterly critical, foundational advice I was given in a jobcentre decades ago as I bounced along the bottom of life.

When it's not a challenge I need to face, but something simply thrown at me by life, at a time when I have lost hope, perhaps when someone has died, I still use my step by step motto. Except I don't head in a specific direction. I just try to do something – *anything* – and the sheer act of movement, in any direction, and the simple physicality of putting one foot in front of another starts to provide answers, solutions, and helps bring light into darkness.

To reach the Burmese border, with the right team, mindset, back-up and hopefully an appropriate balance of courage and trepidation, we left the flatlands and floodplains of Bangladesh and headed steadily upwards into forest-covered hills in the remote Indian regions of Tripura and Mizoram.

The north-east of the country is known as the Seven Sister States, much of it home to ancient and diverse forests under attack by subsistence farming, logging and road building.

People we met were stunned by our journey. 'The mainland' was what they called the rest of India. The Seven Sisters are connected to India by a narrow geographic corridor across the top of Bangladesh. It was 1,000 miles all the way round to Kolkata. It could take four days to drive. Yet they had little dealing with Bangladesh, partly because India was steadily erecting a fence and wall along its entire border. The construction is rapidly becoming one of the longest fenced and controlled lines on the planet, a ring of steel, concrete and barbed wire around a country that India already views as a major source of illegal migration. Some fear vast floods of refugees in the future if, or when, Bangladesh begins to sink beneath the waves due to climate change.

Also bordered by Bhutan, China and Burma, itself a melting pot, and with Nepal and Tibet nearby, the Seven Sisters are one of the most linguistically and culturally diverse regions in the world, an area with an almost unimaginable ethnic mix. There are more than 200 languages spoken in the Seven Sister States, and just as many ethnic groups. But then there are also tribes within tribes.

We didn't have much luck in Tripura. We wanted to film some of the remaining wildlife of the region to illustrate what was at threat from the loss of the forests. But even in the Sepahijala Wildlife Sanctuary we struggled to get good shots of elusive spectacled langurs – cheeky, energetic and flighty little monkeys. There were only around 2,000 left in the entire state. Then we were shown two spectacular clouded leopards languishing in small cages at the underfunded reserve, which I found deeply upsetting. They are extremely rare, magnificent creatures, and their pathetic captivity symbolised the endless destruction of their habitat.

I tried to discuss this with one of the directors of the reserve, an earnest conservationist who clearly cared about the loss of forest in this biodiverse corner of the planet. But his accent was incredibly strong. He launched straight into a diatribe in English about how his reserve struggled to get funding. I thought he was saying that American Jews were to blame because they had all the power, influence and money. I was horrified. Behind the camera I could see Jonathan immediately reacting. Andrew the director lowered our boom microphone. Then we all realised he was saying American zoos. I asked him to repeat himself, stressing the word myself clearly as a pointer. But it was still impossible. My benchmark is that if we are struggling to understand anyone when we are with them, especially after spending time in the country and tuning our ears to local accents, it will almost certainly be too much to ask of people watching at home. We want viewers to be listening and understanding, not discussing what's being said and missing the next bit.

Usually I suggest people might like to talk in their own language. We are in their country, after all. It slows things down due to the need for an instant rough translation, and it is more costly later on because we need interpreters to check the conversation with real accuracy, but on the plus side it means we can then have clear subtitles or an actor reading the lines. When we're filming, people often deliver powerful or critical stories in emotionless voices, so actors can also add a tiny bit more depth and dynamism, helping the viewer to understand the importance of what's being conveyed. It's also why I'm so often repeating back what people have said to me with perhaps slightly too much drama. Someone will say '. . . we lost 20 acres of land and two villages to climate change' in a flat voice that sounds as though they're talking about losing a small bet with their neighbour. So I'll bellow back at them: 'You Lost 20 Acres, and Two Villages?! To Climate Change?!'

I'm sure many people watching must think, 'Yeah, duh, that's what they just said.' But I hope repeating it with more emotion reinforces the point. There are people suffering. Our planet is under attack. We need to get more emotional. We need to realise what is at stake. Let me know if I'm wrong.

With the reserve director the situation was hopeless. We asked whether he might feel more comfortable talking in Bengali, his native language, but he said no thank you he was fine with English. Then we asked if he really could talk in Bengali, please, because we were in Tripura, and he said no thank you, English is an official language here. Then I tried talking about the loss of forest and wildlife with one of our guides. He was young, clever and eloquent. But as soon as we started filming him he began using an incredibly sonorous voice as if he was delivering a live war report on CNN. I tried to coach him to relax, but nothing worked. We were stuffed.

We drove on to the centre of a small market town next to a lake we were planning to cross by boat. I was unloading our bags, ready to go and look for someone to take us out on the lake, when I suddenly stopped. Around me, I realised, was one of the richest displays of humanity I had ever seen.

There were people from the Bengali, Mizo, Darlong, Tripuri, Chakma, Jamatia and Noatia groups, wearing shawls, red sarongs, cotton cloaks, bright saris and orange robes. There were priests, monks, tiny schoolgirls in frilly dresses, and a farmer passing a 12ft saw blade up to someone to carry on top of a bright green bus. It was like national costume day at the Methodist church I went to as a kid, and that was in an almost ludicrously diverse area of London, where more than 300 languages are spoken, making it perhaps the most diverse city that has ever existed.

Jonathan was filming the scene while Andrew kindly sheltered him from the sweltering sun under a rainbow-coloured umbrella, appropriately. Anya was off to the side under the awning of a ramshackle wooden hut, asking politely if it was possible to film some tiny elderly women sitting on the ground. It's rude to gasp, of course, but the women, who were from the Brus or Reang tribe, looked astonishing. Exquisitely beautiful, they were each wearing dozens of thick silver metal and glass bead necklaces, with huge chunky metal rings through their lower ears. Two had thick horn-shaped earrings sticking out of the upper ears. We wanted to ask where they were going, but our CNN guide had vanished. A crowd of friendly faces was surrounding us. In desperation, I turned to them and said loudly: 'Sorry, but does anyone here speak English?'

'Yeah, I do,' said a Tripuri lad at the back who introduced himself as Pradip.

He was in his early twenties, spoke several of the tribal languages, and had learned English by watching football and listening to American rap music on bootleg CDs.

'Do you fancy a job?' I said.

We explored the market, then took a boat out on the lake. Much of the forest on the steep hills around the shore looked like the setting for a battle between warring dragons. Thousands of trees had been chopped close to the ground, leaving sharp stumps, and the whole area including the ground was blackened by fire.

'Some of it is still burning,' said Pradip. 'Look, you can see the smoke.'

Pradip explained that villagers practised 'jhum', a basic form of slash-and-burn farming. Unlike in the temperate zone of Europe or North America, soil in the Tropics can be remarkably lacking in nutrients for crops, because Life gets its energy from the guaranteed sun above. So poor farmers chop trees down, burn them, then mix the ash into the soil as a natural fertiliser for the crops they plant.

'It works for a couple of harvests, and then they move on to chop somewhere else,' said Pradip.

It is a complete catastrophe. Vast swathes of forests are being lost around the Tropics to slash and burn, which would be completely unnecessary if farmers were trained how to grow sustainably (as they are in many areas of Cuba, for example), and also, in truth, if there were slightly fewer of us wanting land.

We chugged along the lake towards a village where Pradip thought we might be able to find farmers who could explain jhum to us, but our boat began to struggle through invasive water hyacinths that had spread across the surface of the lake like a mesh. We tried to go on, dangling our legs over the side to push the weeds out of the way, but after another hour it became clear we would never make it, and it was getting too late to turn back. We made it to the bank and found a family living in a long wooden hut. They agreed to let us sleep inside for the night and then began busying themselves with food and fires.

It took us hours to get back to the market town the next day and divert around the lake. Eventually we made it to the neighbouring state of Mizoram, our last stop before Burma. Aizawl, the capital, was an extraordinary place that seemed to consist entirely of three-, four- and five-storey buildings perched precariously on high hills. We were taken to the Aliens Registration Department to sign in to the state. There had only been 381 visitors in the previous ten years. Most of them were Nigerian footballers travelling overland to play in the Chinese soccer league.

We had lugged cases of kit along with us specifically for the next part of the journey, our entry into Burma. It was time for us to prepare for what would become the most nerve-wracking and rewarding part of my journey around the Tropic of Cancer, and one of the most impossible experiences of my life. This is the first time I have written down the full story of what we did and what happened.

In Aizawl we hired an entire guest house and turned it into a forward operating base, then, on advice, taped fabric over some of the windows as blackout curtains so passing locals couldn't see what we were up to. Despite its global reputation as a friendly democracy, there are elements of the Indian state that act more like the Chinese secret police, and we knew that if spies realised what we were doing, we could be in deep trouble, partly because we had satellite phones, satellite photos and incriminating maps marking out routes we were hoping to take east.

Then we spent hours conducting a full inventory of all our equipment, working out precisely what we needed. It was vital to get it right as from that point on there would be no opportunity to resupply or replace.

Our plan was to head towards a remote stretch of the border between India and Burma, cross over, somehow, into neighbouring Chin State, then make our way to a village of the Chin people, somehow, and try to learn what life was like for people in a forgotten corner of the country. Being in the Indian border zone was illegal. Crossing the border was illegal. Being in Burma was illegal. There was plenty that could go wrong.

It was likely we would be travelling on foot, but in what conditions or weather we didn't know. We also didn't know how we could cross the Tiau River at the border or what might be waiting for us on the other side. Nor were we entirely sure where we'd go when we got into Burma, or how long we'd be there. It might be a couple of days, or it might take much longer, especially if we got cut off by troop movements. Much of the terrain was under jungle, which doesn't reveal its secrets to satellite photos or Google Maps, so we had no idea how many rivers we'd have to cross, or if they'd be narrow or fast or deep. Basically, we had to prepare for travelling into a black hole.

What was absolutely clear was that we needed to avoid the Burmese army. They were effectively an occupying force in the Chin region, committing terrible crimes against the population, who are a Christian ethnic minority group. There were dozens of Burmese military bases scattered around on the other side of the border. We had intelligence on all their locations and had them mapped out so we could avoid them. But the Burmese soldiers would go on long patrols into the jungle hunting for armed Chin rebel groups, so there was a serious risk of encounter and capture.

However bad that might have been for us on the team, it was bound to be infinitely worse for Cheery, our new guide, who was now smuggled into our guest house. Cheery was a campaigner and activist from the Chin ethnic group who at that point was living in exile in northern Thailand. She had flown to Mizoram to translate, guide and help us on our mission. I was struck by how young and jolly she was, and short and slight, but also how determined. Cheery is without doubt one of the bravest people I have ever met. Because of her campaigning work, she was on a Burmese military wanted list, possibly even a death list. She knew that if she was caught back in Burma she would be either disappeared or executed on the spot. She was completely realistic about the risks of accompanying us.

'Going to Chin State, and going to Burma, is always dangerous as you don't know what will happen,' she told me. Cheery knew she was doing something exceptionally dangerous. 'They don't want me to be there. They said that I am being empowered by the Western rich nations and now I try to disunite the union of Myanmar.'

I asked her why she was prepared to take the risk and enter Burma. 'Because if we don't speak up,' she replied, 'if we don't tell the stories of the people under this repressive military regime, then no one will know what's happening, and if they don't know, they will not do anything.' I liked Cheery instantly. She had a real warmth and clear honesty in her aura. She was brave, really brave, but she wasn't suicidal. I trusted her implicitly.

There is something strangely beautiful and ancient about trusting someone you hardly know with your life. We live in a time of fear when people can be reluctant to trust anyone, let alone give them responsibility. To get a job stacking shelves in a supermarket when I was younger, I had to go through two interviews and a short personality quiz. With Cheery I had to rely largely on my gut feeling and the instincts of my colleagues. If Jonathan, Anya or Andrew had thought there was something suspicious or funny about anyone we were trusting, we would have pulled out. But finding someone to believe in, someone you can have faith in, can lead to experiences that are revelatory.

Just a few years ago when I was in San Pedro Sula in Honduras – on the same trip when we raced the wrong way down the motorway to the police murder scene – we decided we wanted to meet the leaders of the criminal gangs who were helping to destroy the country. It became clear that most of them were actually locked up in the city prison. I was told it might be possible to go into the jail to meet them, but we were warned the guards had no real control inside. The prison was itself under the control of gangsters who had seized power by capturing the previous inmate ruler, stringing him up and beheading him. Then they cut out his heart and fed it to his own dogs.

It was a hyper-dangerous environment to be entering, and especially to try and film. As we researched the trip in advance from London, I asked one of our guides if our best bet was to go into the prison with a small group of special forces soldiers as bodyguards. There was a hollow laugh on the Skype call and a voice said softly, 'None of you would leave alive.'

We realised the only person who could take us inside, and keep us safe, and get us out, was actually the Bishop of San Pedro Sula. The gang members had faith in him because he was attempting to broker a truce between the gangs and the government. We entered through the prison gate, met the bishop inside for just a couple of minutes, and had to make a rapid decision about whether we could trust him. Not just whether he was honest and true, but whether we thought he was someone the inmates inside would definitely respect enough to keep us safe if we were with him. I remember turning to my friend Matt Brandon, who was directing, and Craig who was filming, widening my eyes at them and asking: 'OK?' with weight and meaning. They knew what I was saying, and said they were good to continue. We followed the bishop, in his starched white shirt and large crucifix, as we walked among men with face tattoos identifying their allegiance to the Sinaloa cartel or the ferociously violent gang MS13. We stuck to the bishop like glue, as if he was the Archangel Gabriel, and he kept us safe.

On our trip into Burma, Cheery was to be our archangel. She had worked out several possible routes we could take and several villages we could visit, depending on army activity in the area. She had contacted village elders using trusted runners and asked if it was appropriate for us to visit. Most importantly, she had warned them about the possible consequences if we were caught with them. They all wanted us to come.

Then we met up with three wiry, muscular young Chin guys from a group called the Free Burma Rangers (FBR), an extraordinary organisation that had been giving us advice and information over the previous weeks. The Free Burma Rangers is, in its own words, a multi-ethnic humanitarian service movement that has worked to bring help, hope and love to people in the conflict zones of Burma, Iraq and Sudan. It was founded by a gung-ho, can-do American special forces veteran called David Eubank, a Texan who grew up as the son of missionaries in Thailand. The FBR trains, supplies and coordinates mobile relief teams who provide critical emergency medical care, shelter, food, clothing and human rights monitoring. One of their driving motivations is certainly religious belief, but in the Free Burma Rangers you don't have to be Christian.

'You can be any or no religion,' Eubank has said. 'You can be a man or woman; you just have to do this for love. And you can't run if people can't run.'

The three Chin men from the FBR were a highly trained undercover unit taking healthcare and medicine across the line into remote areas of Chin State. They were taking a colossal risk. Rangers have been shot, tortured, blown up by landmines and executed by the Burmese military. They intimidate and worry some other relief groups because they operate right on the front lines of conflict, or even covertly behind the lines deep in enemy territory, and they sometimes arm some of their personnel for their own defence. They're what you might get if you crossed the SAS with Oxfam.

We sat talking with the Rangers for hours in the guest house in Aizawl. I was hugely impressed by the men. They seemed much older than their years, with an air of confidence and calm that felt almost supernatural. They talked to us about the risks they faced, and the risks we would face, and the dangers of our entire mission suddenly became very stark.

Our slightly crazy plan was that the Rangers would go ahead of us, cross the border on their own and launch their medical mission, walking from remote village to remote village. We would be crossing later in a different place, but we would try to reach a specific village around the same time as them so we could film what they were doing.

We confirmed with Cheery that contact had been made with village elders and they were happy for us to visit. We suggested that we would avoid filming any landmarks that could identify a village, and that we would obscure faces of anyone who could be at risk. Cheery told the Rangers, and had told village elders by message, that the film would be shown around the world, possibly on the global BBC World channel, but also by other broadcasters in the region. Like Cheery, they were adamant they wanted their story to be told. Travelling the Tropic of Cancer was one of the first times I came across a truth confirmed many times since on my journeys, that people who are suffering terribly will so often take the great risk of more suffering just to experience the free oxygen that recognition can bring.

Whenever packing for a covert mission, one sensible rule, particularly if you are trying to illegally enter a military dictatorship, is best to avoid dressing like a mercenary. Too many travellers, and TV presenters, go for an excessively rugged, military look. But that can create serious danger. There is a terrible story of a group of French backpackers in North Africa killed by rogue government forces because they were wearing cheap army surplus gear and were mistaken for soldiers. I went through all our stuff stripping out any army surplus gear, including a military machete with a camouflage pattern on the sheath.

One vital bit of kit that could get us into a whole world of trouble, but we still needed to take, were two satellite phones. Without them we had no way of maintaining contact with the outside world as soon as we were out of Indian mobile phone coverage. But we had been told by different intelligence sources that if we made a call on the Burmese side of the border, the military might detect the call, assume we were rebels and fire mortar shells at our position. I had friends who had been bombed just like that in northern Burma. We were also warned that even if we ran into trouble on the Indian side and made a satellite call, the Indian army could also triangulate our position, also assume we were rebels fighting against the Indian authorities, and fire artillery shells at the location, as they had been know to do previously. We took our main satellite phone, and another as back-up, but agreed we would only use it in an absolute emergency, and only then while moving quickly so it would be harder to bomb us. I took one, Jonathan had the other, while Andrew carried an emergency position indicating radio beacon – EPIRB for short.

We were following the straightforward mission advice I was given in the Amazon: two is one, and one is none. We all agreed there was a solid chance something vital could malfunction or break. You never want to be the muppet who didn't bring a replacement. You cannot go on a secret mission into Burma with just one of something that really matters, particularly if it's technical. If we only took one camera, and it had broken, then everything would have been for nought. Also, we had no idea how long we were going to be there and recharging our kit might not be an option. So we took extra camera equipment and extra batteries, even though they were really heavy. Everything was sealed inside waterproof bags.

As for what to wear, to operate in the jungle for days or weeks, you start with the naked body and work out the fundamentals of what you need to survive individually, collectively and to film as a team. I had to put my fertility-friendly boxers aside for this trip and dig out my jungle underwear, which looked a little too like hot pants, but was great for holding things together and reducing chafing on long, sweaty walks. As did wearing the seams on the outside.

We went for long-sleeved shirts to reduce the risk of sunstroke and to help us cover the skin from mosquitoes, and trousers that were quick-drying. I planned to walk in trekking trainers, while

Andrew and Jonathan went for jungle boots, which were slightly too militaristic for my liking, but they have drainage holes so you don't need to take them off when fording rivers. The boots come with hard, uncomfortable insoles, but they resisted the temptation to replace them with more absorbent and comfortable alternatives as they would soak up water like a sponge. For trekking in jungles I often tuck my trousers into my socks or boots and then smear thick natural insect repellent cream around them to deter leeches.

I would normally wear a poncho in tropical rain but, although I took one into Burma, I didn't expect we'd have time to dig out waterproof clothing from our rucksacks. We weren't going on a jolly hike, we were heading into what was effectively enemy territory. We needed to keep moving, not pause to put on waterproofs. In a downpour in the jungle, water will always penetrate whatever you're wearing, and anyway we would be sweating buckets. We knew we'd be soaked through after just a few hours, one way or another. But we did take one extra set of dry clothes each in a waterproof bag. At night after a long jungle trek, you dry yourself, put a dab of antibacterial powder on damp feet to protect against infections, get into a hammock wearing the dry clothes and then – the fun bit – put your wet clothes back on in the morning.

Food and hydration were huge issues. Going on a long hike in sweltering heat and humidity meant we would need to drink at least three litres of water per day. But we knew we would be wading through rivers, which at least meant we could use water filters to refill our bottles and bladder bags, dramatically reducing how much water we needed to carry. As for food, we packed expedition meal packs, which have a heating element that reacts chemically to water and provides a hot meal. We budgeted two a day for four days. Although the meals were heavier than taking light dehydrated food, they would need boiled water, which takes longer, and might slow us down. We also carried a tiny stove to heat a pot of something sustaining, if we could find it. To help our calorie intake we took nuts and raisins and, for morale, flapjacks from home.

Our equipment list ran for several pages. It included a fire lighting kit, compasses, a wrist-worn GPS, emergency water purification straws and a medical kit, including Riamet. This antimalarial medicine once saved my life in Gabon and I still didn't feel comfortable in the jungle without it. I took my favourite parang, a heavy-duty machete with a bigger blade that gives a bit more heft when chopping through thick jungle undergrowth, and I took a squash ball. When correctly deployed it's a low-tech bit of kit with a high impact, keeping you dry at night in a jungle hammock when everyone else is getting slowly soaked. In Burma we would be sleeping in Hennessy hammocks, which come self-contained with a bug net and a tarpaulin cover to keep out the rain. But moisture can still travel down the hammock rope and drip straight into your dry cocoon. So you simply put a slit in half a squash ball, slide it on to the rope with the cup facing inwards and bask in a feeling of smugness when it starts pelting down. To carry all this, I had a special ultralight rucksack that had a mesh panel separating the bag from my back, making me less vulnerable to heatstroke.

It was all very well humping all this kit into the jungle. But we knew that in an emergency we might have to ditch our bags and literally run for our lives. So we each had a small survival kit and I had an SOS neck kit with a wire saw necklace sheathed in plastic, so I didn't garrotte myself, which can be used on wood or as a weapon or animal trap. Strung on that line around my neck was a pocket knife, matches, a whistle, a compass and a micro-fishing kit which could also be used as wound thread. My most intimate piece of kit was a tiny waterproof survival screw case the size of a large pill which contained $200. With the tender help of my wife, I taped it just behind my testicles. Initially it felt extremely uncomfortable, until I realised I had other more important things to worry about. We strapped hundreds of US dollars to various parts of our bodies, for every eventuality we could think of and others we couldn't.

Eventually all our equipment, tapes, cameras, kit and food were packed. Cheery took a rather different approach. She was planning to wear jeans and sandals.

'Are you ready?' she asked with a smile. 'Then tomorrow we go.'

CHAPTER NINE

The Tin Basket

We left Aizawl early the next morning. Our two 4x4 vehicles were waiting close to the guest house, so they stopped outside and we chucked in the bags we had already stacked by the door. The idea was that by the time any Indian police agents watching us had got hold of their senior officer to warn them we'd left, we would be well on the way.

We sped south through lush vegetation and small villages full of large but flimsy homes with rusty corrugated roofs, on roads that wiggled and wriggled endlessly around the hills of Mizoram. The highway was easily wide enough for one vehicle, but a tighter squeeze when meeting lorries hurtling in the opposite direction around a bend. Fortunately there were fewer vehicles on the road at that early hour, but farmers were up and out, and long-distance buses were hauling students. On the back of several were lines of bizarre little rattan cages, open on each side and with chickens held tightly inside.

After a couple of hours we paused for a wee break and a wash by a remote hillside waterfall. I felt something under my trousers and found two leeches crawling up my legs. Anya found one crawling in a southerly direction from her abdomen. These weren't sweet little Western leeches, they were chunkier than an index finger and were preparing for a feeding frenzy. We had to prise them off using the blunt side of a knife.

Later in the day we arrived at yet another guest house, which was really just a line of huts standing next to each other behind a village house. Finally the Indian police caught up with us. A couple of men in plain clothes appeared, showed their ID cards and asked us, perfectly politely, what we were doing near the border. The major in charge seemed privately delighted to meet us. He confided nothing much happened in the region and it was rare to have compatriots visiting from other parts of India, let alone an excitingly suspicious foreign TV team. He started talking to us about his time serving on a United Nations mission in Africa, so we tried to keep him sweet and explained we were just visiting briefly to see a little of the landscape and then we'd be heading back to Aizawl. For now, we said, we're dog-tired and hitting the sack early. He bade us farewell and vanished.

The plan was that Jonathan, Andrew, Cheery and I would leave for Burma early the following morning, while Anya and Abhra Bhattacharya, who had rejoined the team to help with logistics in Mizoram, stayed behind to hold the fort, handle our emergency communications with locals and deal with the Indian secret police, who it was now clear were indeed following us. It was time for me to say goodbye to Anya. We had a sweet couple of hours chatting about the journey and our future plans, and then I gave her a letter I had written for my mum, just in case anything terrible happened, and I slipped another little farewell card into her rucksack for her to find after I'd left.

At dawn the next morning we were up and out, stuffing ourselves and our bags into two different local vehicles Cheery had found for us. We were soon enduring the bumpiest drive possible, on what I suspect was the muddiest road in Asia. Still a long way from the border, our little 4x4s got stuck again and again on tiny hillside passes. After our efforts and preparation, we all felt a fear that we might not even make it to the actual border. But with all of us pushing the cars from behind, helped perhaps by determination and desperation, each time we made it through. Eventually we made it to snaking tracks just a final few miles from the river that marked the border with Burma, and we met a couple of local traders coming the other way. They had crossed from Burma and, crucially, they hadn't seen any soldiers on either side.

The closer we got to the border, the more careful we became, almost peering around corners in case we suddenly encountered the Indian army. India sees all its borders as critical military infrastructure. Endless wars with its neighbours over the decades had led to hundreds of thousands of deaths. The borders with Pakistan and, increasingly, China hog the headlines, but the border with Burma was also seen as a hotspot.

Meanwhile Anya and Abhra were having their own adventures. Early in the morning the police arrived again and Anya went to answer their questions in the main guest house. One of the agents started asking where the rest of the team was, and said he would go to check the huts we had just left.

'Oh don't do that,' said Anya with a keen smile. 'They're trying to get more sleep because they're feeling ill.'

But the officer was still walking out towards the back. Realising we might be rumbled when the officer spotted none of us were in our rooms, Anya made a snap decision.

'Look, they're not well, they're staying here ... and it's me who'd really like your help,' she said. Anya told them she wanted to go on a tour of local villages and she needed them to come with her as a security detail. That worked. They forgot all about checking on us, and followed Anya and Abhra on a long tour of village after village. Anya would stop and fake film every possible shot, and then they would move on. Late in the day the major insisted on returning to the guest house 'to check the team are OK', and they had to turn back.

While the major schmoozed with Anya, one of the agents said he was going to check on our huts. This was a tense moment. Still trying to smile along as the major chatted to her, Anya began sketching out excuses in her head for what might happen when his man found our huts empty. He came back a moment later, looking concerned, and said the huts were shuttered and quiet, and perhaps the rest of Anya's team had already gone back to sleep? Somehow he didn't spot that the huts were padlocked from the outside.

'Oh yes,' said Anya, trying to hide her relieved surprise. 'That'll be it. Would anyone like a drink?'

And so Anya poured out glasses of a local poteen we'd acquired and kept the major and his men chatting away, and laughed and talked with them about the English Football League and Korean pop music, which was huge in Mizoram.

The major eventually confided that because India was busy trying to establish closer trade links with the Burmese military junta, it was particularly important that nothing embarrassing happened in the border area.

'You're definitely not here to cause us any problems, are you?' said the major hopefully.

More drinks were poured, and they talked about Mizoram, and the history of the Mizoram people, who the major claimed were originally a tribe in China who fled when they were roped in to building the Great Wall. By the time the conversation moved on to anthropology he clearly felt he'd done his bit, and left with his men. The mission was saved.

Around the same time, many miles away, Cheery, Jonathan, Andrew and I were finally approaching a remote section of the border with Burma. We arrived much later than expected, said farewell to our local drivers a few hundred metres from the river, and then moved stealthily on foot to find a secluded area of the jungle near the river we could stay in. It was pitch black so we could hear but not see the river that marked the border. We couldn't risk checking the river with torches or starting a fire in case that drew in the Burmese military, so we strung up our hammocks and ate cold rice we'd brought as back-up. Then we had a fitful night until dawn.

I woke up and emerged feet first out of the slit in my tight hammock, which felt a little bit like leaving a birth canal. Jonathan and Andrew woke up at the same time and blearily we all took our bearings. The river was wider and flowing more quickly than we had hoped. We were on a gentle curve and could see less than 100 metres in each direction. On the opposite bank of the river, about 40 metres away, were scattered trees and thick bush. We could see there was a small group of men waiting in civilian clothes. They were possibly Chin villagers there to help us, but it was by no means clear. I started idly scanning the riverbank through binoculars and spotted movement in the undergrowth just upriver. It was men. Wearing green camouflage clothes. That was worrying enough, and then I saw the barrel of a Kalashnikov. Was it an ambush? Were the Burmese military setting a trap for us? Suddenly we thought we were going to be shot at, and we took a step back behind the thick trees that were providing us with cover.

One of the men in the first group nearest to us leapt into the river and swam frantically towards us. For a paranoid second I thought they were all going to follow him and come across to get us. Then I thought the swimmer might be escaping from the soldiers advancing with guns. The powerful current pulled him downstream. Cheery ran across boulders and rocks towards him, had a brief chat and came rushing back. She couldn't see properly but said the villagers on the other side were friendly and were trying to warn us soldiers were coming. We crouched down and started looking behind us for an escape route back into India.

This all happened in moments. But soon it became clear it was a case of mistaken identity. The soldiers were actually fighters from a Chin rebel militia, and posed no threat to us. Quite the opposite – they were on Cheery's side.

Next we had to work out how to cross the swollen river, which was far too wide and fast for us to wade through with our kit and cameras. We had been warned that October, just after the monsoon, was not a good time of year to attempt a river crossing. I had brought two long lengths of climbing rope from the UK, plus carabiners and a Petzl double pulley in case we had to zip-wire across this river, or any others we might find. Although I'm a strong swimmer, I don't normally have to swim against a powerful current, so I had been training, doing pool sprints for a good month beforehand. I had also been practising my knots, which I'm hopeless at, so that I could take the rope across the river, tie it to a tree and then pull the team across.

I was tying one rope to a tree and the other round my waist and preparing to swim across when the swimmer, a man called Tong, said there was an old cable tensioned across the river a short distance upriver. The villagers produced a battered flat tin basket from bushes on the other bank, attached it to the cable and a tiny chap hopped on board and was pulled over to us, which at least meant it was tested in front of our eyes. We took a closer look and could see the tray, handle, wheel and cable were all riddled with rust, but the villagers reassured Cheery the basket would easily carry multiple sacks of rice. I was hoping to be saved from a dunking and said I'd go first, but both Andrew and Jonathan strenuously disagreed. For a couple of minutes everything stopped while we had our one and only row. They argued that it should be them crossing first in order to film me arriving in Burma. But I was adamant that viewers had to see me genuinely going in, not following on the coat-tails of my brave and burly camera crew. It was the simple style of my programmes, something I insisted on, but I was also worried about the possibility of an ambush.

'This is on me,' I said. 'If anyone is going to get captured on the other side it should be me. If you need a shot of me I'll take a camera, hold it between my feet and point it at my face.'

It was only a short ride, but it felt like so much of my life up to that point had been preparing for that moment: sitting in a bit of ramshackle tin attached to a thin rope and sliding on a make-shift pulley across that turbulent river.

The greeting on the other side was cautious. The villagers were smiling, their hands were out and they didn't appear to have weapons. I called back and one by one Jonathan, Andrew and Cheery came over. Even if it would not be for long, she was going home.

'We've arrived,' I said. 'We've travelled from the world's largest democracy on that side of the river to one of the most repressive countries in the world on this side.'

Cheery didn't know the villagers well, but they knew her. She asked them about their community and their families, who had told them to come, and whether they had seen any Burmese troops on patrol. When she was happy with their answers and had identified the Chin village we were now going to aim for, we set off with them through the jungle, with a couple of pack horses to help carry supplies we had brought for whichever community we might visit. Some of our guides went ahead as undercover spotters to signal if any Burmese soldiers were on the way, using an astonishing array of cries and whistles mimicking birds and wildlife.

We walked quickly and quietly in single file, trekking at speed, but always alert to noises coming from the jungle. It felt like a hostile land. There were thousands of Burmese troops and dozens of their army bases in the area. Twice in just the first few miles there were moments where the villager at the front of our line froze and behind him we all dropped to the ground.

The journey took us through genuine *Bridge on the River Kwai* country, with densely forested hills and valleys. Much of it was heavy going and the villagers set a relentless pace. The most unnerving sections of the journey were when we had to wade across more rivers, of which there turned out to be about five, because while crossing them we were quite exposed. Eventually Cheery's sandals fell apart, and I had to gaffer-tape them together. I asked her how it felt to be back. She had a sobering answer.

'A bit fearful,' she said. 'The Burmese troops are not so far from here. It's why the villagers are always careful and scared of the Burmese troops. Whenever they are there it involves forced labour, extortion, sometimes rape against women and child labourers.' It was a powerful reminder of the story we were trying to tell.

After a day of walking at speed, in late afternoon we emerged into a small clearing on an incline and could hear the voices of children playing ahead. At the top of a slope we started to see huts built on short stilts. We had made it to the Chin village. Dozens of people came out to see us. Men, women, barefoot children, from the very old to the very young, all pushed forward to shake our hands.

It was welcoming, friendly and extremely moving. I choked back tears. I could not believe we had made it. After all the preparation and planning, and the trekking and tension, we were actually there. I gave a brief speech of thanks to the villagers who had assembled in front of us, which Cheery translated. Again they greeted it with smiles and laughter.

'We are so happy to see you too,' one of them said.

A wiry old man with a little grey goatee asked Cheery about the camera Jonathan was holding. He had never seen a camera before, nor a European. It all bore out her description of villagers in Chin State being a forgotten people in a forgotten land.

I glanced around quickly. Most of the villagers were wearing the local longyi, a Burmese sarong, or loose, baggy trousers, along with hand-me-down shirts and T-shirts. We were on an unmade track between two lines of homes, each large enough for an extended family, built from wooden planks, woven bamboo, and with roofs made from bits of corrugated tin and local bamboo thatch. Chickens and ducks were running around. Pigs were kept in pens under the houses. There were clothes drying on a couple of lines slung between homes, but there were no overhead cables or phone lines piping power and the outside world into the community. The only real evidence of modernity I could see were a couple of pieces of rudimentary farm machinery. These people were off the map.

Rather to my amazement, our plan to be in the village at the same time as the Free Burma Rangers actually worked. They appeared from the jungle, vanished into a hut to treat a woman with fever who was too ill to move, and then set up an instant clinic outside in a village clearing. They spread their first aid kits and drugs out in front of them as around 20 patients gathered.

We watched as the Rangers went about their critical work, dispensing advice, pain relief and antibiotics to people. Joshua, their main medic, treated a child with vomiting and diarrhoea. One woman was in agony with a broken tooth. The Rangers glued it back together with a filler. A middle-aged man was breathless. The Rangers talked to him, listened to his lungs, checked his blood pressure and prescribed anti-coagulants.

As one patient was being treated I asked him when was the last time a nurse or a doctor had been sent to visit the village by the government.

'Never,' he said. 'I have never seen them coming, even once in ten years.' There was no nurse or doctor in the entire area.

The Free Burma Rangers didn't just bring medical aid; they also had a camera to film evidence of human rights abuses. I asked Joshua what would happen if they were apprehended.

'If they catch us they will kill us,' he replied.

Through Cheery I asked the assembled group of villagers how many had been struck by malaria. Almost every single hand went up.

'Everybody has had malaria,' said a woman.

The demand for fever and malaria treatment was so high the Rangers had already needed to offload most of the paracetamol they were carrying in another village. We had a bundle in our own medical kit that was supposed to be reserved for treating ourselves. But we had to help. We gave them most of our supply, and I was also able to help treat a child with an eye infection with some of our antibiotic eye drops, which we also gave to his mother to use after we left. It felt good to help, practically, even in a tiny way.

We filmed around the village and some surrounding fields but we had to make sure we did not make the community identifiable. Looking around I knew I was somewhere special and peaceful, a place inhabited by innocent people who, although preyed upon by the military and abandoned by the state, had somehow held on to their core humanity. They seemed to me to be very gentle people who were doing something dangerous and brave by collectively entrusting us outsiders with their story and, to some extent, their lives. It was astonishing, and I felt an enormous responsibility to both understand a tiny bit of their experiences and also to carry it out of that forgotten corner of Burma back to the outside world.

Then Cheery came over to tell us that she had been talking to a village elder. He told her the Burmese military had not visited the village for a couple of weeks and were due back. If locals were caught hiding us they could face execution. Realising our time was limited, we had to hurry to film as much as we could. We were taken to a nearby home to meet the Chin elders.

The last rays of the setting sun were shining through the woven walls of the hut, which was virtually bare inside except for a large, low round table and some tiny stools. In the corner was an open fire and two huge pots cooking rice and soup, tended by an elderly woman. A tiny girl proudly showed off her pink dress and the flowers on her old flip-flops.

Some of the senior men and women from the village came and joined us. I thanked them for receiving us and then announced we had brought 40 large family mosquito nets as a gift to the village, courtesy of the pack horses. Cheery had said the nets were the most useful, moral and also safest gift we could offer. They were all bought from local markets and were appropriately grubby. Brand new mozzie nets brought from abroad would have aroused huge suspicion if the military found them in a house. The villagers agreed they would keep some of the nets and distribute the others to families in other villages who needed them most. It was a good present to give, certainly much better than booze and cigarettes.

It was dark now and we switched our cameras to night vision. With Cheery interpreting, I asked the villagers to describe their treatment by the military.

'We are all scared of them,' said one elder. 'Whenever we see their faces we are frightened.'

The Burmese army have raped, murdered and tortured their way through ethnic minority areas of the country like Chin State. They would steal, rob and force peasants and villagers to work as slaves for them. Every encounter with them could end badly for the Chin.

'If they get angry,' said another, 'they slap us and shout at us. They tell us off and threaten us. Then whatever they want like rice or chickens they would just take it.' He had been asked for money by soldiers and then beaten up, three times, when he had nothing to offer. 'We don't see them as our government. For example, if the smallest ones were hungry then a good government would feed them. A good government would help those who are in trouble. But this government is totally the opposite. Instead they take whatever they want away from what we have.'

Hearing this I felt a deep sadness, anger, but finally also a degree of understanding about their situation. It was only by being there, by feeling a fraction of the fear they lived with, that I could begin to comprehend what it was like to live under occupation, like being in Nazi-occupied France during the Second World War.

'We will not forget what you have all done for us by taking this risk and spending your time and energy to come and visit us in this remote part of the country,' another elder said to us, patting his hand on my knee and smiling. I was completely taken aback. 'All you have done is very precious and meaningful for us and we will not forget you.'

I struggled not to well up at what they were saying. And then, very suddenly, everything went wrong.

A breathless runner burst in among us and started blurting something. I had no idea what was being said but there was a palpable change in the atmosphere. The villagers looked scared. Even Cheery, who is remarkably unflappable, seemed frightened. She quickly explained the runner had come from another village. The Burmese military had just arrived there. It was only a short, fast march away.

'They might be on the way here right now,' she said.

Suddenly we were all in grave danger and we had to decide what to do.

The Free Burma Rangers could immediately melt into the undergrowth, which they were used to doing in emergencies. They could take off their T-shirts and blend in. We didn't have that choice. The villagers talked among themselves and quickly suggested we could hide in secret compartments they had under their huts, or in the jungle nearby. But it felt a huge risk to rely on every single villager keeping quiet. What if the military already knew we were in the area and began beating people up or even torturing them to find out where we were?

Cheery spoke to the villagers: 'What we are worried most is for you and of course our team just in case the soldiers know and arrest the people – they won't spare the old people, even the women and children.'

We were all absolutely shattered and our sleeping bags were laid out in a corner of the hut. But we had to decide what we

Exploring Dartmoor with Obi was a tonic for the body and the mind during the pandemic. It's hard to be grumpy, let alone depressed, when you're around such excitement, such positivity, such unconditional trust and loyalty.

I have Anya to thank for introducing me to the wonderful Greek island of Symi, just off Rhodes. Symi has a lovely compact feel about it, along with great food, fantastic swimming, and to my mind the finest harbour in the entire eastern Mediterranean.

Anya and I travelling in Madagascar on an early adventure together, with both of us writing and filming.

Getting some advice about picking a good camel from one of the most successful Tuareg camel dealers in the Sahara.

With the lads on my stag weekend in Spain. Never go paintballing somewhere hot. It was too warm for thick clothing and I had bruises that lasted for weeks.

Anya and I loving a bit of a dress-up for a party in a remote country house in Devon. We had such a good time we decided it was the perfect place to get married.

Trekking on foot into western Burma to meet the persecuted Chin people, on one of my most dangerous missions.

With Carlos Enrique Zaens, the head ranger of a national park in a troubled region of Colombia. I had huge respect for Carlos, who was battling to protect his precious corner of the planet from guerrillas, right-wing paramilitary death squads, drug cartels, poachers, the army and illegal gold miners. On my early travels I realised that Carlos, and other conservationists like him, are front-line heroes, unarmed warriors in a just war.

The secluded little island of Moyenne in the Seychelles, where I met Brendon Grimshaw, the Yorkshireman who bought it, lived there, and planted thousands of trees to turn it into a magnet for birds and wildlife.

Learning how to play the ancient full-contact game of Kabaddi with Tanjilur Rahman, an inspiring and wise guide in Bangladesh.

Anya and Jonathan Young, a brilliant cameraman and one of the small team I have travelled with around the world. We were at the Ubari lake in southern Libya, a stunning desert oasis in the Sahara, so perfect it looked unreal.

Jake finally appeared after the most exciting, exhausting, impossible and bizarre journey of my life. I'd dreamt about that moment, even mythologised it in my head as a transformative rite of passage, but I never fully anticipated the enormity of having a child.

The Casspir, a type of bullet-proof, mine-resistant armoured vehicle which has given me sanctuary several times on my travels. The Casspir has a V-shaped hull designed to direct the force of a roadside bomb away from anyone inside.

As much as I love my travels, nothing in life has given me the same deep joy and profound experiences as becoming a father. This shot of Jake and I was taken while we stayed with friends in the Devon countryside, on the day Anya and I realised we needed to move somewhere green and wild.

My first major trip as a new father was to Somalia, a country riven by conflict. I'm on the front-line in Mogadishu with Jonathan, talking with Lieutenant Colonel Paddy Ankunda, a senior Ugandan soldier, and trying to make sense of the fighting.

Of course there's lots of this on my journeys, but that just makes them more memorable.

Talking with Marie Saleem, a conservationist and scientist, on a stunning island in the Maldives that felt like the culmination of my own impossible travel journey.

Jonathan and I with some of the cases and bags, containing camera equipment, supplies, medical kit, tools, food and, of course, tea bags, that we need for our travels.

Anya and I swinging the lad. We had gone Full Devon, living partly off the grid with Obi, our own huge hound.

Helping to move a giant and ludicrously heavy concrete block into the sea off India to thwart bottom-trawling fishing boats annihilating life in our oceans.

One of my favourite photos with Jake, taken on a boat off the Greek island of Symi. I hope I've always been there for my son when it mattered, and I tell him that I love him, every single day.

The latest addition to my little family. Lyla has joined Obi on our treks and travels with the boundless energy of a Duracell Bunny. Whenever I walk with the dogs, I spend almost the entire time with a grin plastered across my face, an intoxicated smile of love for both of them, and pleasure because I get to share their joy and close connection to nature.

Varanasi in India, one of the oldest inhabited cities in the world, a place of faith for 30 centuries, where I learned two critical lessons that have stayed with me and deeply affect me to this day.

I place such a huge value on time spent in nature. I want Jake to have meaningful, real experiences, and I hope with all my heart that he grows up happy, confident and wild.

were doing. I said although we had hoped to spend several days in Burma, what we had already filmed had given us some insight into life under the military regime. It was better than nothing. Then I wanted to hear from the others, so I asked Jonathan if I could take the camera from him, and then I asked him and Andrew for their thoughts. They were a bit taken aback to be filmed, but I thought it was a unique situation that warranted showing viewers behind the scenes. I wanted people watching to actually see these brave guys I had travelled with, who had put up with risk and an exceptionally difficult situation. I was proud of them, proud to be with them and I wanted viewers to see that we made collective team decisions, especially in a moment of crisis.

'I think our luck so far has been good,' said Andrew, thoughtfully and carefully. 'We've made it here. I think we probably weren't sure that we were going to make it this far, so I think we should probably bank what we've got and stop taking chances now.'

Cheery was in the greatest danger of anyone. I trained the camera on her and asked what she thought. She turned her head to me and calmly but firmly said: 'I think we should go back.'

It's not always simple to come to such a quick conclusion democratically. Sometimes it's easier if someone wearing epaulettes calls the shots. I remember a feeling of pride that there was no panic, no flapping. We grabbed our sleeping bags, threw our kit into rucksacks, and strapped survival kits to our waists. To lighten our loads we had to leave some tech stuff, clothing and food sachets, and agreed that the villagers would bury everything until long after the army had gone.

Before we could even ask, some of the villagers insisted they would guide us back through the jungle towards the border with India. We stood outside putting our bags on our shoulders.

'You have come a long way. We cannot express how grateful and thankful we are to you for doing this,' said an old man to me.

'You humble us with your words,' I said, my emotions in turmoil. 'I will never forget you.'

They smiled, I waved goodbye, then another teenager came running down through the village shouting. Somebody else said in broken English: 'They're coming, they're coming.' We turned and ran into the jungle, heading back towards the border with India. This time round, the trip through the bush and back across the rivers could not have been more different. It was dark, the tension was intense, and we had to travel without lights and as silently as possible. I could hear my heart racing.

We knew we had to get out with all of our footage otherwise it would all have been for nothing. We walked, trotted, jogged and a couple of times we ran. I fell, over and over. A sharp broken branch on the ground skewered my rucksack strap. A few centimetres either way and it would have been a deep spear wound.

The camera could never adequately convey the tension and danger as we raced to the border. Normally we might try and get an up-and-pass shot, where Jonathan will go ahead with his camera and I would walk past looking serious. There was no bloody time for that. We had to flee. Jonathan snatched shots on the move in the dark without a light.

The jungle at night is a cacophony of noise, which seemed to provide us with cover as we moved at speed. But it was also terrifying. Every sound and rustle could have been an ambush.

At four in the morning, after trekking at high speed non-stop for hours, we drew closer to the Indian border, and we walked more slowly, in a line, and as quietly as we possibly could. One of our guides went ahead of us to check if there were any

Burmese troops down by the river. Everything was silent for a moment. Then suddenly we heard voices.

'People are coming,' whispered Cheery, sounding frightened.

It was one of the worst moments of my life. We thought the Burmese army had been lying in wait for us. We thought it was an ambush, and that we were trapped. Time seemed to stop. We tensed our bodies, ready to run. But where?

Then another voice called out. Cheery relaxed. 'That's our guys,' she said.

It was some of the other villagers we had met earlier, who had come back to the river to help us across.

'Bloody hell,' I said. 'I thought we were screwed then.'

The pulley system on the cable over the river had been broken. The locals had been repairing it using what looked like clothes hanger wire. But we had no choice but to take the chance and use it. Soldiers could be behind us. We had to get out.

We said goodbye to the village guides we were leaving behind. It was an emotional farewell. Then it began to rain hard, and I went over first. I had no idea whether I was heading into the arms of Indian border guards, who have a terrible reputation for shooting illegal crossers, and I had no idea whether the tin basket would survive the ride or drop me into the water. I had to hope for the best, while preparing to swim.

For a moment the Burmese riverbank disappeared into the darkness behind me, and the Indian side was still invisible. The pulley stopped for a moment, and I was just left hanging there, stuck between repression and democracy, between two dark unknowns. It felt completely surreal. Then I jerked forward and a moment later landed in safety. The coast was clear on the Indian side, and I signalled with my torch for everyone else to follow.

We had made it back to India. Although we were on an emotional high, physically we were wrecked and needed to grab some rest. Up went our hammocks and we were out like a light. Then two hours later I was woken by something hard prodding at me, which, when I emerged blinking from my cocoon, turned out to be a shotgun barrel wielded by a man wearing a Sheffield United top. It was our driver in Mizoram, who had been worrying about what might happen to us in Burma, and had recruited a rescue party to come and look after us. The rest of his posse had bows and arrows, with which they were planning to defend us from the clutches of the Burmese military.

It was almost suicidally brave of them but, for farcical life experiences, this was right near the top of the list. The Sheffield United shirt provided the finishing touch to the whole crazy picture. It had been given to him by Jonathan, a committed fan who brought ten kits with him on this leg of the journey to hand out like a Yorkshire ambassador. We would have spent more time enjoying the comedy element of our situation if we still hadn't needed to get out of the dangerous border zone. With our wonderful rescue posse we jumped into the back of our getaway vehicle, a dirty old tractor and trailer, and we escaped.

CHAPTER TEN

Plastic Beach

We drove away from the Burmese border on country tracks to try to limit the chances of meeting border agents or the police major, then reunited with Anya in a quiet village and swapped stories about our respective adventures. There was a huge sense of relief, of course, but also a sadness for those we had left behind.

It had been illegal to enter Burma, but it had also been illegal to leave and then re-enter India, so we couldn't entirely relax. We all felt a small nagging concern we might be stopped, questioned, and have our footage impounded or confiscated. It was a small risk but with large consequences. I didn't feel our footage was completely safe until we had left Indian airspace. As we boarded the plane in north-eastern India, it tickled me no end to find that the restricted items for the hand luggage included guns, ammunition, scissors, pepper spray and also jars of Patak's lime pickle.

Anya and I then had some time off to rest and recuperate before we started the final leg of the journey around the Tropic of Cancer. I was already feeling overwhelmed by the scale of my travels, and more than anything by the people I had been meeting. But there were still lessons to learn about the planet, poverty, our treatment of wildlife, and even food.

East from Burma the line travels straight through southern China, but the government in Beijing was battling with foreign

TV crews and effectively prevented us from entering the country. So instead we decided we would divert slightly to the south, through Laos and Vietnam, before following the Tropic across the water to the island of Taiwan, and then leap across the Pacific Ocean to the islands of Hawaii, a suitably impossible ending to my journey.

I could still see the influence of China everywhere in northern Laos, where we started the final Cancer journey. We headed for the very centre of the Golden Triangle, where Burma, Thailand and Laos meet. Long a lawless region notorious for bandits and drug gangs, it was now falling under the sway of Chinese money. The best evidence was a massive new entertainment centre growing out of the forest on the edge of the Mekong River. A flash casino and luxury hotel resort had opened only weeks before, costing developers £100 million. I met one of its bosses, a smartly dressed young man called Han Zhigang, who assured me that this was an investment, not an invasion.

'We are not coming to occupy,' he said, 'and we are not a colony.' His various phones kept trilling as he arranged helipads and ordered road expansions to create a Las Vegas in the jungle, on 100 square kilometres of land, all part of a wider multi-billion-pound Chinese plan to industrialise northern Laos.

In the years since the resort has grown hugely, even though the London-based Environmental Investigation Agency (EIA) has described the entire zone as 'a lawless playground' and a free-for-all 'illegal wildlife supermarket'. In 2015 it issued a report describing wildlife shops, boutiques and restaurants in the zone selling ivory, tiger skins, tiger meat and tiger-bone wine taken from a liquor-filled tank containing a complete tiger skeleton. A photograph of the tiger bones was even allegedly included in a brochure for the zone. Then the United States government announced sanctions against the chairman of the firm behind the casino zone, saying he was running a transnational criminal organisation that engaged in an array of horrendous illicit activities including human trafficking and child prostitution, drug trafficking and wildlife trafficking.

Even in Laos many saw China as a dangerous influence. An emerging superpower with imperial ambitions, I for one am not blind to its influence, power, pollution and catastrophic impact on global wildlife. But other empires and superpowers have already inflicted their own horrific legacy in the region, and particularly in Laos.

During the Vietnam War, the US Air Force dropped more bombs on Laos than they did on Germany during the Second World War, the equivalent of three tons for every man, woman and child. Laos is the most heavily bombed country in history, and my route along the Tropic took me over stunning mountains and into the most intensively bombed part of the country. It is believed millions of bombs still litter the countryside, and inevitably children out playing are among their many victims. To understand more I stayed in a hill village with a sweet and welcoming family for whom the war still cast a long shadow. Our host Mr Pansad lost three brothers in the conflict, and his wife explained she often still found bombs while digging in the garden behind the house. They even found a huge unexploded bomb under the actual property. They had customised the casings of several cluster bombs, a horrific weapon that scatters scores of bomblets over a wide area, and turned them into pillars holding up the upper floor of a farm building.

The next day I went to visit the Mines Advisory Group, a UK-based charity that does brilliant work in former conflict zones all around the world, clearing up the terrible aftermath of fighting, and we went out to do some de-mining. I was driving with John McFarlane, a Canadian former army officer, to a foundry where locals would bring bombs to be decommissioned, melted down and turned into valuable scrap metal. We were only a short distance from the gates of the foundry when John suddenly stopped the car and peered forward. Right in front of us on the road, on the tracks where we would have driven, he had spotted a live cluster bomb. John said it had probably fallen off a truck taking it for scrap, or been uncovered by heavy rain. It had a lethal radius of roughly 30 metres.

I was awake late that night just thinking about what might have happened if John hadn't spotted the bomb. People in Laos will be finding American cluster bomblets for decades to come, and they will not necessarily have the same lucky escape.

We hit the road again in Laos, very carefully, and chose a route that took us through the city of Luang Prabang, the ancient and sacred home to more than 30 temples and monasteries. Anya and I rose early to sightsee at a couple of gorgeous tourist sites and say a few more prayers for our own fertility. Then we arranged to meet a local celebrity chef for breakfast. It was a chance to have a bit of fun, but also an opportunity to use food as a window into the culture and geography of Laos, a poor, forested country where people eat what crawls, slithers and scampers in the woods. Joy, the chef, specialised in turning forest food into gorgeous meals in his lovely restaurant. Unfortunately I met up with him in a street market, and gave him the tricky brief of finding our meal.

Joy, a sweet and earnest chap, picked his way around the market carefully, and then chose a bamboo pole stuffed with live wriggling grubs for our starter. He fried them up himself in a corner of the market and, I have to say, they were pretty crunchy and creamy, almost delicious. We are still strangely reluctant to eat insects, but how else can we hope to feed the ridiculous number of people on the planet? For our main course Joy made a slightly strange choice. He claimed it was spatchcocked squirrel, but it looked more like a rat that someone had splatted with a hammer, around the time Stonehenge was built, and had then left preserved in a peat bog. It was possibly the least appetising thing I have ever seen. But I was there for telly, so I had a bite.

The 'squirrel' didn't taste any better than it looked. I told Joy that I thought it tasted quite ratty. He breezily confessed that's what people called it. So it looked like rat, it tasted like rat, which I've had to eat before, for goodness' sake, and the name for it in the local language was rat. I think it was fair for me to make a certain assumption. I tried to palm it off on to a scrawny market dog, and even that wouldn't touch it.

We crossed the mountains in Laos towards Vietnam and one of our drivers insisted we stopped at a local shack of a café, where he ordered a plate of what looked like steaming spinach. It turned out it was a plate of buffalo poo. But at least it was memorable. We have to try the strange foreign food. Often it's not that bad. Sometimes it's delicious. Roasted sheep's eyeballs, which I had to eat in Saudi Arabia, really do melt in the mouth. While I was in Madagascar my guide innocently mentioned that she liked nothing more than a bowl of penis soup. Of course my TV team insisted that I try some. My guide's point was that it's a poor country, and they can't afford choice cuts of meat wrapped in cellophane. They eat all of an animal. In a dirty café the owner produced a shockingly long penis of a zebu, the horned cattle you see throughout the Tropics, and chopped it up into a soup.

In truth it wasn't great. It was very gristly, and very chewy. But we have to try the local food. It's a window into the culture. We learn so much about a people from what and how they eat. I actually quite enjoy the strange food. It's never too awful and it gifts a good tale.

So don't eat in restaurants that have pictures of the food outside. Don't order the club sandwich from a menu when you're away somewhere interesting. Ask what's exotic and unusual, but of course never, ever endangered. Never waste a meal eating something boring when you could be trying something exciting. That's part of the joy of travel, because food is such a brilliant way of racking up great memories. And remember, it's hardly ever going to kill you.

It took ages for us to cross the border into Vietnam because the police were so suspicious of our endless bags of equipment. As a result we were running late and tried to book into the first jerry-built concrete hotel we passed on the other side. They asked if we really wanted to stay overnight.

'Normally people book by the hour,' the nice lady at reception said, who then looked rather confused when Anya walked in. Suddenly we realised why there was a group of young women lounging around.

Anya and I had to pick up several used syringes in our brothel bedroom, and then I whipped out an emergency bin bag I carry with us, slit down the sides, in order to cover an unidentifiable liquid on the mattress. The slightly sub-optimal hygiene experience continued the next morning in a nearby café. We were having breakfast when a guy emerged from the kitchen with a rat in a clear bag. It was unclear if this was pest control or a takeaway.

The Communist red star was still flying over Hanoi, the capital of Vietnam, but you wouldn't know it to walk around the streets that bustled with evidence of private enterprise. The weirdest example of the new class of moneyed elite, at least to me, was the existence of a manicured golf course caddied by women in traditional Vietnamese hats. The club catered for anyone who could afford the modest joining fee of $18,000. The average income in Vietnam at that point was no more than a few dollars a day. There's even a Ho Chi Minh golf trail, a grouping of courses named after the former Communist leader, who must be spinning in his grave.

As people in Vietnam, China and neighbouring countries were becoming richer, many of them were being seduced by the maddest extremes of traditional medicine. We all know that rhino poaching in Africa has been driven by a disastrous demand for rhino horn in Asian countries, especially China. It is less well known that Asian moon bears, as well as sun bears and brown bears, have long been held captive in Vietnam, in horrific conditions, and subjected to a procedure that is so invasive and so revolting that when I first heard about it from a friend I had to ask them to repeat what they'd said.

The bears are held in tiny cages, often so small they cannot even turn around, and are effectively milked for their bile, a bitter secretion found in the gall bladder. The bear is stabbed on its side and a ten-inch needle or tube is inserted into the gall bladder, and then usually just left there with a pump attached. The bile contains an acid used in traditional medicine to ... well, who cares what it's used for. It's completely mad and completely obscene. One small consolation is that the resulting bile that's often sold in traditional medicine is contaminated by pus, blood and faeces. Perhaps bile users, with more money than sense, get what they deserve.

When I visited Vietnam, the abuse had been banned, but it was still legal to keep bears and the practice was still continuing. We drove to a notorious area where bear bile was farmed. The buildings were not much more than small, dark warehouses that opened directly on to the street. I shouldered my way into one of them and found tiny cages with forlorn-looking animals locked inside. The shifty woman who ran it claimed she kept the bears for conservation.

Perhaps one day things will change. When I physically pushed my way past a metal door she was trying to close so we could film the grotesque scene, I was egged on by our government minder who blocked her door with his foot to help me. Normally their job is to stop you filming such things. He was one of many people in Vietnam who are horrified by the treatment of the bears.

Seeing the bears suffering made me rage. Many are put into the cages as cubs, and are then left to grow inside, never being allowed out. They can get so big in the small cage that the bars compress their bones and bodies. It is a thought that gives me nightmares.

I was deeply upset for the bears, and I was also deeply upset for our species. How can human beings do this? How can the same species that built Hagia Sophia, that loves with such tenderness, be responsible for such atrocities?

The farms are occasionally raided and the rescued bears are taken to a sanctuary and hospital run by the group Animals Asia in tree-smothered hills outside Hanoi. I saw one bear being wheeled into their clinic who had been kept in a dark cage for 13 years. Miso had a deformed face from an injury sustained when he was first captured, and he had rotten teeth that mostly had to be removed under anaesthetic. As he lay supine on the operating table, his midriff swam around like an old man's blubbery gut. It was like touching a waterbed. One vet who had been working on bears for three years said his was the worst mouth she had ever seen.

After that it wasn't hard to leave Vietnam and we crossed the South China Sea to the island of Taiwan, which is like nowhere else on the Tropic of Cancer. People there are richer and freer than almost anywhere in the entire Tropics, the poorest region of the world. In the most popular shopping area of Taipei, all the major international brands lined the brash neon-lit streets, and the pavements teemed with well-groomed youngsters positively glowing with prosperity. The Taiwanese will live longer, are better educated, wealthier and healthier than almost any other people in the Tropics. But just like us, education and prosperity will not protect them from the environmental devastation caused by the human race.

Mankind's impact on the planet was much on my mind as I headed towards my very last stop along the Tropic of Cancer, the end of my three circumnavigations around the globe. Five thousand miles across the Pacific Ocean from Taiwan, I finally set foot in the one part of the US to fall within the Tropics: Hawaii. This tourist mecca was one of the most gorgeous places I had visited. Famously it has the sun, the sea, the surf and the skirts. It also has wealth. We think of Hawaii as a paradise for holidaymakers and the natural world. But Hawaii is actually the extinction capital of the world, and nearly 300 species have vanished within living memory. At a bird sanctuary I discovered that half of the islands' native species were extinct, while the rest were severely endangered. The culprits included climate change, pollution and newly introduced species, to which native animals and plants had no resistance. The situation had grown so serious the only option left for conservationists had been to capture some of the few surviving birds in the wild and protect them in captivity. One such species was the Hawaiian crow. It could not boast exotic plumage – after all, it's a crow – but with only 67 birds left it was the most critically endangered species in human care in the entire world. The inspiring Brit leading the last-ditch conservation effort was called Richard Switzer. He was basically Noah, and his centre was an ark.

'When a chick's hatching we stay up,' he told me. 'Every egg is sacred.'

The whole experience chilled me. Is that what it's come to? Were other species I had encountered on a similar trajectory? Was that the future for orangutans, for example?

I boarded a helicopter for a bird's-eye view of a tropical paradise. In one sense it made for an uplifting finale. The breath-taking spectacle took in mountains carpeted in forest, waterfalls trickling off craggy cliff faces, and volcanic lava spewing out of craters to produce pillars of steam as they met the ocean.

Then we landed at Kamilo Beach, two hours' drive from the nearest village on the southern shore of Hawaii's Big Island. My guide was Professor Sam 'Ohu Gon, a Hawaiian conservation biologist. Before we even reached the beach proper we started to stumble across random items of plastic. Old plastic toothbrushes, plastic combs, plastic shoes, plastic belts and plastic mouldings, plastic containers, plastic bottles, a plastic helmet – it was everywhere. In the middle of nowhere, with the ocean stretching away for thousands of miles, I had set foot on a prime candidate for the dirtiest beach in the world. And this was after a recent clean-up in which 70 volunteers had removed tons of garbage. As fast as the beach was cleaned, it filled up again with a seemingly endless supply of mainly plastic rubbish. With objects covered in Cyrillic, Japanese and Chinese lettering, very little of the tons of plastic debris came from Hawaii, but had been washed in on the Pacific's swirling current.

The larger pieces of waste could be collected by hand. But 50 per cent of the beach was actually tiny little plastic pellets. Known as nurdles, these are the raw material that factories warm, shape and mould to form the almost infinite number of plastic products that surround us in our lives. Dumped, lost or washed out of factories and into our seas in their trillions, the nurdles would be difficult to remove from the beach even with a giant sieve. Yet the real shock came when Sam told me to dig into the sand. Plastic doesn't biodegrade; instead it breaks down into smaller and smaller pieces. Among the individual grains of sand, and to a depth of several feet, were billions of tiny plastic flecks, which friction and the pounding of the sea were gradually reducing down in size. As I dug, a chill went down my spine. It was difficult to escape a horrible conclusion, that the sand was being replaced, and the plastic was not just polluting the beach, it was actually *becoming* the beach.

This was the experience that brought home to me like never before just how polluted our planet really is. It transformed my understanding of the modern world. It knocked me sideways. If one of the richest countries cannot hold back the vast tide of plastic garbage, then what hope is there for the rest of the planet? It was a troubling end to my journey. I'd visited 18 countries, seen amazing wildlife and met some wonderful people. But more than anything, it had made me realise that we're running out of time to protect life on this beautiful planet.

However I'm proud the *Tropic of Cancer* series was one of the first times a programme like mine featured plastic pollution. I feel I can hold my head up when the next generation asks, 'Well, what did you do?' I can say we found out about that place, tracked down the right people to take us and went to that remote spot to show how the oceans were vomiting up plastic waste. As depressing as it was to end the story there, to this day it remains one of the most profound examples of the impact of humanity I have been able to help show on television.

Yet still we use more plastic. The problem of plastic pollution hasn't even stabilised or plateaued in the years since I filmed at Kamilo. Around the planet it just gets worse and worse, and Western governments are completely useless at combating the problem. Plastic particles have been found in the remotest corners of the planet, in the deepest marine trenches, in the air, inside food that we eat, and in the depths of our own bodies.

I compare it to nothing less than milking bear bile. We drill deep into Mother Earth and pump out crude oil, this planetary bile stored there by our ecosystem, which has not seen light for millions of years, and then we use it to power our vehicles, but we also turn it into plastic products that form the stuff of our entire lives. Everything now seems to come in plastic, is served in plastic, is cooked in plastic and is doubtless contaminated by plastic.

In a sense, just as my Tropic of Cancer adventure was ending, my own plastic journey was just starting. Kamilo Beach launched me on an arc of discovery. In the years since I have come across more and more evidence of the scale of the plastic catastrophe. Wherever I have been in the world since I have seen plastic pollution.

In the years to come I would find an island off the Kenyan coast swamped by washed-up flip-flops. Women there simply couldn't comprehend where the plastic had come from. They had begun gathering some of them and refashioning them into ornaments to sell to tourists, even into a half-size dolphin.

Off the coast of Europe I have met fishermen pulling more plastic out of the sea than fish. At the southern tip of Italy I met a couple of conservationists who had set up a turtle rescue centre in a converted ticket office. Turtles are dying in the Mediterranean at an ever-increasing rate, many thanks to plastic pollution. They had recently rescued Raoul, a male turtle who had lost most of a flipper after it got tangled in plastic. Then they tipped out a mass of junk they'd found in his intestine, including plastic fishing cord and ripped shreds of plastic shopping bags, which, when floating in the current, turtles mistake for jellyfish, their favourite meal. In another turtle they found an empty packet of rigatoni, for goodness' sake. It was more clear evidence of the consequences of the modern world for marine life and I had an emotional moment when Raoul was released back into the sea to try again. I hope he's still out there, but it's difficult to be optimistic about his chances.

Further around the Med, in southern Spain, I flew up in a microlight to see the plains of Almería where our fruit and vegetables are grown in plastic greenhouses all year round. It was an astonishing sight. Almost as far as the eye could see in every direction, white plastic roofing smothered the land over more than 100 square miles. The farms are mainly staffed by migrants from Africa working and living in horrendous conditions, which doesn't seem to trouble the British supermarkets who are among the farmers' biggest customers.

The human impact of this story was awful enough, but the environmental one is apocalyptic. Much of the plastic sheeting is chucked away rather than recycled, and an expert in marine pollution took me to a dried-up riverbed where the greenhouse sheets were becoming integrated into the soil like geological layers. In heavy rains they were washed into the sea. I felt utterly disgusted by the obscenity of the negligence. Spain has failed to regulate and stop this plastic pollution, but so has the spineless European Union, which has never adequately addressed the issue. Our filming produced a huge reaction from viewers, and rightly so, because it starkly illustrated environmental crimes. In my office I've still got a scrap of plastic sheeting from Almería as a reminder of the crime. I also brought some home for a couple of friends who are geography teachers to try to help them illustrate a situation whose scale is so hard to grasp.

Back on the Tropic of Cancer in Hawaii I swiftly realised no beach clean or engineering solution could ever solve the problems at Kamilo. The years since have only further convinced me that nobody has a simple answer. You hear of schemes in which some well-meaning youngster has invented a filter to take microplastics out of the sea, but they are all useless given the scale of the problem. Recycling is also not the answer. The only solution is for governments to dramatically reduce how much plastic we are allowed to use, and rapidly phase out the manufacture of single-use, throwaway plastic.

Plastic pollution is the consequence of uncontrolled consumer capitalism and completely inadequate regulation, which allows companies to churn out trillions of plastic products for billions of human beings to buy, consume and chuck away. The beach in Hawaii was just the visible result. What we find on our sand is a fraction of what's floating on the surface of the seas, which is itself a fraction of what's sinking to the bottom.

We think we can learn everything on the internet, but that's not always true. I needed to go to that remote corner of paradise and dig down below the surface to find those tiny multicoloured shards of plastic, so I could begin to comprehend the scale of the challenge humanity faces, and then try to convey that to people watching back home. On a planet where everywhere has been explored, I felt I was harking back to an older time, a time when people would go abroad and come back with new stories. In that moment, on that beach, I felt I did my tiny bit to keep that tradition alive.

CHAPTER ELEVEN

Our Spartan

There were no celebrations or bunting waiting for us at Heathrow when we landed back after completing the *Tropic of Cancer* series. We had travelled around the planet and been moved, upset and delighted by experiences in some of the most beautiful places on earth. But I'm sure another 10,000 travellers shuffling through the airport that day felt just the same. Returning home to normality can often be a tricky anticlimax. Yet I was getting used to that. Anya and I took a taxi back to our flat in north London and dumped our bags on the floor. Then, before we could even unpack, I had to rod out the sewers. People in an upstairs flat had been putting tampons and hair extensions down the toilets. It was a heavy bump back down to earth.

Editing and preparing the whole *Tropic of Cancer* series took a few months. Five to six weeks are needed to edit each of my programmes, but because we had different directors for each shoot, they had been shaping the individual episodes while I continued on the road. After they were cut, edited, graded and polished with composed music and maps, Sam the executive producer and I collaborated, discussed and argued while shaping the scripts, which I then wrote and recorded. As planned, the whole journey was turned into six programmes, one hour each. But as always I was slightly stunned by the reduced length of the final product. Epic experiences were compressed into short sequences. Our entire Burma mission was just 20 minutes long. But we were all delighted with the end programmes, the BBC seemed happy, and the viewing figures were great. Then I had a much more important set of personal numbers to celebrate.

I had stuck to my new healthier regime, particularly sleeping more, cutting drinking and smoking, and avoiding plastic and crap food. We had continued trying naturally for a child, endlessly, but with no luck, and I went for more follow-up fertility tests. I felt a sense of resignation about my own chances but was really starting to enjoy the thought of adopting, perhaps from a country where I had seen the difficulties of life for orphaned and abandoned children.

I remember opening my test results while I was eating toast, almost at arm's length, prepared for the bad news. The sperm headmistress had said I would never be able to conceive naturally, and that IVF was not an option. But as I glanced across the letter I could see there were numbers, where previously there had only been zeros. There had been a transformation.

My test results lifted me into a band of 'normal'. I wouldn't be donating pints to help anyone else, and they still weren't amazing, but they were completely viable. At a shot, we suddenly had a chance. The sperm headmistress who had told us there was no hope and no chance of improvement had been shown to be completely wrong. As Anya had said, change *was* possible. There was hope.

We had been talking with fertility specialists about attempting a relatively new type of IVF called ICSI, where a sperm would be directly injected into a mother's egg, thus avoiding the tricky issue of my morphology. But my test results were so good that ICSI wasn't necessary. IVF wasn't necessary. My sperm were capable of doing their own thing, and wriggling their way through Anya's tubes until they found an egg.

Obviously we celebrated in the only way possible. And for several weeks. But then Anya had some tests that showed her fertility levels were dropping. Now she was the issue. We had taken two steps forward and one step back. Anya went to see her GP, who explained that with IVF at our age we might have a one-in-four chance of conception during a monthly cycle, significantly better odds than trying naturally. But the longer we left it, the longer the odds would become. The GP also explained that, where we lived, IVF was available on the NHS up to the age of 40, and beyond that it would start to get expensive. There are countless stories of similarly desperate couples using all their savings and selling their homes to fund endless rounds of private IVF treatment. I can completely understand their desire. I felt the same.

Anya's inclination was to wait and leave it up to nature. But she wasn't adamant. If we were using our slightly batty scale of one to ten, she was a six in favour of waiting. I wasn't certain, but I didn't want to wait. I felt we had left it up to nature for long enough. Why not give our old eggs and sperm a helping hand? Also we both felt there was something deeply reassuring about doing it on the NHS, while it was still possible, rather than through a profit-making clinic. The NHS had always been there for me during life, at each stage protecting, saving, repairing and looking after me. I was a level ten for wanting a child, and an eight for trying IVF.

'But it's up to you,' I said to Anya. 'It's your body that has to go through all of this.'

Perhaps if we had waited we might have got pregnant naturally. Perhaps we would have tried for years more and nothing would have happened. We'll never know.

We registered with a fertility clinic at Hammersmith Hospital in west London, which I knew well from growing up nearby, and started a cycle of IVF. It was definitely not an easy option. Anya had to endure multiple injections of hormones that encouraged her ovaries to produce multiple eggs. They were then removed, or harvested, as Anya put it, and then I had to provide my crucial little elements, which were added to a dish containing the eggs and left on their own overnight to swim towards destiny.

They were put together on a Tuesday, and we bit our nails. The following 24 hours were critical. On Wednesday the clinic called us to say that five had fertilised. We punched the air in delight. Rather than bunging them back into Anya immediately, the embryologists asked our permission to wait a few more days for them to become a slightly larger bundle of cells called blastocysts. That would give them time to grow and strengthen, hopefully increasing the chance they would survive the transfer from dish to body. But there were huge risks. Wait, and perhaps they wither in the clinic. We took their advice and waited.

The transfer back into Anya was set for the Sunday morning. The clinic rang us every day with an update. By Friday three fertilised eggs had survived. By Saturday two were left. The following morning we arrived at the clinic, not knowing whether either of the remaining two eggs were still alive. We tried to stay calm. One egg was still going strong. That tiny fertilised egg was a survivor, a fighter.

'That's our Spartan,' said Anya.

I had sat in Hammersmith Hospital A & E many times when I was a lad. It's right next to Wormwood Scrubs, an open patch of ground and track where I used to go as a teenage boy racer. I had travelled a long way since then, in every sense. For some reason as Anya was lying on her back, legs up, ready for the single egg to be transferred back inside her, we both had a fit of giggles. The whole situation just seemed so madly alien. It couldn't possibly work. We couldn't stop laughing. At least she was relaxed.

'Maybe that will help,' said a clinic nurse with a smile.

It takes a while to find out whether an egg has survived the transfer. We knew that the odds were not in our favour. Most people have to go through several rounds of IVF treatment to get lucky. The average patient has three rounds, but many then stop, exhausted and drained by the emotion and expense. Many never get lucky at all.

We went on holiday to Denmark in the summer of 2010. It was exactly two years after my brother James had visited us there to tell us his wonderful news, throwing me into the tailspin that changed everything. Professionally we were in a great place. *Tropic of Cancer* had been broadcast earlier in the year and we were hatching another epic journey. Personally we were left crossing our fingers, hoping for good news on the baby front. But a couple of weeks ticked by and there were no feelings or indications of success. Anya wasn't tired, or tender, or nauseous. Both of us were disappointed. We felt hope slipping away.

Then, one sunny day, Anya suddenly had a sense, almost just an inkling, that she might be pregnant. She took a test. But no, it was negative. It didn't look like we were going to be lucky with a pregnancy, at least that time. My dark clouds started to gather, along with a gnawing feeling that even becoming the father of one child was a hopeless journey.

The next morning I was still asleep in bed, buried in a pillow, when I felt Anya shaking me awake.

I just opened an eye. She looked at me and said, 'You know I said I wasn't pregnant . . .?'

She lifted up a pregnancy test stick and pointed at the line. It revealed what it hadn't shown 24 hours earlier. Anya was expecting a baby. We had hit the bulls-eye. And everything changed.

I presume I physically used my limbs to get out of bed but my memory is that I actually floated to my feet. It's rare to feel your mind and your body experience such a sudden change in perspective. In a heartbeat I stopped being someone who was probably never going to be a dad, and became someone who possibly was. If there were a barometer to measure such things, the level of my excitement would have read 'dangerously high'. I was flooded with joy and hope to an extent that felt overwhelming. However much I tried to stay calm and be sensible and keep a bloody lid on it, the elation was intense. I was so thrilled, so ecstatic, so hopeful.

It had seemed so impossible. I had been *told* it was impossible. Could I really be this lucky?

Anya kept taking tests because she also couldn't quite believe it. They were all positive. In early August we went for a scan and, like millions of other expectant parents, we heard the incredible, elemental, beautiful sound of a pea-sized heart beating loudly through tinny speakers. I was stunned. I wept.

Back in London I noticed a change in myself when we saw my brother and his toddler Alice. All of a sudden it was easier to feel pure joy while with my little niece now that I no longer had to stifle a yearning voice bleating that I wanted one of my own. I could revel in and relish this beautiful little girl who stroked Anya's hair and kissed and rubbed the tummy where her cousin was brewing.

Both Anya and I felt overprotective of our Spartan in those first weeks and months. We did everything slowly, and carefully, partly because we had a ridiculous fear the egg could be disrupted, or knocked off its perch. On a bus, Anya would even lift herself up in her seat to minimise the impact of potholes.

She suffered terrible morning sickness in the first months, but we passed the three-month benchmark into the less risky period of the pregnancy and the scans kept showing everything was developing as it should. A little version of Us was growing inside. We started going to parties again, and dancing, which Anya said helped to grease the hips, at nightclubs with good vibes. But we would leave boringly early and only I would be wobbling.

Our mothers were nearby and helping out during the pregnancy, so Anya and I both thought it was time for us to get back to work, and that I should start trekking around the planet again. We discussed whether Anya should come with me, but we both decided it was best for her to stay back at base and work on the adventures from home. She had already gifted me the most important element for my next major journey.

CHAPTER TWELVE

Sharky Cave

As I tumbled down through the cool waters of the Indian Ocean off the coast of South Africa, I twisted my body around and kicked my legs desperately to level myself and control my descent to the bottom. Then I shifted my scuba tanks against my back, slowed my breathing, and signalled to my guide Gail Addison, an expert diver and member of the conservation group Shark Angels, that everything was fine. I could see her eyes shining with a smile behind her face mask as she turned, and I followed her towards a dark hole on the ocean floor known as 'Sharky Cave'.

I was a rookie scuba diver, on my very first open-water dive. Like many of us I had grown up fearing sharks, an apex predator in our seas. I watched *Jaws* at a friend's house, far too young, and then even as a kid swimming in Studland Bay, near Bournemouth, not exactly a hotspot for sharks, I worried about them. When we were aged roughly eight and ten, my brother James and I once spent an hour on a dinghy holding each other tight, terrified by the dark shadow of a shark under the water, which we realised much later was a large clump of seaweed. Travelling around the Indian Ocean I wanted to get closer to sharks so I could swim towards my own demons.

Although the thought of swimming in shark-infested seas was horrifying, Gail promised me she had not lost a single customer in 15 years, and she even took her eight-year-old for regular swims with sharks. She had a warmth and confidence that was inspiring. We slipped into the cave, moved into a good position, and waited. Clouds of smaller fish teemed in front of us and then suddenly they were pierced by the sharp snout and flat head of a ragged-tooth shark. And then another. They swam right across me as I held my place against the rocky wall. They were hungry and looking for food, but it was immediately clear they were not remotely interested in the humans wrapped in neoprene. Instead of being on a menu, I had a thrilling, close-up experience as a whole shiver of sharks gathered around us, sleek and agile with pointy noses and an absolute faceful of jagged jutting gnashers.

For the first time in my life I choked back emotion underwater. It was utterly exhilarating to be so close to such magnificent and maligned creatures. The sensation of being in a new world, and the transformative encounter with a creature that had always terrified me, made this a truly life-changing experience. All those fears that Spielberg had fed with *Jaws* just melted away. Instead I was overcome with wonder and awe, even glee.

I was in South Africa to start a new journey, and a new television series, and it was all Anya's fault. We had been trying to think of new projects and adventures for months after the *Tropic of Cancer* series had been aired, and one afternoon, just before we found out she was pregnant, she slapped down a single sheet of paper in front of me. It was a simple map of the Indian Ocean she had printed out from Wikipedia.

'There you go,' she said. 'That's the one. I've checked and nobody has done it.'

She was right. The Indian Ocean was a region of utter beauty, but also trouble and trauma. As a title and a name, it had incredible exotic appeal, and it also really mattered. There were huge stories and issues surrounding the water and along the coast. The idea was for me to travel around it in a huge semicircle from South Africa up the East African coast, then around India and back down the side of Asia to south-western Australia. It had a wonderful simplicity, and I couldn't believe none of the other telly travellers had thought of it. I went in to see the controller of BBC Two for a catch-up and a chat, armed with nothing more than that sheet of paper.

'What about … the Indian Ocean …?' I said to her, in a whispery tone meant to convey a sense of the exotic, and I popped the map on the table in front of her.

'Ooooh yes,' she said. She got it immediately. She knew exactly the adventures it would entail, and what it would offer on TV. It was, dare I say, a brilliant idea, much better than anything I deserved to be doing in life. I left the meeting with a commission for an epic six-part series. I couldn't believe my luck. It felt like a lottery win.

Why nobody else had ever done it before I have no idea. Perhaps they were put off by the scale. The Indian Ocean is 6,000 miles wide, covers 13 per cent of the planet's surface, has more than 44,000 miles of coastline, stretches across seven time zones and almost half the world's latitudes, and is surrounded by countries that contain a third of the world's population. There were bound to be astonishing stories to tell around its coast. Looking at that massive sea on the map, the great challenge was to live up to the title.

But you can't tell the story of the Indian Ocean without spending a lot of time out on a sea that teems with marine wildlife. It has 5,000 species of fish, many in dire need of protection. I not only had to get on to it; I also had to get in and go under it. Which meant I had to do something I had always avoided: I had to learn to dive. As a strong swimmer who represented London as a youngster, admittedly at breaststroke, I had previously thought snorkelling and freediving gave me enough of a connection with life under the waves. I was also under the impression that scuba diving with tanks was too much of a faff.

After we started researching the Indian Ocean series it became clear I needed to change my mind. I needed to spend time underwater. So I booked myself on to a scuba course in the UK, which was cheaper than doing it somewhere warm, but on the other hand was inevitably rather lacking in coral reef glamour. I learned about pressure gauges and diving rules round the back of a diving shop next to the North Circular in London, and then started training in a council swimming pool. Horrendously but also magically I completed the course in Stoney Cove, a flooded quarry in Leicestershire, where the visibility was awful and I felt colder than I have ever been in my life. In such circumstances, peeing inside your hired wetsuit provides just a brief, localised moment of comfort.

But it was worth the minor pain to qualify for my basic PADI open-water certificate. The joys of diving were immediately apparent to me the first time I wore scuba tanks and sank into the ocean with Gail. Learning to dive has become one of my top recommendations for travel, and even for life. It gives you a whole new dimension to explore, as close as most of us will ever get to visiting another planet. For anyone even mildly considering it, I urge you to get out there and do it, but if you're a cold-water wuss like me, make sure you get a thick wetsuit. Even the southern Indian Ocean, churned up with cold currents from the Atlantic and freezing ones from Antarctica, is not as warm as claimed.

Sharks were to be a major theme of the first part of the series, on a journey that endlessly opened my eyes to the wonder and majesty of our oceans. The truth, of course, is that lightning kills more humans than sharks do. But the statistics somehow don't seem to matter, or break through, because we have a hard-wired fear of the creatures. Sharks have an unfair reputation as mindless killers, with terrible consequences for the species, as I discovered in the water off the South African city of Durban, a holidaymakers' paradise that draws hundreds of thousands of people from across the world to surf and swim. They travel there in the knowledge that the water is safe, because Durban spends millions of pounds defending its tourists from sharks.

I was taken offshore by Geremy Cliff of the Natal Sharks Board to inspect the first line of defence, a system of nets introduced after a series of attacks in the 1950s that killed seven people. They act not as a physical barrier but something more proactive: rather than deter sharks, they are meant to catch and kill them. The nets snag other marine life including rays, turtles and dolphins. But that is a price Durban is prepared to pay to keep shark phobia at bay.

Geremy was happy to show me the huge jawbones of some previous catches. He was cagier about allowing us to film a freezer full of shark carcasses, but I had a peep inside. It was a horrifying sight, like entering a morgue full of dead lions. It just felt deeply wrong. Although Geremy wasn't willing to reveal the full scale of the carnage, as a concession he did bring out a juvenile great white. It was hoisted up on a meat hook like a side of beef. I've rarely seen the conflict between tourism and the natural world more starkly and depressingly illustrated.

'The last thing we want to do is see dead white sharks like this,' he told me, 'but unfortunately we've got a job to do.' Geremy was a perfectly decent man, a scientist with a conscience. I wondered if he was actually trying to make me appalled at what was having to be done to keep tourists coming to Durban. It worked. I felt repulsed by the sight of those dead predators.

Far from being a menace, sharks are to be revered, not feared. They are crucial to the health of our oceans. Their role at the top of the food chain is to keep everything underneath them in balance. If they are removed, the ecosystem starts to collapse.

We travelled on from South Africa to Mozambique on a huge container ship, another first for me. Hitching a ride in Durban, for two nights we travelled on the Italian-owned *Jolly Bianco*, which was 200 metres long and weighed 27,000 tons. She had started in Genoa, had come down through the Suez Canal and stopped off in Jeddah, Dar es Salaam and Mombasa. On the route home she was transporting 600 shipping containers that held, among other things, sugar, paper, foodstuff, tiles, paint, roof tiles, fruit juices, anthracite, mining equipment, milk powder, tin plate, ethyl alcohol, canned food, cotton lint, ceramics, loo rolls, steel, seeds, tobacco, ingots, rubber, hides, electrical accessories and large mining vehicles. In short, the stuff of life as we know it. Walking among the containers lashed and locked together was like being in a cross-town street in New York City, tall and narrow with only a sliver of sky visible overhead.

Below decks there was a whole car park of military vehicles. Wedged in nose to bumper were more than 250 cars, trucks and armoured personnel carriers. It was enough to equip an entire army or, in this case, a peacekeeping force. Painted white and stencilled with the letters UN, the vehicles were being shipped up the coast to Sudan for the United Nations mission in Darfur. But there was now a deadly threat at sea as well, partly sparked by the booming trade along the sea lanes, which were criss-crossed by oil tankers from the Middle East and ships carrying consumer goods from China. In all, 40 per cent of the world's shipping traffic passes through the Indian Ocean, and it had attracted an age-old enemy: pirates, who were operating from the lawless coast of Somalia.

I quizzed Francesco Vanacore, the jolly captain of the *Jolly Bianco*, about this, and his charts showed dozens of attacks by Somali pirates just in the previous two months. The *Jolly Bianco* was heading for some of the most dangerous waters on earth. A printout on the bridge offered advice in the event of pirates boarding. 'Try to remain calm. Offer no resistance. Co-operate with pirates.' To prevent them boarding there was a simple perimeter of razor wire on both port and starboard, and the crew would put cardboard over the windows so pirates couldn't see them when they passed at night. Simple but effective, though I wouldn't get the chance to test their efficacy as I disembarked in the Mozambican capital Maputo. We only found out later that just a fortnight earlier the ship had been chased by pirates in a small boat powered by two 40HP engines and crewed by six men with AK-47s and rocket-propelled grenades.

I wanted to look further into the story of marine conservation in Mozambique and was invited by my guide Carlos Macuacua to travel to his village 300 miles up the coast. Carlos, a marine conservationist, was a hugely impressive tall and handsome young man, somehow cool and warm at the same time, with a lovely smile. I'm six three and he towered over me.

We sped north and at first the roads were tarmacked and we made good progress. Carlos assured me we'd be there in three hours. Fat chance. The road vanished and we soon got stuck in sand. The only way to get through it was to let air out of the tyres, stand on the back bumper and bounce the cars out. It took many hours of jumping up and down to rock heavy four-wheel-drive SUVs out of deep, sucking drifts. When we made it to a guest house in the small hours of the morning I was spent, and my body ached in every limb, joint and muscle.

The reward was to stand on the beach early the next morning and experience for myself the stunning beauty of coastal Mozambique, and a sharp light, strong sun, wide beach, crashing waves and powerful blues. One writer described Mozambique, entirely appropriately, as a veranda on to the Indian Ocean.

Carlos took us for a short walk along the coast until we found a village where he knew a fisherman who specialised in a very particular catch. Nelson, who was also tall, young and muscular, was just waking up when we appeared, but he had soon roused three other kids who crewed a tiny rowing boat that he pushed off into the surf. Just a short distance from the coast they began tugging on a line, hauling something out of the water. Initially Carlos and I couldn't really see what it was, but gradually we realised they had caught an enormous adult female shark. I was completely taken aback. For a start I was amazed something so huge had been just a short distance offshore. But it also seemed inconceivable to me that something so majestic and powerful had been caught on a simple fishing line. But sharks have to keep moving in order to breathe. Trapped on their line for hours, the adult female had drowned. It was a hugely upsetting sight.

Nelson and his men were hunting sharks because they wanted to harvest one of the most valuable fish products on earth. Back on the beach I watched as Nelson produced a long knife and began carefully slicing off the shark fins and tail. It was painful to witness, like seeing a trunk being cut from a murdered elephant.

Without the fins to stabilise it, the huge corpse of the shark began to roll around in the surf, pushed by the waves. It was pathetic and shocking.

Nelson wasn't a wealthy fishing magnate. He lived in a little hut. For him and his crew the shark represented much-needed income. He would sell the fins for £40 a kilo to a middleman. Eventually the almost tasteless cartilage was likely to end up swimming in a bowl in China, the key ingredient in expensive shark fin soup. Sharks were victims of the economic growth of China, because delicacies that used to be available to just a few were in huge demand to a growing new middle class.

What I witnessed on that beach was one more instance in the vast international slaughter of a species. Even with a little rowing boat, a few fishermen in Mozambique can catch hundreds of sharks each year. But the real damage is done further out to sea by industrial fishing fleets that catch sharks, slice their fins off, and then often tip them back into the sea still alive. More than 100 million sharks are killed each year, and there are now thought to be just a few thousand great whites left on the planet. I'd only been travelling along the coast of the Indian Ocean for a fortnight, and within that time my view on sharks had done a 180-degree U-turn. I had gone from being fearful of them to being fearful for them. The appalling reality is that a creature that has been around since before the dinosaurs faces extinction.

Carlos was doing everything in his power to stop the apocalypse. We walked back into Nelson's coastal village and Carlos produced a couple of footballs. A few kids gathered and he drew in more with a kickabout, which turned into an exhausting football match. Then the kids helped us set up speakers that Carlos had brought, and, firing up his Apple Mac, he began blasting out Mozambican dance hall tunes which, with not a lot else happening in the villages, lured yet more people in. Once they'd had a good time, and after darkness fell, he showed them films about the wonders of the marine life of the Indian Ocean.

'If we take away all the sharks,' he explained in Portuguese, 'there are some kinds of fish that will breed out of control and they will eat the fish that we need. Then we'll be left with no fish.' This was more or less what Gail had told me in South Africa, and it was beautiful to see people who had never been told their sea was special learn, with evident pride, why it mattered.

But as he worked the crowd, Carlos then said something that really made me think. He told the villagers there are ways they can profit from the sea while helping to protect it. Have you seen foreigners enjoying our beaches in their swimsuits? he asked. Remember they have to sleep and eat somewhere. We can benefit from tourism.

It was so important, and so true. And in those few words, Carlos was making a key point that we need to remember about modern travel. Tourism can give people in poorer parts of the world an economic incentive to protect what we all treasure. It was the start of a whole new education for me about the need for tourism, and the value of it.

It was also a presentation masterclass. Carlos is a remarkable man who uses his winning charisma to help spread the message of conservation in a powerful, personal and imaginative way. He helped me to realise that what I was seeing just off the coast of Mozambique was a catastrophe affecting not just the Indian Ocean, but all of our great seas around the planet. Humans are annihilating sharks and threatening the health of the entire marine ecosystem. If only we could clone Carlos and tour his lecture through every fishing community in the whole of the Indian Ocean, then the sharks might have a fighting chance.

CHAPTER THIRTEEN

Manta Rays

At the age of 12, with some of the first money I ever earned, I went to Woolworths on Acton High Street and bought a poster of a tropical palm-fringed beach. I stuck it up on my ceiling and stared at it while lying on my bed, escaping into it during my teens, when life was dark and there were problems at home. I was mesmerised by the strip of white sandy beach, the vivid green of the beautiful, drooping palms and the shimmering turquoise of the sea. Never in my wildest dreams did I ever, ever imagine I might one day visit such a place for real. It was a fantasy island far beyond my reach and life expectations.

But on my journey round the Indian Ocean, I found impossible places that matched my poster. And when I set foot on an island that actually topped it for beauty, I am not ashamed to admit I shed a tear and said a prayer of thanks. Because nothing really prepares you for the beauty of the Indian Ocean when it puts on a show. Its islands have a light that lures painters and photographers, dreamers and romantics. It is so sharp and hypnotic you can almost feel it opening your mind, polishing your retinas and giving your soul a deep cleanse. At times I felt it was too much. The sights were so overwhelming my brain felt like it could not process it all. But it's not just me. Technology struggles too. The rich palette was sometimes more than my camera could cope with, and I had to turn down the colour saturation. It was almost as if the islands of the Indian Ocean were too good to be true.

I had my first real vision of tropical Indian Ocean perfection on the south-west coast of Madagascar. We were on a grinding journey, heading towards a remote fishing village, during which we repeatedly had to get out of our 4x4 vehicles and push them through sand and mud. I was totally knackered, but we rounded a corner and there, suddenly before us, was The View. Bleached white sand met the sea, with the irradiated blue-green of the shallows turning darker towards the horizon. Low shrubs and sun-bleached driftwood lined the foreshore. It was the Indian Ocean of a holiday brochure, and encapsulated everything I was trying to conjure up when I suggested the journey to the BBC.

Travelling with me on that leg of the series was Eric McFarland, a youngish assistant producer from Northern Ireland. Over the years I've worked with a small pool of brilliant documentary makers who are all committed, keen and willing to put up with me. Sometimes new people have joined the journeys, and although I'm sure they are impressed by what they see as we travel the world, they can still seem reluctant to show too much enthusiasm. Not Eric. He's a wonderful chap, one of the loveliest human beings it's possible to meet, who has since gone on to become a superb documentary director in his own right. We still travel and work together, luckily for me. But back in 2011 he was a relative newbie with a wide-eyed enthusiasm that was truly infectious. I found it so helpful. If there was any risk of me getting even slightly blasé about what I was seeing and experiencing, Eric was a constant reminder of the thrill and the privilege. He had fresh eyes and no ego or embarrassment that stopped him reacting naturally to a situation. He would 'wow!' even more than me at my most wildly excited, or express wonder at how white a beach was, and astonishment that in Madagascar we could see people pulling rickshaws ('in the 21st century!'). It was a reminder for me to keep my own enthusiasm levels high, and react in a similar way, because that was hopefully how many viewers would see it as well.

A priority as we journeyed around the islands of the Indian Ocean was to capture the beauty on film. Along with Eric, the fantastic director Dominic Ozanne and me was Craig Hastings, a very visual and arty cameraman. Craig loves to shoot. He has a passion for capturing beautiful images on a film camera and on a stills camera as well. I've long said he should publish a glossy coffee-table photographic book. Every time I heard his stills camera click I would turn to see what he'd shot, because I knew there would be a glorious image. Craig also has an astonishing work rate. He would capture a star shot at night, then get up just a few hours later and shoot the dawn. There were rich pickings for a brilliant cameraman in Madagascar, which is completely different to anywhere else on the planet. Madagascar separated from the rest of Africa 165 million years ago and has been inhabited by humans for only the last 2,000 of them. They arrived not from the African mainland but, in one of the great feats of navigation, from far more distant corners of the Indian Ocean – Malaysia and Indonesia. Imagine their shock upon arrival. With a land mass twice the size of Britain, 1,000 miles top to toe, the fourth largest island in the world is one of the most biologically diverse countries on earth. For almost all of its history it enjoyed a parallel evolution that resulted in unique and spectacular landscapes, colours, flora and fauna, which you can feast your eyes on for hour after hour, mile after mile. But sadly even more spectacular species have now gone. The first human arrivals came across an elephant bird that was an astonishing three metres high, and giant jumping rats. There were even massive lemurs as big as gorillas. Having flourished without a human presence they are now extinct.

But there are still spectacular survivors. The star primates include the aye-aye, a nocturnal critter with huge bat-like ears, yolk-yellow eyes, knife-like gnashers, a ratty face and a weirdly long middle finger. Little wonder locals think it's evil. Then there's the indri, a large lemur weighing 10 kilos, which travels among the treetops in leaps as long as 10 metres. As for the rest, there are 200,000 species of flora and fauna, more than 90 per cent of them endemic. Almost all its reptiles and amphibians are found only on Madagascar, including more than half the planet's species of chameleon.

In such relative isolation, many of the people have come to be as distinctive as the flora and fauna. The Malagasy follow a set of taboos known as fady, which may be eccentric, perhaps forbidding: passing eggs from hand to hand, or eating bread from a red plate, or insisting chores should be performed standing on a Wednesday but kneeling on a Thursday. But there are also dark superstitions. In one part of the country, twins are said to be evil and, like figures in a Greek myth, until recently could be abandoned in the forest. The dead are also venerated. Important corpses are left out in the tropical sun and the juices that are emitted from them are collected in a cup and passed among the relatives. Some Malagasy express their respect for ancestors by removing them from tombs, giving them a new shroud and parading them around the village.

The south-west of Madagascar, where I started my Indian Ocean travels on the island, was a place of fady, great beauty and also poverty, the poorest region of a poor country. Three-quarters of Madagascar's 27 million people live on less than two dollars a day. After digging our 4x4s out of endless sand, we eventually arrived at the village of Andavadoaka and took boats to an island off the coast.

The nomadic Vezo people living there depend entirely on the Indian Ocean for their survival, and I went out with them on thin catamaran canoes to freedive and watch as they harpooned their food. They seemed to have lungs the size of barrage balloons and could happily stay underwater for five minutes. Although they didn't get much of a haul, that night I sat down with the village chief who shared the biggest catch. He explained that it was getting harder to find the fish to feed his family.

'You have to work hard every day,' he told me. 'Before we would only go out for two or three hours to catch a lot of fish.' And he needed a large catch to feed his family. I asked him how many children he had and he couldn't quite remember. His wife certainly knew. She butted in to answer: seven. You know a population is exploding when a dad doesn't even know how many kids he has. There were dozens of youngsters running around in the village. More than 50 per cent of the village was under 15. Madagascar has one of the fastest growing populations in the world. There in that village was a microcosm of a problem facing all of Madagascar and many communities around the Indian Ocean. Too many fishermen, with ever more young mouths to feed, meant overfishing and a consequent decline in fish stocks.

The challenge of helping coastal communities to rebuild tropical fisheries and protect the precious coral reef in the area had been taken on by a conservation charity called Blue Ventures. Its dynamic young founder Dr Alasdair Harris, a marine biologist, was quietly confident and inspiring. We talked about the need to shift the focus away from educated outsiders coming in and telling local people what to do. Conservationists need to empower, Alasdair said, not impose. It's a problem I'm constantly aware of, and when possible I prefer not to put white European outsiders on screen when we're in a far-flung corner of the world. We need to identify and encourage local people who are creating and leading change. I never forget that moment in the movie *Gandhi* when the enthusiastic English vicar asks Gandhi what he can do to help, and Gandhi says, effectively, 'You need to leave, because we need to do this ourselves.'

When Alasdair first arrived in Madagascar, he decided the solution to overfishing was to permanently close areas of reef. Fishermen needed to fish less. But for impoverished locals that wasn't an option. Instead, after studying the situation more closely, attention focused on stocks of octopus, a critical seafood in the area but which was declining in numbers. The octopus could grow incredibly quickly, doubling in weight in just a few months. So perhaps closing even just a small area of reef for a brief period of time, giving the octopus a respite in which to grow and breed, might help. The Vezo became completely involved in that idea and closed an area and invoked their ancestors to discourage anyone from poaching. When the reef was reopened six months later, octopus had grown dramatically and their numbers had exploded and restabilised. Vezo fishermen and women were able to fish less, but earn more, while still maintaining biodiversity.

It was an idea that soon spread further along the coast, partly by word of mouth. Seeing the benefits of conservation, Vezo leaders from Andavadoaka joined with more than 20 neighbouring communities and created a larger protected area along a huge stretch of coastline where fishing with fine nets and poison was outlawed and fishing was halted in some sensitive and critical areas like coral reef and mangrove forest on the coastline, a nursery habitat for breeding sea life. They created something spectacular: a Marine Protected Area managed by the local community to help protect fisheries and marine biodiversity. Within five years they were managing more than 200 square miles of ocean, in which they banned destructive industrial trawling.

Absolutely key to the success of the Marine Protected Area was the fact local people were running and benefiting from it. But the local and foreign team at Blue Ventures also realised they couldn't hope to protect the environment without doing something to address the population boom, two major causes of which were high rates of illiteracy among women and a lack of access to contraception. So another initiative the group organised was a family planning programme covering thousands of people in villages in the area. Women from the Vezo community would travel to communities up and down the coast in a giant pirogue named *Captain Condom* advising women to use contraception and showing them how to roll condoms on to a sort of wooden cucumber. It was a radical project for a conservation charity.

I have often found that conservationists are afraid to discuss the impact of human population growth on the environment. But our numbers have more than doubled since the early 1970s, increasing by more than 4 billion. I am convinced this staggering increase is often a catastrophe for the natural world. How can it not be? How can the staggering increase in the number of human beings not be affecting our climate, other species with which we share the earth, and every corner of the globe?

I adore us, and meeting people and spending time with them is the reason I love travelling. We are the most wonderful and incredible creature that has ever existed, but we are also a crea-ture that transforms landscapes and destroys habitats. We need balance. There are too many people on the planet. In that corner of Madagascar, Blue Ventures was bravely doing something to help stop the numbers growing still further.

I was given a lift up the coast in *Captain Condom* while the rest of the team travelled in a boat with a proper engine. Needless to say I was involved in yet another boat-related near disaster. We took on water. Then our engine overheated.

A deeper problem when travelling around Madagascar was the rain. It was monsoon season, and the roads turned to thick mud the minute the heavens opened. At one point our vehicles got stuck and the team and I, plus a dozen local guys, had to push us out, wading knee deep into a riverbed. There has always been flooding during the rainy season in Madagascar, but the problem was getting worse thanks to the blight of deforestation. The trees of a tropical rainforest would help to soak up flood waters but there just weren't many left. The landscape had been completely denuded of its natural forests.

More than 90 per cent of the forest in Madagascar has been chopped, logged or burned. That is an astonishing statistic. Yet I found it hard to convey exactly how significant the problem was, and the scale of it, because even though trees were missing from the landscape it was still the right colour. As soon as the rich canopy of forest was destroyed, other shrubby, scrubby plants and bushes rapidly replaced them. At first glance nobody would think there was a problem, because the landscape still looked green. But it supported just a fraction of the biodiversity a tree could harbour and nourish.

We are victims of what's called 'shifting baseline syndrome', where we fail to recognise how much the natural world has been degraded or destroyed by human behaviour, because our 'baseline' changes with each generation. We know what we see. We fail to understand what the natural world looked like when our grandparents or great-grandparents were alive. What we see today as a 'natural' or 'wild' patch of the planet, our ancestors would know is a pale shadow of the glory they enjoyed. We have lost so much, so quickly.

It was left up to me and Charlie Gardner, an expert from the World Wildlife Fund, to try to paint a picture of what's happened. Charlie explained that there would have been 200 species of trees just in the area where we were standing. He told me local people had cut the forest for fuel, or to clear land for agriculture. Poor farmers in Madagascar practise slash and burn, or tavy as they call it, the same basic form of agriculture that was destroying vast areas of forest in north-eastern India, and across the Tropics. With axes and cheap Chinese chainsaws, people would clear the forest, burn the trees and mix the ash into the ground as a cheap fertiliser.

I travelled to the south of the island to visit the famous Berenty wildlife reserve, established by a Belgian plantation owner in the 1930s and now a home to Madagascar's iconic lemurs, many of which are endangered. Scientists believe the lemurs are descended from primates that came across the Indian Ocean from the mainland millions of years ago, perhaps washed out to sea during a storm on a log or matted vegetation.

Crawling and creeping through the forest for an hour, we had a thrilling encounter with sifaka lemurs swinging through the trees, and then found ring-tailed lemurs gambolling and playing back around the reserve visitor huts and offices. The reserve has been used as the setting for dozens of wildlife movies over the last few decades. The staff at Berenty told us about a two-man

French film crew who came to film lemurs, spectacularly fell out with each other on their first day, took all meals at separate tables and used the staff to pass messages between them about what they were going to film. By the end the staff had become relationship counsellors.

Many camera crews, even those filming for the most popular natural history programmes, have carefully framed out the buildings in Berenty while filming lemurs. This happens on countless other wildlife documentaries, shot in other beautiful parts of the world, on which camera crews are told to keep out evidence of human habitation in the form of paths, roads, buildings and people. Movies and wildlife documentaries always paint an image of Madagascar as a forested paradise teeming with wildlife. To me this is dangerous and immoral. It results in artificial wildlife porn, giving the viewer a false sense of security about the natural world.

Berenty is tiny. Almost obscenely small. It covers an area little bigger than a city park. And it is surrounded by thousands and thousands of acres of land that was deforested decades ago to clear the way for farming. When I was there the land around was covered to the horizon in sisal, which was being grown, irony of ironies, to provide eco-friendly packaging for Germany. The whole situation had me tearing my hair out.

There is still plenty that determined individuals can do for the natural world, as I discovered when we moved on to the picture-postcard paradise that is the Seychelles, where the marine colours went up another notch in tone. The Seychelles are what you might get if a Caribbean country was plonked in the Indian Ocean. It was more laid-back than I expected and less honeymoony, with a relaxed vibe to the restaurants and bars. The sea was as clear as a swimming pool painted by David Hockney, and the main island Mahé was a stunning peacock display of shimmering beaches and forested crags.

It was glorious to see how not just the seas but the trees had been protected. Strict environmental legislation had turned the Seychelles into a world leader in eco-friendly tourism, with nearly half its total land mass under conservation. I hopped into a boat and headed towards a secluded island called Moyenne. Unlike many of the Seychelles' 115 islands, some of them owned by billionaires, Moyenne had none of the grandiose paraphernalia of high-end tourism, such as jetties thrusting out into the sea, and secret retreats fit for a Bond villain. Surrounded by a coral reef, Moyenne looked wild and uninhabited as we approached. Then a lone little wooden bungalow could be spotted peering through the trees. The boat pulled into the shallows and I disembarked to be greeted by a Yorkshireman in his eighties called Brendon Grimshaw.

Brendon's story really belongs in an uplifting movie. In 1962 he bought Moyenne, an island of only 22.5 acres, for £8,000 and found scrub so dense that coconuts couldn't fall to the ground. It had just four trees. Brendon had since planted 16,000. We walked up the hill to his simple home, with a sheltered verandah, where there was another surprise. Brendon shared the island with more than 120 giant tortoises. A whopper was sitting on the steps. A mini-army of them seemed to fill up all the space so there was almost nowhere to put your feet. Though indigenous to the Seychelles, they had been killed off on most islands. Brendon reintroduced them, giving each tortoise a number and a name, which he painted on their shells. One was called Four Degrees South after Moyenne's latitude. As he replanted the island he also successfully introduced indigenous birds, some 2,000 of which flocked there from around the Indian

Ocean. They gathered to feast on rice from the five 50kg bags Brendon put out each week, gifting a magnificent sight.

Outside his home I spotted a sign: 'Please respect the tortoises. They are probably older than you.' In fact some were youngsters. The youngest giant, a tiny little critter just two weeks old when I visited, was born in Brendon's bedroom and was now living on his verandah. It's astonishing to imagine that it may live to be 180 and survive on Moyenne until the end of the 22nd century.

Brendon had gone a little bit native himself. We had been warned in advance he would often greet visitors while wearing his island uniform – a pair of the very skimpiest budgie-smuggler Speedos. Fearing this might alarm viewers, or at least distract them, we needed to persuade him in advance to pull on a pair of shorts. I've never heard anyone squirm on a phone call quite so much as when poor Eric tried to politely ask this favour. Then at the last moment Eric thought of a decent excuse. We needed to hide his microphone pack somewhere. Happily, when we disembarked I was greeted by a lithe and tanned man with a Dewsbury accent who was dressed entirely respectably.

It is easy to believe we are impotent in the face of environmental catastrophe, but Brendon's story proves otherwise. He didn't save a wilderness the size of Devon, but he did what he could, stubbornly transforming an area of the Tropics into a protective haven. He embodies that line from the book *Schindler's Ark*, which I read at school and mentioned in *Step by Step*: 'Whoever saves one life saves the world entire.' It is so vitally true. Just because we can't do everything, it doesn't mean we can't do something.

A Saudi prince once offered Brendon a blank cheque for Moyenne. Brendon turned him down.

'The only reason somebody would want to buy this island is to build a big hotel,' he told me.

Brendon has died since I visited, but what he achieved as an accidental conservationist has had ripples far beyond his own death. His island was made a national park, perhaps the smallest in the world, so that its flora and fauna are protected in perpetuity.

There is hope for conservation on a much larger scale in the Maldives, an archipelago of 1,200 islands scattered over 35,000 square miles of the Indian Ocean.

I knew the country would be beautiful, but I saw it as an expensive and one-dimensional honeytrap for soap stars, honeymooners and first-generation Instagrammers. We couldn't do a series about the Indian Ocean without going there, but I didn't expect to have the extreme experiences I crave.

As we flew across the outer islands I started to feel genuine excitement. Many had nothing on them. I could see the coral and the cays glistening with life. The reefs form protective barriers around islands, creating atolls with turquoise lagoons. It was the Indian Ocean at its most beautiful.

We landed and transferred to a resort called the Hilton Conrad Rangali, which looked like a spectacular vision of pristine paradise, and were ferried to reception down a long straight jetty on a golf cart. I didn't have to lift a finger. Suddenly I was catapulted into a very different sort of journey. This was glorious luxury and my room was more like an apartment. The bed, surmounted by a ceiling fan, was entirely surrounded by floor-to-ceiling French windows that let in the gorgeous Indian Ocean light. Outside, the garden boasted a raised plunge pool shaded by a roof of reeds and enfolded by exotic fronds, and through a gap in the foliage a beach beckoned with the clearest sea I have ever seen in my life. Bloody hell, I loved it. It was absolutely gorgeous.

I met Marie Saleem, a Maldivian conservationist and scientist, for lunch at a stunning underwater restaurant at the resort, which felt like being inside a fish tank. Calling Marie a local expert might suggest she had a narrow outlook. But Marie went to school in the Himalayas, studied marine science in Australia, gained a Master's degree in Protected Area Management, then worked as a reef ecologist on shark conservation with NGOs around the world, and won the global Seacology Prize for her work in preserving environment and culture. She was diligent and clever, of course, but also wise and funny, and she taught me so much about our blue planet. One of the great privileges of making my programmes is the direct line it gives me to people who are brilliant and keen to share what they know and care about with both me and the wider world.

Marie explained that the entire Maldives archipelago is made up of coral islands, one of the most extensive reef systems in the world. It is a magnet for life across a huge swathe of the Indian Ocean, and its reefs are a nursery for many young fish and a crucial habitat for hundreds of unique fish and marine invertebrates.

Shark fishing had been banned in the Maldives and protection had also been granted to other species including dolphins, turtles, Napoleon wrasse and giant clams. Crucially there are more than 40 Marine Protected Areas in the country, akin to having national parks in the sea.

We took a boat to the Baa Atoll UNESCO Biosphere Reserve, strapped on scuba tanks and dived down on the world's seventh largest coral reef. As soon as I ducked below the surface

I was greeted by a vision I will remember for the rest of my life. Everywhere I looked was colour and life. Marie led me as we swam slowly with bright yellow and white butterflyfish, angel fish, smiling orange clownfish, wrasses, eels and a curious turtle. Life flitted and flapped all around me, with giant shoals of tiny fish parting at the movement of my hand. Then there was the coral. More than 250 types are found in the Baa Atoll Biosphere. Colours we only see through the fizz and flash of advertising flared in every direction. There was sharp iridescent red, burnt orange, fluorescent purple, yellow and deep dark blue, on coral the size of dinner plates and dining tables, and representing every colour on a paint chart.

They might be less than 1 per cent of the global marine environment, an area just half the size of France, but around the planet coral reefs provide food and shelter for more than a quarter of all marine species. Never have I been so glad I learned a new skill. Diving had taken me to a place of utter extremes. It was exactly what I needed. My brain raced to process and store every sight. Every sense was tingling.

Reefs are not just there for lucky folk like me to gawp at. They form a fundamental part of the marine environment. Yet three quarters of the world's coral reefs are at risk to a combination of climate change, pollution and overfishing. I was aware of coral bleaching, where huge areas of coral can die rapidly because of our changing climate. But I hadn't understood just how vulnerable coral actually is. Marie explained that even a rise of one degree Celsius spells disaster.

She took me to another area of reef to see what can happen when coral bleaches. It was like swimming through a marine graveyard. The coral was ghostly white, as if all life and meaning had been sucked out. Which is, in a sense, exactly what had happened. Even the water around the dead coral, which stretched over football pitches of seabed, felt slightly stagnant compared to the sharp sea over the live reef.

In recent decades, around the world, vast areas of coral have been subjected to extreme bleaching events, as we poison our seas and unbalance our climate. We can see the consequences with our own eyes, as gorgeous vibrant reef is destroyed.

I am so often reminded of what I was later told by the Australian running the Great Barrier Reef tourism organisation. 'The reef is a shadow of what it was 20 years ago,' he said to me, 'but it's a lot better now than it will be in 20 years' time.' We have lost so much. And still we lose more. Whether the Maldives will survive the coming decades is another tricky question. The country's highest point is roughly nine inches higher than the top of my head, so it is fantastically vulnerable to rising sea levels.

Travelling around the Indian Ocean I wanted to learn more about fishing, and especially the story of tuna. In Mauritius they wouldn't let us film in the huge port where the tuna industry has its base, even after we'd acquired the correct permits. It's as if someone wanted to cover up the truth that the industry is stripping the seas of fish.

In the Maldives half the workforce is employed in the fishing industry. Marie took me to look round the commercial fish market where fishermen brought their catch. Based on the small size of the tuna they landed you'd never think tuna fishing is a multi-billion-pound industry in the Indian Ocean. We met one fisherman who explained that's because during the 30 years he'd been out on the water, the larger foreign fishing boats, which operate over the horizon in the lawless international waters, had increasingly been using huge nets to catch vast quantities of larger fish. Some nets can be seven miles long. They weigh tons. Six of the nets, I was told, could cover the area of the entire archipelago.

After overfishing our other oceans to near annihilation, the giant European and Asian industrial fishing fleets have begun targeting the Indian Ocean, hunting sharks and fish like tuna with vast nets that scoop up entire shoals, but are so indiscriminate they drag up and kill turtles and dolphins as well. It is an astonishing scandal. Far too often the nets are snagged and discarded, or lost, and left to drift in the ocean as ghost nets, killing marine life. It baffles me why this has been allowed to happen. I can just about understand that the Chinese government doesn't care about life in the Indian Ocean, or perhaps anywhere else, even though they claim to think long term. But why have European democracies, or the EU, Taiwanese, Japanese or Koreans, not prevented their fleets from threatening life in our seas? It's not as though we haven't known what's happening. Countless reports, documentaries and movies have revealed the full scale of the disaster.

There are alternatives to industrial fishing, and the next morning I went out early to find out how to fish sustainably, on a large, open-topped wooden fishing boat. The sun' was soon baking down. One of the fishermen was pulled through the water off the side of the boat, his body fully in the water and his masked eyes looking for tiny sprats. We hauled in a shoal, and then when we spotted tuna the sprats were chucked back in again as live bait, and the fishermen began casting hooked lines into the water on the end of long poles. As soon as they had a bite they would swing the fish in and skilfully flick them over their heads into a holding tank in the centre of the boat. I loved how they genuinely, enthusiastically believed in this viable method of fishing. They caught only what they needed to bring them a solid income while leaving the rest of marine life undisturbed. It was as if they'd been sitting in on the lessons that Carlos delivers to villagers up and down the coast of Mozambique.

Four and five kilo tuna began flying through the air. I was only hit once, but it felt like being whacked by a brick. Eventually, after trying for ages, and while the men around me pulled dozens of fish out of the water, I finally caught a skipjack tuna, and I caught it sustainably, which felt even better.

All the while I was falling for the Maldives, hook, line and sinker, and overcoming my initial prejudices about the place. More than a brochure come to life, it felt to me like a genuine community. As such, it was not immune to problems afflicting everywhere else on the planet. Marie wanted to draw back the curtain and show me more of the reality. So she took me to Thilafushi, an island near the capital of the Maldives that few other locals, let along foreigners, were ever able to see.

As we approached the island across the water the air grew hazy with smoke. We overtook a vehicle ferry heading in the same direction, transporting trucks loaded high with rubbish. There were boats crowding the shore, dirty great rusting hulks I hadn't seen elsewhere in the Maldives. We came round the back of one rotting old ship and suddenly Thilafushi came into view. It was an apocalyptic sight.

Every square metre of the shore was covered in rubbish, multicoloured plastic detritus in blue and green and yellow that spilled off the edge of the island into the water like molten lava. Further inland were hills of rotting trash letting off foul smoke and a toxic smell. I was almost dumbstruck. Never have I seen a more jarring sight. In a place of near perfection it was a vision of fetid horror.

Only 20 years earlier, Thilafushi was just another unspoilt coral island. But then the government decided to use it as the waste dump, and up to 300 tons of waste began arriving every day. The sheer visual shock of finding so much rubbish was profound. There were smoking slagheaps of it. We walked down one path and on one side was a football field of plastic bottles, on the other a bunch of oil drums with contents leaking into the ground, eventually to seep into the sea. Everywhere there was rubbish: great bags, sacks, piles and hills of it. On this apocalyptic island the dust was more toxic, the stench more foul and the thousands of swarming flies more crazed and aggressive than I've ever experienced.

It is worth pointing out no one stopped us from visiting Thilafushi. Indeed I heard that people in the government who knew of our presence felt an international spotlight might actually help nudge the authorities to sort it out. It's also worth saying that the Maldives was doing what almost everyone else does. It's just more of an affront when you see Bangladeshi workers torching plastic with flame-throwers in a place that otherwise looks so perfect.

Thilafushi was not the Maldives I had anticipated. But the islands exceeded my expectations at both ends of the scale. To give me a sense of real luxury in the Maldives we transferred to the Four Seasons Landaa Giraavaru, which still remains my benchmark for a stylish resort. My room was now a whole villa, so insanely luxurious that I took pictures of it before I sullied it with my dusty clothes and weathered kit. Indecent surfeit of fluffed pillows? Check. Four-poster bed? Check. There was a bath the size of a plunge pool, I had my own swimming pool and massage deck and my own private bit of beach, plus hammock. It was all a bit much for a lad from Acton, but I just about coped.

When night fell, the team and I walked towards our evening meal along sandy tracks lit by braziers scented with perfumes. That, and the bicycle they gave me with my initials as a wooden number plate, linger in my memory as the cherry on the cake. And I say that as someone who, while in Turkey, stayed in the penthouse suite of what may be the most expensive hotel in the world, just after the King of Saudi Arabia, waited on by my own butler. That night at the Four Seasons in the Maldives, ever so slightly drunk on cocktails, I pedalled back to my palatial accommodation along a wide sandy path, wobbling, singing and swaying, until I crashed through the bushes into someone else's villa. They came out very happy and inebriated themselves, picked me up and sent me on my way.

Of course I was tempted to sit by the pool the next day. But only briefly. My journeys are never a grind or a treadmill, but they certainly aren't a holiday. I have a responsibility not to relax, and that suits me fine because I'm hungry for experiences. Every moment needs to be used. It's not a bad motto for life. I can completely understand if you want to lie on a lounger by a pool topping up your tan. But I promise you that getting up, getting out and trying to extract every bit of juice from existence is the way to feel like you have actually lived.

So that morning Marie took us to a spot in the nearby marine reserve where she predicted we would see an astonishing sight. It required us to be in the right place at the right time, and it very nearly didn't happen thanks to an epic sequence of technical failures. Marie moored our boat near where she thought we needed to be, but before Craig and I could get into the water our first camera failed. With our second back-up camera we swam most of the way to the allotted snorkelling spot across a strong, energy-sapping current. Then the second camera failed. We were running out of time and swam back to the boat in a panic. Back on board we loaded another camera into an underwater housing and tested it and immediately it started to leak. We were trying to film one of the wonders of the underwater world and three cameras had gone down like skittles. Thankfully, Marie lent us a camcorder.

We swam back across the current yet again and arrived just in time to capture the heart-melting sight of manta rays arriving on their monthly commute, led by a new moon over hundreds of miles, to gorge on plankton. The rays are huge creatures and yet so graceful. They seemed to fly through the water, flapping giant wings that can span between five and seven metres, as wide as a van is long. I ducked underwater and watched as they opened their mouths and performed somersaulting aquabatics. It must count as the most elegant feeding frenzy on the planet. At one point they turned and swam inquisitively towards me, ten mantas stacked in a perfect formation like a Bolshoi corps de ballet gliding in slow motion. I was so enraptured by the moment that my snorkel fell from my mouth and my brain forgot to tell my lungs to breathe. It was a priceless experience.

As we came back to the surface and swam back to our boat, I passed near some tourists who were playing around in the water. I told them the mantas were nearby, but when I pointed to where they were, they looked at me like I was asking them to row the Atlantic. They missed the chance to see one of the great wildlife spectacles of Planet Earth because they weren't willing to push themselves. They couldn't be bothered. I regularly think of them when I'm on a trip or a holiday, and someone mentions there is something splendid to do or see. Always say yes. Always go to have a look. Never waste a moment.

There was also a uniformed ranger from the marine reserve bobbing around in a small boat, making sure tourists were behaving themselves and not damaging any of the reef. Marine life needs that protection because the Maldives is a wildlife ark. The archipelago is the oceanic equivalent of an African watering hole where animals cluster in vast numbers. Those tiny pinpricks on a map of the Indian Ocean attract marine life of extraordinary abundance from thousands of miles around.

Because we were visiting the reserve we paid an entrance fee, just as people pay to visit national parks in Africa or Asia, whether they are aware of it or not. Often it's bundled up in the price of a holiday. That money helps to pay for the ranger in his boat, it helps to pay for an anti-poaching patrol, and it helps to ensure that wildlife on land and sea is protected.

In the Maldives tourism is a critical part of the economy. It employs a huge proportion of the workforce. That gives an economic incentive to people to protect and preserve the wildlife. It means fishermen are less likely to try to poach the manta rays, or hunt sharks, or fish on reefs. They have a personal financial desire to protect life, because they, or no doubt someone in their family, will depend on tourism for their income. If we don't visit these national parks and marine reserves we will lose them, because locals will lose their income and turn to more destructive ways of providing for their families. Precious wild arks will be fished to death, or logged on land and turned into palm oil plantations. Tourism creates huge problems for the environment, of course it does, but it needn't just be about exploiting and ruining. When it's run right, it can really help to protect and preserve.

The high point of my time in the Maldives came when Marie took me on a liveaboard boat to a remote island she had been renting for research and conservation. I was amazed to discover you can lease a patch of paradise as if it's an inner-city flat. We moored offshore the night before and the next morning I wandered out to look where we were going while I brushed my teeth. It was a moment of serious emotion. There in front of me was a perfect tropical island, ringed by light golden sand and topped by palm trees waving in a gentle breeze, a place that equalled and exceeded in beauty the sacred beach in my bedroom poster.

Throughout the troubled years of my teens, a tropical beach had stared back at me from my ceiling, a vision of an impossible place I could never hope to reach. Back then I was a very lost young man, helpless and hopeless. The memory of who I had been, and the distance I had travelled in the years since, was almost too much. I sat on the deck of the boat, holding my toothbrush, and felt my emotions swing, from a lump in my throat all the way through to a proud thump in my chest.

I was trembling with anticipation when we got into a dinghy and motored towards the island. Everything about the island and the sea was more beautiful, I can honestly say, than anything I'd imagined. The light was so startlingly sharp, and the colours so overwhelming. The sea was an otherworldly cerulean. I'd seen a similar rich blue on tiles in an Islamic school in Uzbekistan, achieved, I was told, by mixing pigment with human blood. I feel genuine sympathy for anyone who has not experienced such colours. It felt to me as if I was discovering what my eyes are actually for. That's what the Maldives meant to me.

As I set foot on Marie's beach, scrunching the sand between my toes, it was as if I was returning to my childhood bedroom, but successfully, confidently, as an adult with a present and a future. That beach, in that moment, as much as anywhere before or since, marked the full arc of my own impossible travel journey. It felt like the culmination of a redemptive quest to reclaim my past.

CHAPTER FOURTEEN

Little Squid

It was while I travelled through Mozambique on the first part of the Indian Ocean journey that I realised how little I actually knew about childbirth, or about having children at all, for that matter.

Anya was back in London and growing rapidly. I was spending hours on the road and thinking about the littler who was on the way. Our birth was imminent and I was struck by the thought, like thousands before me, how astonishing it is that in Britain you have to register with the government to keep cattle, and take a test to drive a car, both quite rightly, but are not required to undergo any form of preparation before taking charge of your own small human being. I'm not suggesting everyone needs some sort of training or certificate when they become a parent, or at least I don't think I am. Actually, perhaps it isn't such a terrible idea, at least for guys like me.

In wealthy countries with nuclear families we can easily live in a bubble that involves little or no fundamental contact with children before parenthood. I loved kids, wanted my own, and had bounced a lot of kids on my knee, but I don't think I had ever put one to bed. The only nappies I had changed were on young orangutans. Whenever a baby or child I was holding would start to moan or cry, which wasn't always, I'll have you know, the default position in the West seems to be hand them back, just as parents also reach out to take, partly to avoid the social embarrassment of a complaining littler bothering someone else. These are newish developments in the so-called developed world. Even our relatively recent ancestors would not recognise this way of life, and I'm often struck by the difference with other cultures.

When we were in the village in Mozambique where Carlos started the football match and showed his shark video, groups of children and families had gathered to watch and listen. I noticed, as I have on every visit to a remote village or indigenous community, how even small children were caring for those slightly younger than them, and how teenagers were given the responsibility of caring for a larger group. Children were not segmented within a narrow age range. Ten-year-olds weren't just hanging around with other ten-year-olds. They all mixed together. Parents arrived, and babies were passed around between different aunties and uncles for a hug and a hold. When a baby or child began crying, they weren't automatically handed back or taken by parents. Unless the child needed mother's milk, other adults would soothe and distract them. There was no danger of any young adult in the village not knowing how to look after a child. In communities where people live closer together, anyone can be handed a child to look after by a stressed parent, or an uncle might have to distract two five-year-olds as they bicker over a remaining piece of food.

We in the West are too often segregated or shielded from the realities of life, from the start and the finish, from babies but especially from old age and death. Wherever I go in remoter parts of the world, by choice and tradition older family members are also kept near at hand, and people are appalled and mystified to learn of the existence of our old people's homes. Often they cannot understand why such a thing could even exist.

Carlos told the Mozambican villagers that congratulations were in order because my wife was pregnant. They were all lovely about it and we clinked local beers to celebrate, and I was emboldened to ask them what women did when it was time for them to give birth.

'What do you mean?' they said.

'Does the mother go to the hospital?'

'The hospital is hours away!' they hollered in chorus. 'They only go there if there is a problem. Usually they stay at home or use the trees over there.'

'What do you mean the trees?'

'The trees women hold on to when they're giving birth.'

I admit I was a bit jolly by that stage of the evening but that doesn't quite explain my failure of imagination. I'd so internalised the Western concept of clinical hospital childbirth that I couldn't picture a woman holding on to a tree while lying down to give birth. Carlos explained to them how birthing was generally done in Europe. The villagers said women there would lie down, walk around and often also squat while holding on to a tree.

'We want the child to come out,' one said. 'We don't want to pull it out.'

I am open to the idea that in the West we might not always do things in the most sensible way. With apologies for tacking across here to an adjacent area of the anatomy, I'd travelled enough to realise that squatting to void the bowels puts infinitely less stress on your internal organs. But I'd got to my late thirties without ever really thinking about the act of childbirth.

Back home I felt more confident armed with my new knowledge when we started going, voluntarily rather than due to a government training order, to prenatal classes run by the National Childbirth Trust (NCT). At our first birthing class after I returned from East Africa, they pointed out that women only started lying down to give birth when male doctors became involved in obstetrics. Men couldn't be bothered to bend down. Up to that point, in older and ancient depictions of women giving birth, they are generally standing or squatting upright, often holding on to a tree, and using gravity to assist. On the flip side, Western medicine has of course dramatically improved the chances of a mother and baby surviving childbirth, which can't be guaranteed in a Mozambican village.

The NCT classes were brilliant. Although you're not required to attend them, it's a good idea, not least because you begin to understand how the pelvis works and just how an adult woman is able to birth a melon. Neither Anya nor I had any idea about this, and at the classes they didn't just tell us; they had a model of a skeleton and showed how part of the bones move down so the new little human can fit out. In my ignorance I thought it was just push and squeeze. But no, it turns out the architecture changes.

We decided we wanted a hippy home birth and went for the full monty, with a huge inflatable water pool, candles, washable nappies and a doula, a trained companion who supports you through childbirth. They don't replace a midwife, but help almost like a friend, to guide a mum through a birth, particularly their first, which can be a staggering shock and involve difficult decisions about drugs and pain. We found a lovely woman who had helped countless other expectant mums, and Anya started plotting out a birth plan with her. I went and rented a pool, which filled the entire living area of our basement flat when I pumped it up. We were ready.

But sometimes it turns out life has alternative intentions. Around the time of the due date we were in a sweaty pub cellar celebrating a friend's birthday when Anya's contractions started. We made our way slowly home as a huge moon filled the night sky. It was the closest the moon had been to the earth in 18 years. Our doula had told us babies often come on a full moon, so perhaps ours was being pulled out by lunar magnetism. Back at home, Anya's body began shaking uncontrollably. She called the doula and explained.

'Don't worry,' said the doula soothingly. 'Your body has gone into shock.'

'Why?' said Anya.

'Because it knows what it's about to go through. Your birth has started.'

Anya asked when the doula might be coming round. We knew it wouldn't be soon as we were just at the start of labour. But we weren't expecting her reply.

'I'm really sorry,' she said, 'but I'm actually in hospital now with another mum.'

We'd been double-booked. And then dumped. Anya could have been really upset, but stayed calm and collected. We still had our birthing pool and our candles and, thank goodness, access to NHS midwives.

The moment came for Anya to enter the pool. I had filled it with a hose and by pre-boiling vats on the stove I managed to get the temperature to just the right level of warmth. A Bart Simpson towel covered a giant stack of pillows and cushions to provide more body support if required, and we had borrowed a giant yoga ball that Anya could drape herself over. I'd even jokingly tested the strength of the door handles in case she wanted to hang off them during contractions. Everything was ready. I lit a couple of candles and Anya slipped naked into the warm water.

'Temperature OK?' I double-checked.

'It's lovely,' she said, with a grimace and a smile.

She was only in the pool for 20 minutes. And then the bloody thing started leaking.

It was a complete disaster. Six hundred litres of water began seeping out around the back, spreading beyond the protective matting and on to the wooden floor. For a moment I thought sod the flat, a baby is on the way. But it was Anya's flat and I needed to start baling.

Anya climbed out and moved over to the bed. As I started lugging buckets of water to tip down the loo I did briefly have a moment to reflect that at least this was a familiar situation; after all, 50 per cent of the boats I'm in start to take on water. On quick inspection the hole turned out to be a long way below the water line, which meant I couldn't bale fast enough. So I decided to reverse the flow in the hose and get a siphon running. Unfortunately I failed to check the water first or use the debris strainer provided. I started sucking on the tube but something stuck and impeded the flow. I sucked harder. The blockage cleared and whatever it was, I'd really rather not know, went down my throat. I started choking, reached for a chair to perform the Heimlich manoeuvre on myself and just about managed to swallow it down. I have never come closer to asphyxiation. I remember thinking, well I've nearly died about a dozen other times. Is this it?! What a way to go, just as another life arrives . . . Not content with having just one accident, I then fell over a chair and hit the side of my head on the bathroom step.

Anya was on all fours trying to breathe in the correct rhythm. In between the agonies of labour she managed to shout out, 'Are you OK?' And I thought I've really screwed this up. This is not how it was meant to go.

I carried on baling and three lovely midwives arrived. Not one, not two, but three. It was quite surreal to have them populate our tiny flat with chatter. I made tea, shared biscuits and conversation, but eventually Anya thought I might be too focused on hospitality rather than helping with her contractions. My defence is I was trying to keep them distracted. Otherwise after every contraction one of them would bear down on Anya and prod her with a cold hard implement known as a Doppler in order to measure the heart rate of the baby inside her uterus.

It took forever. Anya went into labour at 8pm. By 6am – ten hours later – her uterus was only five centimetres dilated, whereas the baby needs ten centimetres to fit out. At one point a midwife suggested Anya walk up and down the stairs to advance the contractions, which achieved nothing except to make her violently sick. After 16 hours Anya had eaten nothing and was getting weaker. The midwives' shift was due to end, so they gave her a choice: either she could stick it out with a fresh lot of midwives, or go to hospital. Anya viewed the prospect of three more midwives chatting loudly while I served them tea as the less attractive option, and gave up on her dream of a home birth.

Two female paramedics arrived in an ambulance and insisted on carrying Anya up the stairs in a special chair. I wanted to help but was told I wasn't qualified. The staircase, inserted to gain access to an 18th-century cellar, was narrow with a wicked twist.

'Oh my God,' one said. 'It's like carrying her out through a birth canal.'

With siren blaring we were transferred down the road to the Royal Free Hospital where, slightly amazingly, we were the only parents having a baby that night. On the labour ward we were greeted by a no-nonsense obstetrician who whipped out something that looked like a knitting needle and broke Anya's waters without even asking. Her pain levels moved up a notch to something close to unbearable. Next came an epidural. Anya had to lie dead still during waves of excruciating pain while the doctor inserted a needle into her spine.

By now Anya was in the care of a warm and hugely experienced British Nigerian midwife, a mother of six herself, assisted by a young male trainee doctor. They were both brilliant. Anya says I took my first nap in 32 hours while her mum sat with her, but my main memory is spending three hours turning myself into a human pouffe while she leant against me, then draped herself over me and gripped my arm with her nails so hard I actually bled. But it seemed to help. We were getting close.

Anya later told me that she'd always imagined I'd be at the head end during the actual birth, stroking her hair and holding her hand, because she worried I'd never be able to relate to her in quite the same way again if I saw everything happening at the business end. But I was fine about it. Her mum did the hand-holding and I held up a leg. The young doctor took the other one.

'Come on Anya, puuuuush,' urged the midwife.

We were all there for a while. Two hours, to be precise. The crown of a little head appeared and my heart was pounding out of my chest. But instead of slowly emerging, the head almost seemed to be stuck. The midwife started telling Anya that the baby's hair was red. *Eh?* I thought. Was there a mix-up at the clinic? I looked more closely. I could see with my own eyes it was dark.

'I'm trying to make her angry so she pushes harder,' the midwife whispered to me. 'Always works.'

But the baby refused to make an appearance.

Anya decided enough was enough. She had two blokes holding her legs up, the midwife goading her on, and her mum pinching her ears in a loving but misguided attempt to distract her from the pain. She turned around so she was on all fours, gripped the railing on the back of the raised bed, went into a squat like she was in a Mozambican village and engaged gravity.

Then something incredible happened.

A tiny baby was born.

However much I'd dreamt about that moment, even mythologised it in my head as a transformative rite of passage, I never anticipated the enormity of it. I wasn't remotely prepared for the moment it became a reality. For all my deep belief in the gifts travel can offer, no experience around the planet before or since can match the power or thrill or beauty of having a child and becoming a parent. I knew that as an experience it would be massive, but it was still far bigger than anything I could have projected. It was an eclipse. It put all else into the shade. It was the culmination of the most exciting, exhausting and bizarre journey of my life.

Anya was overjoyed, but utterly spent after 25 hours of labour; she also just thought, *Thank feck for that.*

Initially I thought she had given birth to a squid, or possibly an alien. The head was long and thin. But within seconds the shape reformed itself as a human.

My mum and Anya's dad, brother and stepmum all visited. Then the newborn baby on her stomach began to nudge his way up her body in search of a nipple. When he began to feed for the first time, after all she'd been through, my wife finally experienced the transformative power and beauty of nature doing its thing.

Looking back, do we find ourselves wishing for that tree in Mozambique? I think not, given the complications. What I do wish is that we'd been a bit less starry-eyed. We hadn't imagined anything going wrong. If I'm honest, I gamed out the Burma trip more thoroughly. Especially after I nearly choked, I was grateful we could call on the expertise of people who really knew what they were doing.

But muppetry aside, we had crossed the threshold into parenthood. There's a scene in the movie *Paddington*, when the expectant mum and dad arrive at the hospital as happy hippies on a scooter promising childbirth won't change them, then come out wearing beige and drive off in a Volvo with side impact protection bars. In an instant, like them, we became the hilarious clichéd overprotective parents of a firstborn child.

Perhaps this instinct expresses an insecurity that, as first-time parents, you have no idea what you're doing. Intensely aware of this ignorance, we overcompensate and swaddle the child in protection. I remember feeling astonished that we were allowed to walk out of the hospital the next day with a baby. I kept thinking security would stop us and ask to see our permits. All the medical team wanted to see was evidence we had a car seat. I couldn't believe I was allowed to leave the hospital with my son.

Although we had known a boy was on the way, we didn't have a name ready. A minor row about what to call him had rumbled on for a while. Anya was keen on a Danish name and at one point genuinely suggested we call him Bo. I put my foot down and said he'd never survive going through any school with a name that means body odour. Finally we agreed on Jakob, on the grounds that it works in multiple cultures, and could be shortened to Jake.

I was instantly devoted. Jake made himself all the more lovable by being no trouble at all, apart from feeding every two hours and having colic. He was really quite compliant, slept a lot of the time, cried a bit but was, in essence, fairly easy to manage. Admittedly as a heavy sleeper I was less exposed to the grumpy small hours of the night when Anya would wake every time he even squeaked. What I didn't realise was this was the phoney war that lasts for a few months. It's a total illusion because in due course he started crawling, and from then on our hands were forever full.

I was stunned by what a character he was from almost the beginning. After just a few months Jake was a real little human: funny, clever, and, like both his parents and all his grandparents, wonderfully stubborn. Finally I was able to practise dadding on my own tiny lovable ball of joy. I was hands-on and completely involved, mastering nappy changing to the level of a Formula One pit stop within a week. There were a few minor mishaps, but no disasters. Jake loved being swung around and chucked in the air. I never dropped him, but I did quickly learn not to tickle him while he sat above me on the edge of a table, because he threw up all over my face. It even went into my eyes.

You hear so many people say that life is going to change when you become a parent, but I had no comprehension of how dramatic it would be. There was a before and an after. We became different people living a different life. Within a month of giving birth Anya turned 40. We played rounders on Hampstead Heath with a group of friends and then hired a house in Devon and had a big party to prove to ourselves we could still have a good time. We thought we were the kind of parents who could shove Jake under the table in a pub or let him fall asleep at a festival. Reality came into sharper focus when we went to another birthday weekend in Deià in Majorca where we were the only couple with a child. We all went to a fancy restaurant one night but couldn't fit the pram through the front door. The staff joked nobody had ever brought a baby on to the premises. Then we shuffled off to the loos while everyone else clinked mojitos. I came back beaming and announced a little too loudly that Jake had managed to do a proper giant poo in the toilet. There and then I realised our world had changed.

Some parents start out hopeful but are faintly disappointed by the reality of having children. For me, the actuality was more profound and meaningful than I'd ever imagined. Of course it was life-consuming and draining, but that was a small price to pay for the joy of staring into Jake's eyes, an elemental pleasure the fertility tests had told me I could never experience. And yet there he was.

I knew I had been fundamentally altered when my sleep started to change. I'd always wanted to fly in my dreams. Perhaps my unconscious was telling me something was missing in my life. After I met Anya I could take off and fly in my dreams and my sleep was enriched by vivid journeys. Then, a few months after Jake was born, I could suddenly control my flight, which had never happened before. I was piloting my dreams, choosing whether to swoop or soar. There couldn't have been a more perfect illustration of the state I was in. I felt content and complete.

So although I was in the middle of the Indian Ocean series, I certainly wasn't mad keen to go back on the road. It meant leaving my baby son and Anya behind. If I'd been born with money, maybe I could have stayed at home. But Anya and I didn't have that luxury. I consoled myself that I had managed to get far more paternity time than most new dads. On the other hand, most new fathers don't head straight off into a war zone.

CHAPTER FIFTEEN

Blast Boxers

Leaving the secret base felt like exiting a walled medieval castle. We strapped heavy armour around our bodies, tightened the straps on our ballistic combat helmets and climbed into the back of a giant bulletproof, mine-resistant armoured vehicle. The sandy-green-coloured, four-wheeled Casspir had a machine gun poking from a roof turret and a V-shaped hull designed to direct the force of a roadside bomb away from occupants. As we started to move towards the base exit through the first of a series of security zones, passing guards manning machine-gun positions behind concrete barricades, the army officer we were with told us not to get too comfortable. Militants had started using shaped charges that could send an explosive projectile through the floor at our feet, destroying the interior and melting everyone inside. Suddenly we didn't feel quite so safe. Then we left the base and drove out into Mogadishu, perhaps the most dangerous place in the world.

My first major trip as a new father was to Somalia, a country riven by conflict since a civil war started in 1991. Warlords had taken over when the government collapsed. Their battles laid waste to much of the city, then Somalis had to endure the devastating suffering of a long famine. The United Nations and foreign governments had all tried to intervene, but fighting and suffering continued. At least 1 million people had died. There was a fledgling government, but it had little power and its troops were fighting battle-hardened militants from al-Shabab, a heavily armed and exceptionally violent Somali Islamic group that has close ties with al-Qaeda. Piracy flourished in the power vacuum and rippled out to affect the entire western Indian Ocean.

The question of how to get to Somalia was something we looked at from every angle. I'd hoped we could arrive by sea, but the ocean off Mogadishu was full of pirates and I met several experts and sailors who thought going on a ship was completely mad. In Kenya I was looking around Mombasa, the busiest port in the whole of East Africa, and found myself welcomed aboard a Pakistani cargo ship that had arrived via Somalia, carrying 800 tons of cargo including rice, sugar and cooking oil. The captain told me his boat had been boarded by pirates pointing rocket-propelled grenades (RPGs) at him and the crew.

'Take food, telephone,' he said. 'Sometimes take clothes.' I asked him if he thought it would be safe for me to head towards Mogadishu by boat. He said definitely not, and told us that on his most recent visit there was a suicide bombing in the port.

But eventually we found a shipping company who were willing to give us passage on one of their cargo ships that was heading towards Somalia. It would have given me a dramatic insight into the fears and dangers facing sailors and boat crew operating in the area. But at the last minute the shipping firm changed their minds.

In the end I flew to Mogadishu on a cargo flight from Kenya with two magnificent colleagues, the sturdy and stalwart cameraman Jonathan Young and courageous director Andrew Carter, whom I had travelled with repeatedly before and entered Burma with on the *Tropic of Cancer* series. Both were willing to accept the risk of going to Somalia in order to highlight the story of people living there. I trusted them completely. There was nobody I would rather have walked with into a danger zone.

For our last supper before departure we went to the legendary Carnival restaurant in Nairobi where Andrew, a vegetarian, graciously agreed to leaf through a menu mainly containing farm-reared zebra and crocodile. Atmospherically it was all a bit TGI Fridays except with meat served on huge skewers and carved by great machetes. As a bonkers preamble to Mogadishu, it felt somehow appropriate.

Uncertain about internet access in Mogadishu, that night I video-called Anya. She thrust Jake's startled face towards the camera and I took a snap of our three faces on the screen. When I look back at it now I wonder how I could have left him for an hour, let alone weeks. With hindsight I fret about the risk I was prepared to take as a new father of a beautiful tiny son, leaving him in order to enter a conflict zone.

It was not a journey I undertook lightly. But to tell the story of the Indian Ocean, and the people who live around it, I felt I had no choice.

The advice we were given before going was pretty stark. We were told that all of Somalia was a hostile environment and that threats came from 'armed conflict (small arms and heavy weaponry), indirect fire, suicide bombings, roadside bombs, sniper fire, kidnap, terrorism'. I wasn't nervous for myself, but I did always have pangs of concern about leaving Anya with our little lad, and I was well aware that I was going off on a journey while she was stuck behind juggling baby care at the same time as working on the logistics and research from our office. But the fact she'd travelled on the journeys was a huge reassurance to Anya. She knew what I did, why I did it, and whom I was working with as well. It was our job, which we both loved. The dangers Jonathan, Andrew and I were facing on the road were all further spelled out in documents that gave background logistical and medical information about where we were going, which we all studied in case we were separated, shot or kidnapped. One key section warned that 'medical care throughout Somalia is extremely limited'.

'They don't say,' I said to Jonathan.

In Mogadishu there was just one clinic that might be able to help us if we were badly injured, staffed by doctors who were primarily serving soldiers of the African Union, which was running an armed peacekeeping operation in Somalia, fighting the al-Shabab militants for control of the city and the country. 'It has an ambulance converted from an armoured car, though access to this cannot be guaranteed and it will not risk travelling to all parts of the city,' said our report. None of that sounded entirely reassuring.

I had been to Mogadishu before, early in my TV adventures, and wrote about it in *Step by Step*. During that trip a couple of colleagues and I had been the only foreigners in the city, which was completely anarchic, and we were escorted at all times by a dozen heavily armed local mercenaries. To illustrate the state of collapse we had been to the main market and I bought a genuine Somali diplomatic passport in my own name, and with my own photograph in it, from a man called Mr Big Beard. I would like to say that Mogadishu didn't seem quite as Mad Max as on that previous visit. But when we landed at the airport, even though it was in a zone controlled by the African Union peacekeeping forces, the atmosphere simmered with tension and several men suddenly began fighting among themselves.

'Well you don't see that at Gatwick,' said Jonathan.

Local officials were trying to carve out their own little zones of power, and they were brawling over who should be checking in visitors and taking their visa money.

'Welcome to Mogadishu,' I said to Jonathan and Andrew.

Soldiers from AMISOM, the African Union peacekeeping force, met us at the airport. They looked genuine and official. But foreigners had died in Mogadishu because they'd been hustled away by kidnappers or militants pretending to be police or guards. So we rang a security line to confirm their ID and treble-checked their passes. In a situation like that you just don't know who you can trust. Running through our heads was a list of questions. What vehicle are we in? Are we driving through hostile territory? What's going to happen when we get where we're going? Mostly though, who the hell are you and can we trust you?

We climbed into an armoured SUV with doors so thick and heavy they were opened and closed by a huge internal lever. Then we drove to a remote corner of the airport security zone and into Bancroft Camp, passing through tall barrier walls and more armed guards.

Bancroft was a bizarre place. It was a secretive base run by an American development group that had initially specialised in clearing landmines, but was expanding its work to train AMISOM soldiers from Uganda and Burundi in advanced urban warfare. There was a sense of enclosure about the place; a constant awareness of mortal danger just beyond the perimeter. It felt besieged.

The base was a temporary home to a weird array of people. We were met by a bubbly, enthusiastic and beautiful young Kenyan-Somali UN official. From a wealthy exiled family, she was a valuable kidnap target. She had taken a great risk in volunteering to work there and was forbidden from leaving the base. She checked us in, explained the rules, and impressed on us that we weren't allowed to film there, so as not to give potential infiltrators any location information. I was sitting at a table with her when she answered her mobile, and after a moment started blowing raspberries down the line. Then she swore sharply at the caller in English and, I presumed, in Somali, put the phone down and continued chatting away as if nothing had happened, before she saw my look of curious amusement.

'Oh, that was the militants,' she said breezily, as if she'd just had a slightly annoying sales call from an insurance firm. 'Someone at the phone company keeps selling them lists of our mobile numbers, and we all keep getting these calls where they tell us how they're going to kill us.'

We were sitting in an outdoor communal work area. Around us there was a bar, pool table, dartboard, and people having hushed meetings and using laptops on plastic garden tables in dappled shade. Among the other guests lounging around were ex-soldiers and special forces guys from around the world: skilled snipers, engineers, weapons specialists. There was a war photographer, a couple of burly Americans in wraparound sunglasses ('CIA,' said Jonathan after chatting with them), drone operators, and some private military contractors or PMCs (aka mercenaries), who were doing God knows what. Some were willing to chat, others wanted to keep a distance.

A contingent of buff young French special forces guys had been there for a few weeks. They looked like the Chippendales in fatigues. They were there to rescue a French hostage being held captive by pirates or militants. Another French official, apparently an agent from DGSE, the equivalent of MI6, was also being held captive in Mogadishu. The senior French officer, a captain aged about 30, would go to the beach in his Speedos most afternoons and come back brandishing a huge fish that he cooked up for us and his men. When we talked he struck me as earnest but surprisingly naïve about the kidnappers.

'We 'ave tried to meet with zem, but zey just lie and keep changing ze demands,' he said, sounding completely shocked. He leant forward: 'You know, zese pirates, zey are completely untrustworthy!' He sounded so surprised. I felt old.

We were billeted in shipping containers that had been converted into basic, functional rooms. They were topped by sandbags to protect against mortars and their walls were re-inforced externally by floor to roof sand-filled bastions known as HESCOs. Basically a huge rectangular sack that can be filled with earth at speed, these are a brilliantly simple invention that could limit the explosive power of mortars, RPGs or even surface-to-surface missiles. Jonathan was delighted to remind me they were the brainwave of a fellow Yorkshireman, who could persuade no banks to help fund his idea apart from his local branch, where he deposited the millions he then made. The HESCO changed modern warfare, enabling armies to quickly build front-line defensive positions. They were helping AMISOM to not only stay safe in their base but also to move the front line forward as they tried to drive militants out of the city.

The thick walls and protection were reassuring, but we had been told there could be militant spies infiltrating Bancroft. While we were there a suicide bomber managed to get over the fence, and we heard shots and explosions. It's why one of the simplest bits of kit I carry with me is a thick rubber door wedge. Really ramming that under a solid external door is a last line of defence.

The next day we had arranged to leave the relative safety of the base and head out into Mogadishu with a group of Ugandan soldiers, led by a lieutenant colonel called Paddy Ankunda, a very calm senior officer. The AMISOM troops weren't just running a peacekeeping operation; they had been tasked with driving the militants out of Mogadishu, and out of Somalia. We were heading into a full-on war.

Jonathan, Andrew and I absolutely had each other's backs, but we didn't know about anyone else. We were reliant on the Ugandans for security, but beyond professional courtesy they had very little motivation to risk their necks for us. At least they viewed us as a useful means of letting the outside world know what they were doing. But I certainly didn't feel completely safe.

For our protection we had each bought our own combat helmets and class 4 flak jackets. These are heavy and constricting, with ceramic plates that slot into marsupial-type pouches front and back. Ironically the plates can crack easily, potentially even when our luggage is chucked around at an airport. Yet they can absorb the elephantine force of a Kalashnikov high-velocity round and prevent your lungs from being pierced or crushed. Our most intimate piece of protection was armoured underwear, a pair of Blast Boxers with a Kevlar fabric around the crucial zones of the groin and upper leg. They're designed to stop small bits of shrapnel from wiping out the undercarriage. Wearing the same pair, day in, day out, was not exactly ideal from a hygiene perspective, but we had bigger stuff to worry about.

As soon as we climbed into the Casspir there was no turning back. With another armoured vehicle behind us, we drove out into Mogadishu.

The city had been completely hammered by incessant fighting. Refugees moved around, trying to stay out of the path of the conflict. Skinny donkeys pulled old water carts. I don't think I saw a single building that was not pockmarked by bullet holes.

Many looked like they had been sprayed with bullets, and had huge gaping holes left by RPG strikes. Roofs were missing. Trees had been blown apart. Some shops were still clinging on, their jolly hand-painted signs advertising a barber or vehicle spare parts, but buildings had collapsed, almost exhausted by the fighting. Everywhere there was rubble. Whole sections of the city looked like Stalingrad during the Second World War.

At least if we stayed in the parts of the city controlled by AMISOM there was less chance of being hit by a roadside bomb. But Paddy warned us in military parlance that the front line was 'fluid', meaning we might stray into an area where we didn't want to be. In case anything like that happened, there were firing portholes along each side of the Casspir and loaded Kalashnikovs were pegged to the roof of the vehicle.

'Do you guys know how to use them?' he said.

We took them down and had a quick Kalashnikov refresher lesson, just in case everything went to blazes.

At one point we actually did take a wrong turning and strayed into enemy territory. A look of concern appeared on Paddy's face. Everyone stopped talking. I eyed the assault rifles. Another couple of turns and we moved back into a safer area. Then five minutes further on we pulled up sharply.

'We're here,' said Paddy. 'This is the front line.'

It really is a hell of a thing to approach a front line, to go in search of a conflict. You approach from safety, and make for a point where blood is being shed, where people are being killed, and on both sides.

The transformation was incredibly sudden. The giant South African armoured personnel carriers had air conditioning, thick quadruple-glazed bulletproof windows and a steel door at the rear. On one side of it I was in a sealed container and outside sounds were muffled. When I opened the door I felt like I was stepping out of a spaceship. I jumped down and it was like leaping on to the surface of Mars. Intense light and scorching heat hit me. And then there was the noise – the loud rattle of gunfire was all around. Having been in an armoured womb, in an instant we were vulnerable.

We had arrived on the outskirts of the city, at a front-line position of trenches and barricades on higher ground over-looking areas still under the control of the hardcore militants of al-Shabab. Their tactics were extreme. They'd even taken to using donkeys as mobile mines. Until just a few weeks before my visit, al-Shabab held most of Mogadishu. Scores of AMISOM soldiers had died to capture the high point. We crouched down and jogged towards the barricades marking the front line. I peered out through barbed wire and a high wall of sandbags towards a road cut through scrubland by the militants. Then we looked through binoculars for any fighters moving around on the other side. Paddy was describing the area we were looking at when a soldier just to our side started machine-gunning a car in the distance. They said it was a ve-hicle belonging to al-Shabab.

Empty shells littered the ground, yet there was a strange sense of normality at the front line. Shooting would suddenly break out, and some soldiers would duck for cover, but others carried on drinking tea. Soldiers there were spending their days watch-ing, ducking, shooting, sniping, killing and dying, but that could still become a humdrum routine like that of anyone else.

We filmed and talked to the soldiers, waited and watched, and then after a couple of hours Paddy began to worry that al-Shabab might target our position with gunfire or artillery, and we climbed into the Casspir and drove through the city.

Along with the constant sense of danger, it was deeply depressing to drive around a place in which almost every building looked like a hollowed-out skeleton. It must have been like this after the bombing of Dresden. On one sortie we were taken to the national stadium, a dismal and ghostly place, which, until recently, al-Shabab had used for public executions. They would bury their victims up to the neck and stone them to death.

Yet there was still beauty to be found in Mogadishu. Down by the seafront I walked up a couple of floors inside the flayed carcass of a war-damaged building to look out at a spectacular view beyond, taking in an impressive arch, a minaret and a Renaissance-style church built by Italian colonisers. Somehow these pockmarked remnants of a less chaotic past had survived into the nightmare of the present. That felt like something of a miracle because destruction really was everywhere.

By the old port I met Mohamed Nur, a one-time business adviser to Islington council who had become the mayor of Mogadishu. He seemed a decent chap with good intentions, but I worried about his priorities. He was fixated on the need to repair street lighting, because he thought it would signify a return to normality. He was also worried about plastic in the sea. Now I'm as obsessive as anyone about that issue, but it didn't feel like it should be the most pressing item in the mayor of Mogadishu's in tray. I had grave worries about his ability to lead people out of the disaster. A cameraman was following the mayor around making a film. He seemed in a huge rush, shooting everything. I asked him why.

'Mayors don't survive long here,' he said, slightly embarrassed. 'I need to make this film before they get him with a car bomb.'

I've rarely felt so sad for a place and its people as I did in Mogadishu. In some war zones, conflict can actually be quite localised. But all of Mogadishu was dangerous, and everywhere we went we were at risk, even when visiting one of the city's dozen famine relief centres. We would normally lower our guard in such a place, but we knew it was unsafe even to remove our helmets. 'Watch your six,' said Jonathan, warning us to be aware of what's happening behind our backs.

The feeding centre was full of families driven there by the worst drought in 60 years, resulting in a famine made all the more destructive by the presence of al-Shabab, which had prevented foreign aid agencies from entering the affected regions. Desperate people had travelled hundreds of miles to seek refuge in Mogadishu, often walking with small children. The ones who had made it were the fittest and strongest. The weakest died on the way. I talked to one man who had walked 250 miles.

'The farms are gone. The animals are finished,' he told me. 'We ran for our lives. This is better. We came here to survive and we found food here.' I found it hard to imagine how bad life must have been in the rest of the country for Mogadishu to be seen as a place of salvation.

It felt clear to me that AMISOM could only do so much. As a relatively small force battling a fanatical enemy able to hide among the local population, they were undermanned and under-resourced. They could have done with some of those UN vehicles on the *Jolly Bianco* container ship or, even better, attack helicopters.

The scale of their task was even clearer when Colonel Paddy took us to the edge of AMISOM's area of control in the north-west of the city, where his soldiers were still fighting in close-quarter street battles, and sometimes even in people's gardens. We jumped out of the Casspir and Paddy warned us to stick close to him. It was a situation where the lines had blurred, and you could turn a corner outside a house and suddenly find yourself face to face with a militant fighter.

But I felt we had to get close to the fighting, to get a visceral sense of the conflict. Unless we could see and film what was happening, viewers wouldn't understand the reality. I heard a rattle of fire from a heavy machine gun, tried to work out whether it was incoming or outgoing, and then, totally at odds with my natural inclination, I started running towards the shooting. In no other sphere of life would this be a wise move. I could hear Jonathan and Andrew keeping pace with me, and Paddy a little way behind.

'What are you doing?!' I could hear Paddy shouting. 'They're taking fire over there!' He was herding kittens – in a war zone.

I dived into a machine-gun position with Ugandan soldiers who were shooting at militants running between broken cover on the other side.

We filmed with them for a bit, then moved along the front line, ducking as we ran, to another position that was trading gunfire with al-Shabab. Rounds were thudding into the ground and barricade around us.

I talked with Paddy for a while and Jonathan and Andrew filmed and worked wonders to capture a sense of the scene. At the sound of yet more ear-splitting gunfire, a junior officer ran up to Paddy and told him the fighters on the other side were setting up a barrage of rocket-propelled grenades to launch an attack on our position, probably because we were there. At his insistence we had to be evacuated out.

Paddy told me we needed to run across open ground to the safety of armoured personnel carriers, and snipers would fire low over our heads to provide covering fire. He said it would be best if we didn't film as we ran, because from a distance a shoulder-mounted camera can look like an RPG.

I could see the building where snipers were firing through tiny holes knocked in the side. I went first, running across open ground with sniper fire close overhead, and then heard a strange sound off to one side. I glanced over and saw a bombed-out archway. And there, under the archway, in the middle of the battle, a barber was calmly giving a soldier a wet shave with a Sweeney Todd cut-throat razor, while his stereo pumped out jaunty upbeat music. He must have had a very steady hand. As I came through his field of vision he turned to look at me, a cigarette dangling from his mouth, and a wry smile spread across his face as he watched me running and diving for safety into the back of an armoured personnel carrier. It was a surreal moment, perfectly blending madness and normality.

But then so much of Somalia was a surreal and impossible place. It wasn't easy to sum it all up. The executive producer Sam Bagnall and I talked endlessly about the crazy challenge of trying to explain four decades of conflict and civil war, then attempted it with a piece of commentary in the final programme that could only last for 40 seconds of screen time. Such are the limitations of television.

I left Somalia feeling angry and upset at the suffering, and also somewhat impotent. Although we would do our best to explain what was happening there, I feared it was unlikely to make more than a jot of difference. As I slumped into my seat on the plane out, and sank my teeth into an apple, I felt intense relief to have made it out safely, and a degree of guilt I'd taken such a risk as a new father of a baby boy.

CHAPTER SIXTEEN

Ecocide

Centuries before Christopher Columbus reached America, merchants were trading enormous distances around the Indian Ocean, thought to be the first huge expanse of water humans really explored. Sailors were able to use the annual monsoon and the trade winds, which blow from east to west near the equator, to travel in one direction early in the season and then travel back a few months later. No single power ever controlled and conquered the Indian Ocean in the way the Mediterranean was dominated by the Roman Empire. Less turbulent than the Atlantic or Pacific, the Indian Ocean was used by hundreds of communities and kingdoms around its edge.

Trade was a major driver encouraging exploration of the Indian Ocean, and even around the time of Christ goods were being sold and exchanged between Tamil kingdoms in southern India and Roman Egypt. But our ancestors also travelled for pleasure and work. Carpenters and artisans journeyed from ancient Rome to India for employment. I love the fact a craftsman in ancient Greece, from the island of Rhodes, advertised himself as having a great reputation in India. Another student in ancient Greece was sent to Egypt to study. He decided to go on a trip to India without telling his family, who thought he was missing and consulted an oracle. The student eventually returned home to discover the oracle claimed the student had suffered a violent death and the family had killed his slaves in punishment.

It's always assumed that Europeans did all the travelling and exploring. But countless cultures developed around the Indian Ocean or used the sea for trade. Zheng He, a eunuch admiral during the Ming dynasty, tried to forge trade routes between China and East Africa in the early 15th century. He commanded a fleet consisting of more than 250 ships, some said to be utterly colossal, as big as 135 metres long by 55 metres wide with nine masts. This claim was dismissed as an exaggeration by scoffing marine archaeologists until they unearthed a rudder taller than a two-storey house. Zheng He's navy left a legacy of DNA that can still be found in East Africa today.

As I circled the Indian Ocean onwards from Somalia, I came across equally surprising evidence of population movement in the north-west of India. We were driving along a quiet country road when we stopped to help an overloaded rickshaw that had broken down. The women in the rickshaw were all wearing bright saris, but the passengers were Sidi people, the descendants of Black Africans who were brought to Gujarat and what is now Pakistan. Some experts think millions of Africans travelled to India, and the Sidis have been in India for at least 600 years. Many were forced to travel as slaves, but often they went willingly as sailors, merchants, mercenaries and traders. There's even thought to have been an African king in central India. The movement of Black Africans to India and Pakistan has not been a major focus of study, but I was fascinated by their presence, and delighted when a local Sidi leader told me his community actually lived very harmoniously with neighbouring ethnic groups. It was a relief to hear that, at least according to him, everyone was getting along just fine.

In order to make the story of the Sidi people work for television, we wanted to find something really visual to film, and we found it when we discovered that a troupe of Sidi entertainers were in a neighbouring village, making money at temples, weddings and funerals as musicians and dancers.

The only problem with music and dancing is that I'm expected to join in. I'm fine with dangerous places, or eating weird foods, but dad dancing on camera is close to my worst nightmare. In truth I have a bit of a dance phobia, even when no cameras are watching. It brings up memories of drinking in the shadows at parties as an angst-ridden teenager. The truth is I never let myself go enough as a teenager to be a true dancer, and I've been reluctant ever since.

We met up with the Sidi musicians and dancers at a small concrete temple that was still under construction. Their band was playing – they had already gathered quite the crowd – and the only way I could avoid being yanked into action by the performers was to grab a pair of maracas. It was a tolerable situation, but then one of the dancers, a toothless old man, leapt up into my arms, wrapped his arms and legs around me in a tight embrace, and began sucking on my earlobe. I tried to laugh and push him off, but then for some reason he stuck his tongue deep into my ear. It was, quite frankly, revolting. And at the end of it all he expected a tip.

We left the Sidis, quickly, and travelled down the west coast of India to Mumbai, the biggest city around the entire Indian Ocean. We timed our visit so we could be there for one of the biggest festivals in the world, the annual birthday celebration for the elephant-headed god Ganesh, the greatest of all Hindu deities. For months before the festival, families and communities had been making giant statues of Ganesh that were then paraded through crowds in their millions and taken to the coast to be immersed in the sea. It was a spectacular and overwhelming event, but by the end felt a bit like being sober in an Ibizan club at nine in the morning when nobody wanted to go home.

We made our way down to Goa and then to Cochin to learn about the ancient lift nets that fishermen use there known as Chinese fishing nets. From the 14th century, Cochin was a major spice trading hub on India's west coast, and the legend is that Zheng He's fleet introduced a new style of fishing to the region in which a huge cantilevered outstretched net would be lowered into the sea from the shore. They were certainly photogenic, if you ignored the quantities of plastic rubbish that seemed to have gathered in a drift just nearby. But they weren't quite the uplifting sunset ending we wanted to film.

We moved on to Sri Lanka briefly and then flew back to India to continue our journey up the east coast of the country. After landing at an airport on the east coast very late at night, we joined one of the slowest travel queues I've ever experienced. Getting through immigration in India is always an ordeal but this was another level. Alongside me were mostly itinerant villagers returning from work in the Gulf and immigration hadn't laid on enough staff to process them. After three hours I finally made it to the front and found myself taking part in a tragic farce. The woman behind the desk, who appeared to be drunk or half asleep, asked me where I was going.

I leant forward just slightly. 'Orissa,' I said, clearly and confidently.

She looked at me blankly.

'Odisha?' I said, trying the new name for the neighbouring state, an area bigger than England.

She put her pen down.

'Orissa?' I said again, less confidently this time. 'Odisha?'

I repeated the name again clearly, and then in several different accents, just in case that was the problem. Orissa is not an obscure village. It was like landing in Manchester and saying you were going to Liverpool.

Still she shook her head. I started to panic.

'It's the next state!' I said.

It was now 5am and I was getting desperate. Fortunately I had formed a bond with the villagers behind me in the queue. The chap at the front said their friend at the back had a map. A ripple went 30 metres down the queue and a ragged paper map was held up in the air. I walked back down the line to get it, but by the time I returned to the front the immigration official was asleep. Properly asleep. Not wanting to annoy her, I knocked gently on the glass, but she didn't wake up. So I went round to the back of her booth, opened the door and with my hands clasped together in prayer I said: 'I'm so sorry, but look here on the map, there's Orissa.' I tapped the paper. She looked up, looked at the map, put her head down again and went back to sleep. I thought I'm never going to get into this country unless I improvise. So I leant across her, stamped my own immigration form and, having returned the map to its owner, made my way into India, to be reunited with my Bengali guide Abhra Bhattacharya.

Our problems with Indian Ocean muppetry did not end when we left the airport. The next day we headed towards a remote fishing port. It took us a full day of driving and the only place we could find to stay overnight for miles in any direction was a 'guest house resort' near the sea. When we got close, some men from the guest house came along the track to meet us and explained that the road went through a river that was flooded. We drew closer. Although it was dark I could clearly see that not only was it dangerously impassable, it also appeared to contain crocodiles. The guest house workers began arguing among themselves. Apparently the honour of India was at stake if we didn't attempt to cross the river. They became convinced we could float the vehicles across. As I described earlier, I had done this once before, in Ecuador when travelling along the equator, but that was in a crocodile-free river with the villagers holding the car in place as water came up to the window. Also, in Ecuador we had 4x4s with vented exhausts on the roof. In India a farmer who lived nearby walked up and sensibly pointed out that national honour would take quite a significant knock if we did attempt and got chomped on by crocs.

The farmer made a hilarious face at me from behind the guest house workers, suggesting they were a bit mad. Then he calmed everyone down and pointed out there was a footbridge further along the river. This seemed a sensible solution. However it meant we had to carry all our heavy bags on a half-mile round trip to the resort, which turned out to be a collection of scattered and barely habitable huts. It was a rare moment when I wished for a bland business hotel with functioning plug sockets where we could charge camera batteries. The guest house staff were all hammered on a coconut toddy made of fomented sap and the next morning we had to pay one of them to go and buy some toilet paper and breakfast eggs. On the plus side they did introduce us to an agile gentleman who shinned up a tree to get some sap for me to sample. It was actually pretty tasty. The downside was as I watched him climb I realised he was in very baggy shorts and had no underpants. I didn't know where to look.

My main focus in the area was fishing. Over on the west coast of India I had visited Veraval, a vast fishing port where almost

4,000 trawlers were moored waiting for calm waters after the end of the monsoon. With the flags fluttering on thousands of masts, the fleet had made for a splendid sight, but that many boats all going out in search of the same catch spelled utter disaster for marine life in the Indian Ocean. They land hundreds of thousands of tons of fish in Veraval every year. But each season they have to sail further out and come back with fewer fish. I went aboard one small boat whose skipper told me that he was having to travel between 400 and 500 kilometres because the waters off western India were empty.

On the east coast I went to a small port called Astaranga and headed out to catch prawns, one of the ocean's most lucrative seafoods, on a small, old wooden fishing boat with a crew of five. India is one of the biggest suppliers of prawns to the UK. The crew cast their enormous net out into the sea, waited until it had settled 30 metres down on the bottom, and then began dragging it along the seabed, aided by huge wooden barn doors that kept the mouth open. The fine mesh nets cause staggering damage, tearing at the seabed and consuming life. It's akin to clear-cutting forests, knocking down all the trees and taking all the birds and animals. Fish have nowhere to hide.

An hour later the boat engines strained and began pulling in the net. I felt completely horrified by what I saw. When the net was back in the boat it only contained a few shrimps and a small amount of bycatch, unwanted sea life caught alongside the target catch. Around the world, prawn fishing is thought to be responsible for a third of bycatch, amounting to tens of millions of tons. Much of the bycatch is chucked away dead, including juvenile fish that have no chance to breed. But what really shocked me was that the overall catch was so pitifully small. Here, after years of overfishing in the area, the ocean was almost empty.

On every level it was a catastrophe. It was also a real wake-up moment for me. I had seen with my own eyes on my journeys how we were targeting and annihilating marine life. I had spoken with experts and read reports and I knew we were fishing our oceans to death. But what I witnessed off the east coast of India, and what I've since seen elsewhere around the planet, is that it isn't something we are still in the process of doing. In many places it is something that has already happened. We have already fished large areas of our oceans to death. We fish not just for ourselves, but to create protein sources for chicken and pig farms as well. Targeting our favourite species first and wiping it out, and then going after another and another, we have killed life in the seas.

The next morning I headed to meet Tuku Vehera, a local conservationist deeply worried about the impact of trawlers on ocean wildlife. As we walked along a vast empty beach, he suddenly noticed a rotting smell and began digging into the sand. A foot down he found the buried body of a turtle. The sight of its head peeping out of the sand was desperate. Tuku said his research had shown that every year, 10 to 15,000 turtles were killed due to illegal fishing along the Orissa coast, but he claimed the government forest department was hiding bodies to lower the tally.

Turtles die when trapped underwater in nets, preventing them from coming up to breathe. Trawling was supposed to be illegal in the area to protect a vital nesting site of the Olive Ridley turtle, one of the largest in the world. But that hadn't stopped the fishing boats. Tuku pointed out to sea to a clutch of trawlers that had trespassed into the marine reserve.

Tuku was a passionate communicator with a wiry physique and cropped hair. He was angry about what was happening and had decided to take matters into his own hands. He had come up with a simple, ingenious solution to the illegal trawling. He had made huge interlocking concrete circle blocks, which were effectively artificial reefs, and then he dropped them off boats on to the ocean floor. The goal was to rip and damage any trawler nets that were dragged across them, while encouraging fish to colonise them.

The only problem was that each concrete reef weighed hundreds of kilos and took eight men lifting it on a pole to carry it from the beach to the boat. Being much the tallest person on the team, I had to take more than my fair share of its considerable weight as we lugged it from the shore on to the boat. My back hurt like hell for days, but it was a price worth paying. We took it out to sea and let it plummet into the water. It felt great to be actually doing something that would discourage or even prevent trawling, and might help marine life.

In a country where conservationists could be imprisoned or sometimes simply disappear altogether, Tuku was taking real risks. I found him inspiring. A brave and brilliant activist fighting for sea life, he is an example to all of us of what needs to happen, and what can be done.

I have no problem with direct action, where campaigners actually do something. We are hammering the planet, and we should all be doing more to confront the climate emergency, the nature emergency and the plastic emergency. If anything, we need more rage. Without anger nothing changes.

In the years since I dropped concrete blocks into the sea with Tuku, we have seen the emergence of Extinction Rebellion. The movement wants to force governments to act and avoid critical tipping points that lead to runaway climate change and biodiversity loss. That seems like a pretty sensible and essential desire to me. Extinction Rebellion uses non-violent direct action and did a great job of getting issues that matter back into the public eye; even if some supporters did spoil it slightly by halting London Tube trains and accepting jet-setting A-listers literally on to their bandwagons.

Personally I completely agree with Extinction Rebellion that we are in a critical situation. Most definitely a climate emergency. We live in an era where the extinction of a species, which would have been considered a desperate event just a couple of decades ago, is now greeted by humanity with a resigned shrug. It's thought around 150 species are lost every day. How can this be tolerated by the planet's most successful creature? What used to be deemed unacceptable has slowly become normalised. We live in a world where humans and their domesticated animals outnumber wild mammals by 22 to one. In order to survive, almost all species in the wild are competing not with one another, but with humans.

Individuals doing small things to save the planet is not the answer. 'Make small changes' is the type of tagline corporations now market to consumers, often to encourage them to buy something. Small changes will not resolve the fundamental problems with the destruction of our planet. I think our only hope now is leadership and the law. We need brilliant leaders with long-term vision who rein in our excessive consumption. And we desperately need new laws. We need laws that require everything we use, import and consume to be produced, created and provided sustainably, and we need to introduce an international law of ecocide.

Ecocide literally means 'killing the environment'. It is not yet a punishable crime, but it could be, and it should be. It would be the crime of causing mass damage and destruction to ecosystems – harm to nature that is widespread, severe or systematic.

Will it happen? Leading lawyers are drafting a legal definition of ecocide as a potential international crime that would sit alongside genocide, war crimes and crimes against humanity. The Pope and French president Emmanuel Macron are among high-profile supporters of the campaign to confirm it as a crime. The French citizens' assembly, a group selected to guide the country's climate policy, has voted to make ecocide a crime. Macron has said his government will consider how to incorporate it into French law, but he's also said: 'The mother of all battles is international: to ensure that this term is enshrined in international law so that leaders ... are accountable before the International Criminal Court.'

A law of ecocide could be defined in different ways, but ideally it would be kept short and clear. If it can be one sentence, it could be used to prosecute all manner of appalling behaviour that humans and corporations are perpetrating to soil our nest and destroy our home. However if ecocide becomes a law requiring a 1,000-page document of caveats and conditions, no doubt rampaging palm oil corporations and giant industrialised fishing fleets that are annihilating life in the oceans and the entire landscape of the marine world will find clauses that forgive and cover them. We need the law of ecocide to be short, sweet and powerful.

We also need to start treating the climate crisis as the emergency it really is. Even if we just look at the Indian Ocean area, we can see that the last year brought deadly floods in Indonesia, catastrophic bushfires in Australia, drought as well as record-breaking rainfall in China, and extreme storms in the Philippines. Scientists believe that global heating is increasing the rate of warming in the Indian Ocean and leading to a rising number of cyclones. Weaker storms are also more rapidly becoming intense cyclones with severe consequences, particularly for India.

We travelled north and around the coast of India to Bangladesh, a major producer of farmed prawns. Demand from Europe and the US is so high that more than 35,000 prawn farms operate in the country. Many of the farmers are villagers who got into the business on the promise of short-term gain, or because other farmers flooded their rice fields. One farmer told me that an acre of land returns about 400kg of prawns a year, and yet he makes barely any profit. But he can't go back to growing anything else because, once his land had been saturated with salt for prawns, it could not be repurposed for growing crops. The result was vast areas of wasteland. I was taken to a village that had resisted the lure of prawn farming, a little patch of plenty where locals grew mangoes, cherries, pumpkins, rice, lentils and other fruit and veg all year round. Prawn farmers in the neighbourhood could only look on longingly and went to them not just for food, but even for drinking and cooking water.

I travelled on to the coast of Bangladesh, an endless series of inlets cutting deep into the land where a cat's cradle of rivers meet up with the Indian Ocean. As I looked out over a muddy inland sea spreading as far as the eye could see, I was reminded just how flat Bangladesh really is, and how vulnerable it is to shifting climate and weather patterns. Bangladesh can feel uniquely unsuitable for human habitation. When so much of the country is a delta, the land is basically silt and there's nothing to make bricks with. Pretty much the only solid building we came across was a cyclone shelter built for the evacuation of humans and livestock during one of the ever-increasing tropical cyclones. As a result we spent an awful lot of time wading through mud. Bangladesh's waterfront communities sometimes seem to be sinking in the stuff. We had to lay planks down when one of us got stuck. At one point Jonathan, yelling 'Save the camera!' had to be pulled out.

Much of Bangladesh is disappearing under water, but not everyone knows how to swim, and children often drown during the frequent floods. We found out about an NGO group that was running a project giving children swimming lessons and were told they would love us to film with them in some outdoor pools less than an hour from the capital Dhaka.

What happened next became something of a model for me of all the things that can go wrong when trying to dash around filming. Whenever a 20-something eager beaver researcher now tells me they've been assured something is half an hour outside Caracas, or wherever, I apologise for being a cynical old git and explain that bitter experience has taught me they might not have been told the truth. An NGO, for example, often has an incentive to bend the facts to encourage us to film with them, completely understandably, because we're an advert for them that can help with funding.

It actually took us more than four hours to get to the location of the swimming lessons, and by the time we arrived in the early evening there was only around an hour of light left for us to film before the sun disappeared. There was also a complicated further set of obstacles in our way. Everyone in the community had been waiting on tenterhooks. No sooner did we show up than the village headman, who I think had already been drinking, tried to drag me into his hut to clink glasses. Meanwhile the NGO was desperate for us to go to a different hut and listen to a presentation about their work. Then they wanted to do the swimming lesson in a pond half an hour's walk away because all the nearer ponds had rice growing in them and nobody had asked farmers if it was OK for us to jump in. The rest of the community thought the carnival had come to town and people had music playing from different huts, plus some musicians had shown up hoping to make money. Meanwhile the children who were supposed to be taught to swim had been waiting for hours and were shaking with hunger.

We rapidly assessed the situation. Someone needed to persuade the NGO that feeding and then filming the kids took priority over their deadly presentation. I volunteered to talk to the headman briefly and drained a glass with him, otherwise he might have stopped us filming. We pooled all our resources, mixing extreme diplomacy and sheer stubborn willpower, and navigated a path through the chaotic situation. We politely but firmly persuaded everyone to manoeuvre themselves into positions where we could film the kids, who didn't drown, while the NGO stayed happy because we listened to them, the village headman had a drink, the musicians were paid handsomely to stop playing and the villagers watched everything and I hope have been talking about it ever since.

And after all that the swimming project never made it into the programme.

After leaving gorgeous Bangladesh, I travelled down the west coast of Indonesia and on to Australia, the last country I would visit on my Indian Ocean journey.

We flew on a small plane across the Kimberley, spread over Australia's entire north-west, an area more than three times the size of England and one of the last great wilderness areas on our planet. Down below, an archipelago of islands and headlands fanned out across the edge of the ocean in a spectacular panorama.

I went there to meet a team of hardy fish farmers breeding barramundi, an Australian favourite, in cages at sea. We motored out on a speedboat into a bay to watch as food was fired through a hose into a cage containing up to 45,000 fish. It looked like the most idyllic job available anywhere in the global fishing industry. A turtle swam up to nibble the algae on the ropes. The sun kissed the sea and the tree-smothered coast. But it didn't take long to pick out an ominous shape cruising through the water.

'He's a small one,' I was assured by Ben the farmer, 'maybe seven foot.'

It was a saltwater crocodile, locally known as a salty. They can grow to more than five metres in length and weigh as much as a ton. Salties were once hunted to near extinction but conservation efforts had brought a recovery in their numbers, so much so they had become a real threat to the workers on the fish farm. One in particular had turned into a genuine stalker, patiently watching and following workers at the farm. Before it could launch an attack they called in a team of croc catchers to apprehend it and move it to a sanctuary.

Catching crocodiles is not a normal job for normal folk. The three blokes who arrived on a boat – Mark, Luke and Marshall – were suntanned, rugged, hairy and touting an icebox full of Castlemaine XXXX they planned to consume for breakfast. On a superficial level you could take them for the classic Aussie cliché. But having visited the country several times on my journeys, I don't buy into Australia's occasional claim that it's just a haven for rough, hard males who only think about sport and barbies. These guys were tough, yes, but they were funny, outgoing, clever and thoughtful and among the best characters I had the privilege to meet around the entire Indian Ocean. They had a vital job to do, helping humans being stalked by a salty, but they were also dedicated to protecting crocodiles, a vital part of the ecosystem.

I went out at night with the croc hunters, and my job was to kneel near the prow of the boat pointing a huge searchlight out into the darkness in the hope of paralysing a croc in the powerful beam, while Mark stood over me with a harpoon.

'Your last line of defence if all else fails,' he told me, 'is to throw the light down its mouth.' He tried not to laugh, but I could see a smile. Mark was a joker, but also a renowned conservationist who ran a wildlife sanctuary further down the coast called the Broome Crocodile Park.

I knelt there on the front of that boat for hour after hour, feeling like a tethered goat. Or at least a tempting mouthful for a peckish passing salty. I don't think any animal actively seeks to hunt or harm humans, apart from crocodiles. Few creatures are such efficient killing machines. A croc will happily lie in wait for weeks, unmoving, until the chance comes to grab its meal. And I hate the way they do it. They take you down, death-roll you until you drown and then lodge your corpse under a branch to tenderise your flesh for a few months so they can chomp you up later. I just had to trust to the croc hunters' expertise and their previous good luck, and I idly hoped that if I was taken by a croc, one of them would jump in and wrestle me from its jaws. Marshall, the biggest of the three, looked like he could take on a dinosaur. He'd watched my programmes on Australian TV and apparently liked them. That would surely motivate him to help. But who was I kidding? It was the middle of the night and the visibility was minimal.

Eventually we spotted the one we wanted. I kept my torch beam on its eyes, the engine was cut and we glided in. It turned and swam away in a huff, but the boat approached again and

Mark thrust his harpoon into the tough skin on the back of its neck, holding it firm, but not harming it. Soon enough they got another shot in and let it work off some energy rolling round and round, before they pulled it slowly towards the boat. At that point it understandably got into a grump and put up a fight. Mark hoiked its head out of the water and the salty's jaws gaped open then clamped shut with a terrifying snap. But helpfully it wrapped its jaws up with rope as it struggled. Marshall, Mark and Luke pulled, and the crocodile came up over the side and into the boat. Luke, the most athletic of the trio, leapt on its back to hold it down and I jumped on its tail. With its gnarled and armoured skin I felt as if I was on top of a flightless dragon.

'OK. We're going to get Simon to sex the animal,' said Mark.

My embrace with the salty was about to get more intimate. Up until this point no one knew if we'd tussled with a male or female, so the guys asked me to find the cloaca, an aperture on its undercarriage between the two rear legs, and insert two fingers. Sexing a crocodile is right up there with the weirdest moments on my journeys. But I could definitely feel some sort of rod-like shape, which meant the croc was a boy, and he'd be transferred to Mark's wildlife sanctuary, where he could live without posing a risk to humans. With that, we went back to the safety of dry land and had an extremely welcome morning beer.

Back on the mainland I drove with Mark to see more of the Kimberley. It has the most pristine coastline in the Indian Ocean, and the scale of the place is mind-blowing. It's easy for an outsider to forget the size of Australia. The state of Western Australia itself is so vast that if it were a country on its own it would be one of the ten biggest in the world. It is a whopping 11 times larger than Britain.

We had hired a white four-wheel drive car for me, and promised the hire company we wouldn't take it off-road. But almost all of the Kimberley was off-road, and considerably more photogenic than tarmac. The team egged me on to race along and kick up clouds of dusty red earth while they were filming. I didn't need much urging. A friend who taught me to drive at 17 told me, 'You're only 10 per cent boy racer. But the other 90 per cent is rally driver.' When we returned the hire car, the chap at the rental firm was not best pleased. He could see there was dirt all over the roof, so I must have been moving at quite a pace. I tried grovelling, but we weren't allowed to hire a car for the next bit of our trip, and instead had to fly down to the west coast of Oz.

This was around the time that new regulations were coming in about taking lithium-ion batteries on board a plane due to safety concerns they might spontaneously combust. Some airlines wanted batteries to be hand-carried and some wanted them put in the hold. We packed ours in bags for the hold and made sure to tell the airline in advance we were a camera crew travelling with batteries, then informed staff at check-in, and even told the people at the boarding gate. Everything was fine, they said.

After we took off I was dozing in a seat at the back away from the rest of the team, but then noticed Matt our director was up at the front of the plane talking with a senior steward. I could see him walking back down the plane to his seat looking white. Our plane gently dipped a wing and slowly started to turn.

One of the airline crew had finally mentioned to the captain that we had our batteries in the hold. He checked his new regulations and decided we had to fly all the way back to the airport we had left an hour earlier to unload the batteries from the hold and bring them into the plane as carry-on luggage. This would have been bad enough even if we had been the only passengers, but the plane was full of scores of horny miners who had been working in remote parts of Australia and were now returning to their wives and families. They were burly blokes, some still in steel boots and fluorescent jackets, and they weren't best pleased. Stewards started telling the miners what had happened, claiming the fault was all ours, and a ripple of anger began to spread.

I kept my head down during most of this. But then the miners began swapping rumours.

'Maybe they've done it deliberately,' said one.

Then I heard a miner say, 'And you know what? I hear they're French.' Which was when I thought, now hang on. That is too much. I stood up and addressed the back of the plane.

'Gents, I'm very sorry but I've just heard the terrible news. I'm part of the TV crew and I assure you we told the airline about the batteries and the people at check-in and again when we boarded, so it's completely untrue if they say we didn't warn them. And just to be clear, we're definitely not French. It's much worse than that. We're British.' Thankfully they laughed and were incredibly understanding. I cannot think of anywhere else in the world where there would be such generosity of spirit. After my colleagues crawled into the hold to find our bags with the batteries, the horny miners actually clapped and cheered them back on to the plane.

We headed further south down the coast. I treated myself to a last dip in the Indian Ocean, and a chat with Professor Jessica Meeuwig from the University of Western Australia. Her research was helping to change our understanding of our seas. She was placing small cameras at depths of more than 500 metres, well beyond the reach of divers, in order to document life under the sea in areas of the Indian Ocean to discover what's down there.

By analysing the footage, Jessica's team were monitoring the size of fish in the deep, because one of the first signs of overfishing is when the fish get smaller. My journey had already shown me that every time a trawler's net was hauled out of the sea, fish populations were collapsing.

Jessica and I talked about what I had seen on my journey, how sharks were being slaughtered in their millions, how Carlos in Mozambique was trying to persuade villagers to protect marine life, and how it was being wiped out off the coast of India. Jessica believed the only answer was creating Marine Protected Areas in the oceans where fishing would be restricted, allowing stocks of fish and life to recover.

'We need somewhere where the fish can go to grow big, old and fat and produce lots more fish,' she said.

Blue Ventures in Madagascar had shown this could work, and in other forms it was happening in parts of the Maldives and Seychelles. Australia was at the forefront of creating marine parks where it was illegal to trawl, or drill for oil and gas. It was an overwhelmingly popular idea in Australia. As I prepared to say farewell to the Indian Ocean, that gave me a clear solution for some of the problems facing our seas, and a measure of hope. Marine parks need to be introduced in biodiversity hotspots across all of our oceans if we are to have any hope of reversing the massive damage that's already been inflicted on the seas through overfishing and pollution.

There is some good news. Roughly 8 per cent of marine areas are within formally protected zones, along with 17 per cent of land and inland water ecosystems. Since 2010, an area bigger than Russia has been added to the world's network of national parks and conservation areas. But these numbers need to rise, dramatically.

In 2010, world leaders agreed to give protection to 10 per cent of our oceans. We now know that is not nearly enough. Shortly after entering office, US president Joe Biden committed to protect 30 per cent of American land and 30 per cent of US oceans by 2030. The UK government has launched the Global Ocean Alliance and is calling for at least 30 per cent of the global ocean to be in Marine Protected Areas by 2030. Greenpeace and other environmental groups are backing the campaign, using the tag of 30x30. At the time of writing, 43 countries, including Indian Ocean nations like Australia, Bangladesh, Kenya and the Maldives, are also on board. It is a profoundly important and brilliant idea that might just help to turn the tide.

I finished my journey at Cape Leeuwin, where the Indian Ocean meets the Southern Ocean, at the bottom of Western Australia. Alongside Craig Hastings artfully manning the camera, and Matt Brandon the director, wearing a very appropriate T-shirt that just read 'Go Outside', I felt a sense of elation as I walked down to a lighthouse on the Cape.

It had been an extreme and exotic dream to travel all the way round the edge of the Indian Ocean. Few people are able or allowed to go on such a great quest. Slowly, over many months, it had gone from inspired idea to reality and now completion. I had finally made it to the end of the Indian Ocean. It still remains today one of the most impossible journeys I have been lucky enough to complete.

CHAPTER SEVENTEEN

Woods and Water

One weekend when Jake was still a baby, we went to stay with our friends Milla and Tim, the couple whose band played at our wedding. They had bought Hayne, a beautiful old house with outbuildings in the rolling hills of mid-Devon, and were busy renovating it and turning it into what is now a gorgeous wedding and music venue – the perfect place to get married. Their life back then was muddy and chaotic and outdoors and wonderful, and one morning Anya and I were snuggled up in their guest bedroom when she turned to me and said this was a life she would love for our son.

We were slowly outgrowing our little flat in north London, couldn't afford to buy a house with a garden, and I was starting to lose faith in the city I was born in. London didn't feel much like home any more. On the one hand many youngsters in poorer areas were disconnected and disaffected. On the other there was so much extreme wealth and entitlement. We had a toehold in a posh area, and when we started taking Jake to a local toddler group, among the other parents were A-listers or their partners, and the nannies of Russian oligarchs. There was too much of a divide in London between the have-nots, and the have-a-lots.

Another pressing issue for me was identity. I'd started to feel I didn't have one. Even back then, many had a sense that a gulf was growing between people rooted in their local communities and a more globalised elite who were usually university-educated. Perhaps the writer David Goodhart crystallised it best when he argued most of us fall into one of two categories. Either we are from 'somewhere' or we are from 'anywhere'. The some-wheres are people with a sense of belonging, to the place where they live and the group they live or work among. They might be a car mechanic in the West Midlands or a farmer in Somerset or a working-class mum in Newcastle. They feel a strong connec-tion both to the place and the people where they live and ascribe value to the idea of belonging in a community. The anywheres derive their sense of self not from where they grew up but to what they have gone on to do as adults. Goodhart says their identity is connected to their achievements and their profes-sional status, and they place value on freedom, openness and social diversity. They are far more likely to have been to univer-sity, and perhaps gone on to live and work in Europe.

Of course this is over-simplistic. But it helps to make sense of why the issue of identity became such a hugely divisive subject across the Western world during the last decade, and nowhere more than in the UK. The somewheres and anywheres stopped talking each other's language. They often struggled to see the other point of view. And, so it's argued, their differences all came to a head during Brexit, when the somewheres came out in droves and voted the UK out of Europe.

I grew up in Acton, a diverse multi-ethnic part of London. Crucially, it was a community, and I felt like I belonged. But then I became a writer and eventually a telly traveller. My world widened. I lost touch with my roots as I became more of a global citizen. It was my choice, but I missed that sense of kinship and belonging.

When Jake was born I was a third of the way round the Indian Ocean. I was often travelling to places where life was desperate, or at least a struggle, but there was also cohesion. After finishing *Indian Ocean* I travelled across Cuba and around Australia, Turkey, Ireland, East Africa again and Vietnam. I played the role of a medieval palace guard in a Turkish soap opera, picked tea in Kenya, cruised in a Bentley with a Vietnamese coffee billionaire and helped a scientist capture a box jellyfish, the most venomous creature on the planet. I was definitely feeling like an anywhere, and our area of north London was full of the global elite; lawyers and bankers who might live in London for a while, then would jet off somewhere else. Too often they felt like people from nowhere. I wanted Jake to grow up feeling he had roots, that he was from somewhere, but could do anything, anywhere.

I also thought Jake should grow up with a positive English identity. When I compare England with Denmark or Greece, two European countries I love and have visited regularly, I'm struck by the way they still have a profound sense of identity that feels meaningful without being discoloured by nationalism. I'm English, and it saddens me that Englishness has come to mean so little, or to be so disputed. It's even seen as something toxic. I would describe myself as proud and patriotic, but more about the people than the institutions and the history. But what on earth is 'being English'? Nobody seems to agree any more. There are times I wish I'd been born Welsh, Scottish, Greek or Danish, because that so often confers at least a little more of a clear and agreed identity.

Although I grumbled about London, the super-rich and the size of our little flat, I struggled to imagine living anywhere else. But it was definitely way past the time I should have joined the property ladder. I'd managed to get to nearly 40 without ever buying even a small flat. I like to jokingly blame one of my friends for this. He was a brilliant young economist and for years, as prices in London rose steadily, he kept telling me not to buy a house because the values couldn't possibly keep going up and up. But like many others he didn't reckon on the government allowing, and even encouraging, thousands and thousands of wealthy and super-rich Chinese, Russians, French and Americans to flood into London and hoover up the housing stock. Prices did keep going up and up, until they were stratospheric and way out of my reach. I felt like I'd missed out, and buying was a dream, at least in London.

While I complained, Anya decided we needed to do something. Partly as a joke she started making me watch *Grand Designs* to try to persuade me that creating and building a home could be a real adventure. She was keen on buying something derelict or difficult and transforming it. But we thought that might be a tricky thing to do if we were also going to be expanding our little family, and the burden might fall too heavily on her if I was regularly away.

Then we went to stay with our friends in the Devon countryside, and even I started to feel that moving out of London was the best thing for Jake. To begin with we adopted a scattergun approach. All we knew to start with was that anywhere close to London was unaffordable. 'Right,' Anya would say. 'We're going to Shropshire this weekend.' So we would drive around the Welsh borders, or Dorset, then Somerset. Or Anya would reconnoitre while I was away travelling. She got heavily into property porn. I joked that she was going to nightclubs and having an affair while I was away, when she was actually on a series of secret missions looking at ramshackle old farms.

Eventually Anya pointed out we needed to be close to main-line trains, so we could ditch the car as much as possible, and I came up with a plan to narrow down the search by looking at national parks, and Areas of Outstanding Natural Beauty. Well at least it resembled a plan. Even then the search felt more theoretical than practical. Perhaps because I was away so much of the time, I may have given the impression I had other priorities, and was perhaps not fully on board. I think secretly the Londoner in me was half-hoping the desire to up sticks was a phase, a fad, and that we'd get over it. We started bickering about moving. Then we had a minor row.

'We're never going to move somewhere green, are we?' Anya said, looking at me with a pained expression.

My arm was being gently twisted, but perhaps it's what I needed. That was the turning point. I had to be reassuring. 'Yes we are,' I said soothingly. I had to mean it. And then the hunt began in earnest.

The options were whittled down until there was only one answer, which had been staring us in the face all along: Devon. It had everything we loved. There was wilderness, coasts, moors and forests, and we knew plenty of friends who had already moved there. The area around Huntsham Court, where we married, was beautiful but too pricey for us. So we started to look around Dartmoor while staying with old friends of Anya's parents who had left sixties London to live and work from an idyllic farmhouse. Even the most urban type would be hard pushed to stay there for a few days and not think it's closer to what human life should be.

Anya signed us up with some Dartmoor estate agents and mentioned that what we loved were woods and water. After a few months one of the tweedier estate agents took on a property and immediately called Anya.

'I think I've found what you're after,' he said. We raced down.

It was a big old barn of a place with acres of land and woodland. We walked through wizened old trees next to a stream, on a bank completely covered in spongy moss just as sunlight poured through the leaves above. It was completely magical, like a secret land owned by fairies. Anya and I looked at each other, our eyes shining. It was the trees we really loved. There were giant beech trees soaring high, along with ash, oak and birch. You can do a lot to change a building, but you can't snap your fingers and suddenly have 150-year-old trees to hug.

The owner was deeply protective of her home and the wild world around it, and wanted to sell to people she trusted. Her daughter was a wildlife documentary maker who had even made a beautiful film around the land. I worried about what we could afford, but it was less than the price of many London flats. Anya asked all the right questions about how to steward the land, while also mentioning her time working on wildlife documentaries. We made an offer and were accepted. The house never even went on the open market.

So we upped sticks. There was no removal lorry groaning with furniture. We were moving from a small flat, and in our transient lives we were used to living out of bags and cases. I hired a van and we speedily loaded our worldly belongings, strapped in our one-year-old son, and drove down. Walking into our empty new home for the first time, we went from room to room marvelling at all the extra space and wondering what on earth we'd do with it.

'These rooms need bodies,' I said.

'What do you mean?' she said.

'Finally we've got space here. We need to have people staying.'

So a couple of times a month we would have family and friends to stay for long weekends, and discovered you get to spend far more quality time together that way compared to meeting briefly for an overpriced pizza and a pint in a city pub.

Our home is buried on the edge of a wood where scores of creatures fly and skip and slither and trot. We have at least 40 different bird species and rare bats living around us. A stream runs through the garden. The house was constructed in the 19th century as a barn, but was only used for a couple of decades before the owners, who lived in an adjoining farmhouse, were forced to sell due to a compulsory purchase order. Their last act before emigrating to Australia was to burn the farmhouse to the ground. The barn became derelict and was used as a potato store during the Second World War, then in the 1980s a man discovered it while walking through the woods, spotted its potential and bought it from the water board. He needed planning permission to convert it into a residence, so for month after month he attended every meeting of the parish planning committee. Eventually they asked what he was doing there.

'I'm learning your ways,' he replied, then submitted a planning application they couldn't refuse. We still thank him for converting it into a family home.

The previous owners kindly left us a whole encyclopaedia of instructions on how to look after the place, ensuring even two relocated Londoners had the tools to survive their first winter fairly successfully. But we also had to deploy some of our survival kit when everything froze solid and we had to get ice from a nearby lake, carry it back through deep snow and melt it. I had a two-stage stainless steel water filtration unit I'd used while staying somewhere tricky. I thought it might come in handy again one day. I never imagined that would be in Devon.

To keep ourselves warm we did the right-on environmentally minded thing and put in an incredibly costly biomass boiler that needs feeding with wood we gather from the land around. I was soon to discover the truth of the saying that wood keeps you warm three times: when you chop it, move it and finally burn it. As the blunt tool in the family, my job became shifting and splitting hunks of timber from wind-blown branches and fallen trees. I use a chainsaw to cut rounds of a downed tree, but I split them all into firewood by hand with a worryingly large collection of much-loved axes and mauls. I sometimes whinge about it, but chopping wood is both workout and mindfulness. There are few things, I would argue, that connect us faster to the lives of our ancestors.

But it was Jake who really benefited from, and deserved, the space outside. From an almost indecently young age he was forced out of the door and encouraged to explore. I would watch as he picked his way slowly through thick undergrowth, dodged clumps of stinging nettles, and crawled up steep banks. His face would scrunch in concentration when he waddled carefully along a narrow high bank near our house.

'Baa baas!' he'd shout as he spotted the neighbours, and his feet left the ground as he bounced in delight.

Watching your very own toddler squealing with delight at the sight of some bored sheep is completely entrancing. And when Jake was a littler every stroll outside, whether through the Devon countryside or over a hill on a Greek island, was packed with adventure and discovery. Like almost all children he would come alive in the outdoors. The air, the movement, the soil and a bit of sun, all combined to lift the spirits. Is there a greater treat for a child than a chance to explore? I doubt it. A soft play centre might offer jolly fun, but it doesn't tantalise the spirit like a stroll.

Our senses of smell and hearing sharpen for both adults and children when we move purposefully outdoors, because our bodies are built for walking. We may bundle them into prams and strollers, sometimes simply because we need them to hurry, but children need to snuffle and sniff around just like a hound, and even the youngest can trek long distances.

Jake had only just turned one when Anya managed to encourage and inspire him to walk his first mile. I was away, leaving him in the best possible hands. With enthusiasm, patience, and by talking to him about the forest around, she would inspire him to use his little legs to totter through the trees.

As well as discovering nature, we were keen for him to accept danger. Our journeys among indigenous communities had opened our eyes to the need for children to embrace risk. In Africa, South America and Asia, we had seen tots picking up knives, or jumping around on sharp rocks while their parents accepted there would be accidents, injuries and tears. The belief we encountered over and over again was that children need to learn tough lessons quickly in life to survive in an unforgiving environment. The words of Lucy, a sage-like Maasai grandmother, stayed with me.

'If we don't let them take risks in front of us,' she said. 'They'll only do it out of sight, where we can't help them if they're injured.' The most extreme example I came across was in a remote village in eastern Paraguay with a group of hunters from the Aché tribe. One of their tiny children started swinging a long, live snake around by the tail. I had no idea whether the snake was harmless or poisonous, like much that crawled and slid through the forests around the village. Instinctively I coiled myself to leap towards the lad, pausing only when I realised at least a dozen Aché adults were already watching him closely.

Most of them were smiling at the playful youngster, a tiny snot-nosed boy wearing ragged pants. Even the parents bit their lips and stopped themselves from interfering.

I remembered Lucy's advice when Jake, aged only two, found my Leatherman knife while I was fixing the boiler. The blade was open. He picked it up and waved it around. I gasped in shock, leapt forward, and clasped my hands in prayer to beg him to put it down, all at once. The look of abject horror on my face convinced him to pause, and with immense relief I was able to grab his wrist. But then I remembered Lucy's advice, and I took him to strip some bark off a branch and cut an apple with the knife, so he could see the power and danger of a razor-sharp blade, under careful supervision and with my hand holding his.

It can be a battle to suppress our natural instinct to cosset and coddle. Once on the beach in south Devon, Jake started clambering barefoot over sharp granite rocks. I told myself it was something he needed to do, and that I couldn't be a stifling, suffocating parent. But at the same time I couldn't bear the thought of anything happening to him. It nearly did when we were on holiday and he fell into a shallow baby pool. I am still haunted by the image of him slipping backwards into the water, but also comforted because as I leapt forward and the water closed over him, his eyes locked with mine and I could see fear, but also trust. He held out his hands, certain Daddy would save him. There was great beauty in that moment as well as sheer terror.

As he got older and started picking up on the modern fear of risk, I started to promise that if he did break a limb I would buy him a big present. Obviously I didn't want him to smash himself up just to get a gift, but I would never want him to be too fearful of leaping off a rock or climbing a tree. If he were excessively foolhardy, I might have a different view. The point is that I want him, as I'd want any child, to take chances. That's how we grow. This can only be done if he spends as much time outdoors and stays away from brain-rotting screens. I want him to make nature his protection, armour and shield.

I still taught him how to avoid daft injuries. We would watch *You've Been Framed* together, which he started calling Plonkers, because it's what I kept saying as another idiot balanced precariously on a wobbly ladder. I told him they were health and safety videos, which has at least a ring of truth.

As he's grown, I haven't worried about him facing risk and danger. Instead I worry about screens, which I find one of our biggest challenges as parents. Anya and I still struggle to decide the appropriate amount of time for him to spend on the TV, our computer or phone. We ration them all and try to suggest or insist on alternatives, but they're not banned. By the time Jake was seven he was pleading to be allowed to download the video game Minecraft, which lots of parents view as a creative world where kids can play and use their imagination to put bricks together and build almost anything. We felt we already had something where he could do that, called Lego. So we kept saying no to Minecraft, but that didn't stop him asking, and it was starting to wear us down.

One weekend we were visiting a local arts and crafts fair, browsing from stall to stall and Jake, having wandered ahead on his own, came back with a hyper, nervously excited look in his eyes. He wanted me to come and have a look at something, and pulled and dragged me over to a stand selling beautifully hand-crafted bushcraft knives. He pointed quickly at a small knife with a red stag antler handle, a short blade and a beautiful leather scabbard. Then he screwed up his nose and his courage.

'If I could have that then I promise I'll never have Minecraft,' he said, all in one breath. It was 15 minutes before the fair was supposed to close.

'Are you serious?' I asked. I had never seen him so maturely adamant. He was processing some huge emotions. He was desperate for Minecraft, but something about this knife had opened a whole new door in his head. 'Why do you want it?' I said.

'It's for bushcraft. I could make spears in the woods,' he replied, looking very earnest.

Now it was my turn to take a deep breath. Bushcraft in the woods and making play spears was exactly what I wanted him to be doing. I leant over and looked at the knife, at which point I realised it cost £300. I gulped, recoiled and started to say 'Whooo …,' but saw Jake watching me nervously, and stopped myself.

It was a proper grown-up bushcraft knife, an heirloom that could be passed through generations. But it was also 300 quid. I absolutely blanched at the price. Buying it was completely bonkers. That was my immediate feeling. Jake knew it was a huge amount, and I could see him biting his lip as he saw my horror.

But in that moment I knew I had to put a value on what matters. I wanted him to be out in nature wherever possible, and I believed he needed to be trusted with serious responsibilities. I had inherited next to nothing and had no treasures or tools to pass on from his ancestors. Perhaps it was a chance to gift him something for posterity. I had also never seen my son so convinced or mature in acknowledging he would go without one thing he wanted to have something he wanted more. I thought for a moment, discussed it with Anya, who was equally shocked, but said it was up to me, and then told Jake we would have to come to some sort of grown-up agreement if he was to get a grown-up knife.

'To make the rules clear?' he said. I nodded.

I took him around a corner and quickly tapped into my phone a jokingly semi-legal contract with multiple clauses, including the requirements Jake must always remember the knife is a tool, and not a toy or a weapon, is careful and sensible with a knife and doesn't show off with it, never cuts towards himself or towards his gripping hand, never holds a knife while walking around – always sheaths it first, never points a knife at someone else, even as a joke, always gives a knife his full attention when using it, and of course, never has Minecraft or similar computer or phone games. He read it through very carefully. Twice.

'OK,' he said, very seriously.

With minutes to spare before the fair closed, I bought the knife and showed him how to use it, sharpen it and pass it to somebody else, how to whittle and cut and slice and secure it back in its sheath. I hope and still believe it was the right thing to do. He uses it regularly, is appropriately careful, and still has all his fingers. Of one thing I'm certain: Bushcraft beats Minecraft, every time.

Perhaps you think writing a pact was bonkers, but I would really recommend it to other parents. I think it showed Jake I was taking him seriously, and it has since reminded both of us what he agreed to and ensured fairness. Obviously I've got no more right to pass on parenting tips than anyone else, but also no less right. Perhaps one thing I do have to contribute is a knowledge of how children are raised in other cultures and countries. My sense is that ours is a nannyish and mollycoddling society that doesn't give children and especially teenagers enough opportunity to take risks or shoulder responsibility. It's not just because we're obsessed with safety. Often it's because we're all moving too fast and cannot spare the time to get a child to take on something that might take twice as long and be done half as well. But it's crucial we set aside the time to allow them to learn skills and make mistakes, even if it involves cuts or breaks.

I've had to learn my parenting by doing it. When I first became a father I didn't have much to go on. As I explained in *Step by Step*, my own dad and I had a difficult relationship. His father had died when he was young, so he had even less to build on than me. But he loved me. He tried. And he worked so incredibly hard for us. I miss him so much.

As for me, I'm very physical and expressive as a dad. I hug a lot. I tell my son I love him. Every day. Work keeps me busy busy, but I'm present and around far more than people often assume. I hope I've always been there for my son when it mattered. Every one of my journeys has been scheduled around Jake's holidays. I've never been away on his birthday, but inevitably, there are life events that I've missed. I was away when snow came to Dartmoor and he built his first snowman, when he had chickenpox, when he got dressed up as a train engine, and when he handled a snake. But I felt I could safely go away on my trips because I was leaving Jake in the care of a wonderful, dedicated, caring and wise mum.

As an extra surrogate father and sibling, we also thought a four-legged friend would help our little family. Becoming a dog dad was quite a turnaround for me. As a child I had a terrible record as an owner of goldfish and gerbils, which tended to die on my watch, and I was always reserved around dogs and the commitment they involved. When I first lived with Anya I would shoo Boris, her mother's Jack Russell, off the sofa. But by the time Jake was five years old he was desperate for a dog. We agreed we didn't want a puppy from breeders or puppy farmers. We wanted a happy accident. Looking through ads for puppies we found one that said explicitly not to even think of applying if you live somewhere unsuitable, or you might change your job or get divorced. We went up to Gloucestershire to meet a family of farmers-cum-undertakers who had a litter to sell, products of an unplanned liaison between a German shepherd and a large collie. I left it to Anya and Jake to pick the right one and they turned around holding a bundle of black gorgeousness and I just melted.

Obi did grow slightly bigger than expected. From early on people would say, 'Ooh, he's got a lot of paw to grow into.' As a puppy he had almost comically large feet ready to take the weight of what is now a nearly 50kg hound. Aside from having a child and persuading my wife to marry me, nothing in life has made a greater difference to my personal happiness than getting Obi. At every stage of his life, Obi has encouraged and inspired Jake and all of us to get out on walks and explore nature. Just being near him lifts my soul and raises my spirits. Often I'll take a moment to lie next to him and just snuggle. He moves his head to mine. Honestly, it's like cuddling a bear.

One of the American Founding Fathers wrote something that has been paraphrased as 'I study politics and war, so my children can study biology and chemistry, so their children can learn art and poetry.' Where do I place myself on that curve? My parents grafted, saved and scrimped to help get me to a point where I could embrace life. It was difficult. I struggled. But eventually I claimed life. I did it myself. I inherited nothing. No house, no land, no loan, no seed capital, no public school education. Definitely no trust fund. But I did have the privilege of gender and colour. And also location. I was brought up in London. I would have found it much harder to carve out a life, perhaps impossible, if I had been raised in a remote part of the country, with less access to the opportunity and luck that eventually came my way.

I want Jake to have more than I had. I want him never to feel self-conscious, forlorn and fearful the way I was as a teenager. I want him to be confident enough to dance like a wild one in public. I want my son to feel part of a community, to take risks, to be loved and happy, to hold eye contact and handle himself confidently in whatever situation he finds himself in, to be independent, and to enjoy responsibility rather than feel it as a dead weight.

For now I watch him playing football with his buddy George, one of our godsons, and I'm so proud and moved by his humour and skill, and I feel relief that even in some small way I've fulfilled my part of life's bargain by raising him somewhere beautiful and giving him experiences.

I certainly haven't got it all right. One time when Jake was four years old we were on the train to London together, happily playing with some old toy cars on a seat, when the train started to free-wheel silently into a station, so you could hear even the faintest rustle of a packet of biscuits at the other end of the carriage. Suddenly Jake froze, sat up, and said loudly with perfect clarity and my weary intonation: 'Oh fuck, I've forgotten my teddy.'

There was a horrified silence, while everyone around us paused to suck in their breath, and then a ripple of laughter spread to guffaws halfway down the train, which a startled Jake completely loved, of course. Clearly I've failed to shield him from my grumps and irritations, but I'm still hoping to make up for it. So far I give myself six out of ten as a dad. Maybe I'm being hard on myself, but of course it's not me who gets to decide the score.

Jake has reached double figures as I write this book, and I am fully aware a different set of challenges are ahead as he edges into his teens. I just hope his trials aren't like mine. When I was a lost, hopeless and helpless teenage boy, I flunked out of school and spiralled down into darkness. I have experienced our cultural failure to lead and mentor young men. It nearly cost me everything.

I don't have a personal road map for raising Jake as a teenager and guiding him as a young man. But as with exposing small children to risk in a controlled environment, I've seen how it's done around the world in indigenous communities where wisdom and custom are handed down from one generation to the next. For thousands of years, in cultures around the planet, older adult males in indigenous communities have helped to guide and mentor younger men. Through words, actions, ceremonies and tasks they would initiate teenagers into manhood, giving roots, purpose and meaning to the youngsters and helping them to become valued and valuable members of their community. Of course some youngsters must find that imposing and oppressive. In the most thoughtful cultures I have visited there is still provision for those who do not want to fish or hunt, or train to be warriors. In a remote community of the Bajo 'sea gypsy' people in Indonesia, who live on water, there was a young man who refused to swim and spent most of the day wearing curlers. He was loved and respected by the community.

But for many, mentoring and initiation help to provide nothing less than a point to life, and a focus for manhood. They train them, teach and guide them.

Anya and I are not raising our son in an indigenous community. But he has good friends around and solid, loving godmothers and godfathers, or guide parents as we heathens sometimes call them. They will help to guide and mentor him when he cannot face listening to his annoying parents. He also has Dartmoor, which through its rugged landscape helps to gift experiences that shape and guide a teen, and is home to a real community.

The very geography of Dartmoor creates social cohesion. It's not a place where people can live and commute daily to London or even Bristol. So people who move here have made a decision to build their lives here and stay here. Ultimately it's the people, more than the place itself, that squashed my prejudices about town versus country. I used to believe that if you left London or any other big city it was often because on some level you couldn't take the pace, and I regarded that as some sort of flaw. I was so wrong. People move to places like Dartmoor precisely because they are successful and confident, and they want a more interesting life or at least a different challenge than a metropolis can offer. They want to live with nature close at hand and feel the seasons on a more intimate level.

Yet I still question whether I really belong among the hills, tors, forest and moors of Dartmoor. On paper I was a very unlikely candidate for moving to the countryside at all. I was London born and bred, and still pine for the exotic urban delights of Acton, White City and Shepherd's Bush.

At the same time I was also a privileged media ponce approaching middle age with a baby, and therefore a perfect candidate for a life crisis. At times the change in my circumstances felt ludicrous. I plunged into a completely different lifestyle from the one I knew growing up on the edge of inner-city London. At nine I was pedalling around Acton on my BMX setting fire to rubbish bins. At 11 I was learning how to make petrol bombs. A few years later I was a joyrider doing doughnuts in Wormwood Scrubs. Now as an adult I have my own small patch of the planet to steward. You could tell friends thought I was going native when, one Christmas, I received no fewer than four different copies of a new book called *Norwegian Wood: The Guide to Chopping, Stacking and Drying Wood the Scandinavian Way*. Although I certainly did not take to rural life immediately, I've come to truly love it.

CHAPTER EIGHTEEN

Good Karma

Amid the parched plateaus and mountains of south-eastern Turkey, there is a truly remarkable place. It was discovered in 1994, when a German archaeologist called Klaus Schmidt was looking for somewhere new to dig. He travelled to the site of Göbekli Tepe, which means Potbelly Hill, to inspect a collection of limestone slabs, previously dismissed as just a medieval cemetery. As soon as he arrived he realised the mound of the hill had actually been shaped by our ancient ancestors, and the site was something truly extraordinary. Intriguingly, further research revealed it could not have been a settlement as there was no water source for miles. Nor was there any evidence of habitation. So what was this impossible place?

Schmidt brought in students and locals and began to dig. Gradually the site revealed first one ring of massive standing T-shaped pillars, then another circle, and another. With the help of ground surveys, all told 200 pillars have since been identified, each up to six metres tall and weighing up to 10 tons. At nearly 12,000 years old, they were erected an astonishing 7,000 years before Stonehenge. The oldest known megaliths on the planet, they are the earliest example yet found of a place that humans congregated. Schmidt believed this was man's first temple, and that it attracted pilgrims who would walk from up to 90 miles away.

Only a fraction of the Göbekli Tepe site has so far been uncovered, but it is probably the most important archaeological discovery of modern times. It could rewrite the history of humanity. Academics have long believed that it was only after we learned to farm and master agriculture that we settled and built our first temples, villages and eventually towns. Schmidt, who has since died, argued that Göbekli Tepe came first, and it was the need to provide for worshippers, builders and long-distance pilgrims that required us to start building human society.

For me, Göbekli Tepe is one of the wonders of the world. I truly believe that ancient and modern pilgrimage, the act of walking and travelling long distances to draw strength and inspiration from a sacred place, is evidence of how the need and desire to travel is almost embedded in human DNA. I'd even argue pilgrimage was the original spur for mass travel. Long before Freddie Laker and Ryanair opened travel to almost all, the only way of freely seeing the world was as a pilgrim. Pilgrimage got Britain on the move. At one point in medieval England, an astonishing 200,000 pilgrims would travel to Canterbury each year, out of a national population of just 2.5 million. Evidence, perhaps, that humans have almost all, almost always, gone on impossible journeys.

So when I was asked if I'd like to trace ancient and current pilgrimage routes for a TV series, it felt like the perfect opportunity to investigate these ideas more deeply, and to go on a different kind of adventure. I am not religious. There was Methodism in my upbringing, which was as much about being part of a community, yet whatever faith I had has since ebbed away. My work investigating terrorism made me wary of religious conviction. On at least a couple of occasions I have been in tight spots with people who thought their beliefs directed them to contemplate chopping my head off. I've encountered Christians, Hindus, Muslims and even Buddhist fundamentalists whose faith, and reluctance to question or harbour doubt, made them dangerously intolerant. But being a traveller myself, I was curious to find out more about the journeys of our ancestors and hear what inspires people today to make similar journeys of pilgrimage. As I set out, I was not consciously trying to be a pilgrim. But the further I went, the more I learned, about belief, about the inspiring people who go on such journeys, and ultimately about the nature of travel itself.

From the start, the journeys were a revelation. Like many of us, I had associated pilgrimage just with piety and blisters. But for hundreds of years a holy journey was the motivation for adventures, against which our comfy modern travels sadly pale.

I began my first journey for the *Pilgrimage* series off the coast of north-east England on the holy island of Lindisfarne, the home of St Cuthbert and one of the first places where Christianity was preached in the British Isles. After visits to Lincoln, Walsingham and London, I stopped in Canterbury, where for more than 300 years pilgrims flocked to worship at the shrine of Thomas à Becket, the archbishop murdered by knights of Henry II in 1170.

One of the things that attracted me to the concept of pilgrimage was the freedom of movement it originally offered. We take our right to roam now as something almost sacred. But our ability to take a holiday or even nip out for a countryside ramble would have been a dream for many of our medieval peasant ancestors, who were often tied to their land and restricted from travel. A medieval peasant had few opportunities for exploration, and if they left their fields they could be punished for vagrancy. But with written permission from their priest or bishop they could escape a life of drudgery and set off on a pilgrimage across the country or continent, on magnificent quests to places of myth and legend. Pilgrimage was a way for ordinary people to see the world. Peasants still ran the risk of being seized as vagrants and sent back where they came from. But if they stuck to an agreed route they had the chance of adventure, and a degree of freedom unlike anything else they would likely experience in their lives.

Imagine arriving for the first time at Lincoln Cathedral as a medieval pilgrim. For decades it was the tallest building on the planet. Tired, probably ragged and hungry, you would have been confronted by a sight that made your jaw drop. It would be like seeing the Eiffel Tower at the end of the 19th century, or the Empire State Building in the 20th century. I found it beautiful and awe-inspiring when visiting on my way to Canterbury. I'm ashamed to admit that I had never seen it before, but for me it's a close runner-up to Hagia Sophia in Istanbul as the finest building on the planet, and would surely have evoked feelings of holy wonder in our distant relatives. Quite apart from the towering height of its hilltop spire, visible for many miles around, nothing a medieval peasant would have seen or heard before could have matched the shock they would have felt on entering its vast interior, with columns that soar towards heaven. Many would have fallen to their knees and cried in wonder.

But visiting Lincoln taught me that medieval pilgrimage was also an industry. Pilgrims would arrive there and find people selling souvenirs. They could buy pin badges that helped to show the journey they had made, just like people sew country flags on their rucksacks today. There was serious money to be made from credulous pilgrims and implausible products abounded. Walsingham, a pilgrimage site in Norfolk, came to be known as Falsingham thanks to stallholders who claimed to sell the Virgin Mary's breast milk. Fake Becket blood went on the market. Inns sprang up along the way to feed pilgrims. One of my favourite moments was meeting up with Caroline Yeldham, a medieval food historian who served me up some of the offerings a pilgrim might have eaten on the way, including fish and vegetable potage and apple fritters, all utterly delicious. Too many of us have a degree of contempt for our ancestors, the lives they led and the food they ate. Often what they ate was fresher, healthier and more interesting than the processed convenience rubbish we heat in microwaves today.

Obviously huge numbers of medieval British and European pilgrims were inspired by religious devotion or fear. But pilgrimage was not just the preserve of the saintly and devout. Many were also looking for excitement, romance and adventure. In the ninth century priests were criticised for going on pilgrimage just to escape their duties. In the 13th century a French bishop complained that people were going on pilgrimage 'out of mere curiosity and the love of novelty'. We may be much less religious in the 21st century but let's face it, they weren't so unlike us, were they?

In some years, a whopping fifth of the population of the European continent was either on pilgrimage or directly involved in the industry of inns and churches and hostels that sprung up around it. The origins of the modern travel industry lie in pilgrimage. It was responsible for spreading thoughts, belief, culture, food and even deeply practical concepts like washing, which fell out of favour with dirty West Europeans until pilgrimage and travel to the East reminded us of the merits of an occasional bath.

Towns were once defined by their proximity to holy sites, and shrines vied to draw pilgrims with tales of miracles and healing. Pilgrimage to such places could be astonishing, enlightening, difficult and dangerous for our ancestors, with thieves and disease a constant threat. It could also involve excitement and temptation, with inns and brothels established along major pilgrimage routes. Being away from home was an opportunity for vice as well as virtue. In Southwark, just over London Bridge, there were around 18 brothels by the early 1500s. Even there the church made a profit. The landlord receiving the rent for the brothels was the Bishop of Winchester. Prostitutes became known as Winchester Geese.

In 1538, the destruction of Becket's shrine, which had been in Canterbury Cathedral for more than 300 years, put an end to the pilgrimage industry in England. The vast majority of people now visit it as tourists rather than pilgrims. And yet some still invest their faith in Britain's holiest city, where the monk Augustine, sent to England by the Pope, first set up a monastery 14 centuries ago.

I was struck by this most at a 12th-century shelter for medieval pilgrims near the cathedral. I found a book where modern visitors had written prayers. One was for somebody on death row in Ohio. Another asked that a baby girl would be healed and not need an operation. As I read these simple but powerful expressions of piety and hope, I felt anger towards those who say there is no place for faith in a 21st century of science and learning. Baiting the Christians of Middle England had become an ugly public combat sport for some leading British atheists. But faith can be such a magnificent and marvellous support in difficult times. I know that if Jake had a problem there is nothing I would not do, no God I would not pray to, in the hope of getting help for him. How dare anyone take that away from people?

Travelling and filming among Brits was a culture shock. As someone who had perhaps spent a little too much time abroad, I was surprised by how much we had to pay for grotty accommodation in the UK. I stayed in some really depressing hotels, almost all of them with a view of a car park or a light industrial park, often in rooms where mould was a decorative feature. It was also difficult to film in Britain. I quickly came to realise that you need more permits than almost any other country I have visited. Finally, although I met many wonderful people, I was taken aback by how in every single town and city centre there were stroppy and aggressive people shouting and screaming threats at one another, and someone would jump in front of the camera or try to stop us filming. Near the cathedral in Canterbury, a lairy lad deliberately barged into me from behind and tried to push me over while I was talking to the camera, then started laughing with his mates. Nowhere else has that happened. 'Welcome to England,' said our lovely director Chris Mitchell, who was filming, and trying to keep gurning and prancing bystanders out of his shots.

It was something of a relief to cross the Channel and set off along the Camino, perhaps the most popular long-distance walking route in the world. A 500-mile trail that snakes over the French Pyrenees and through northern Spain to the beautiful and holy city of Santiago de Compostela, around 200,000 hikers and bikers now complete the Camino in a normal year.

Around half of those walking were no longer religious pilgrims, at least in the medieval sense of penance and suffering. As often as not they looked to me to be adventure hikers, seeking an experience they would remember forever. I started to meet people who were on their own deeply personal journeys. One determined American hiker was a small, tough woman who had been caught in a house fire as a child. The physical evidence of her injuries was still there on her face in old age. She'd endured an astonishing 72 operations. Walking helped to give her more purpose.

There are different reasons to walk the Camino. It can be a time to think, for religious devotion, or for many the sheer physical challenge of completing an epic journey. As I hiked, and as I listened, the journey deepened my appreciation of walking as a restorative healer. The act of putting one foot in front of another, of taking life and its challenges step by step, had been of such immense value to me when I was a struggling teenager. I began to realise how the modern concept of pilgrimage had moved on from its medieval meaning. But it was still an act that had a deep resonance. For those following a pilgrim's path, a long overland quest was so often about self-discovery, and not just about reaching journey's end.

It can be tough to walk the Camino, but nothing like as arduous as the hike that took British pilgrims to Rome. Lying across the path of anyone coming from northern Europe were the Alps. The route between Britain and the Holy See was first mapped in the tenth century and the way over the Alps was via Great St Bernard's Pass, at 2,500 metres above sea level. Weather conditions around the pass are notoriously unpredictable, and there are endless accounts of pilgrims losing their companions to avalanches or exposure. The snow around the pass can be 10 metres deep in winter, and the temperature drops as low as minus 30 degrees Celsius. In the 900s an Archbishop of Canterbury froze to death there while on a pilgrimage to Rome.

The story of pilgrimage deepened my respect for the resilience and adventurous spirit of our ancestors. Before mod cons and Gore-Tex, it took genius as well as sturdiness to survive extreme weather. One of my personal favourite travellers, Ötzi the iceman, was found encased in ice by two German trekkers 3,200 metres above sea level in the Alps between Austria and Italy in 1991. More than 5,000 years old, his leathery corpse is the only example of an almost perfectly preserved prehistoric man, complete with tools, clothes and belongings. Europe was still only sparsely populated with Stone Age tribes, the Pyramids were just being built in Egypt, and the Mesopotamians were just discovering the art of writing. But incredibly, among Ötzi's tools were 17 different types of wood, each with a very specific purpose. There was viburnum for his arrows, yew for his bow, a tinder fungus for lighting fires, birch bark containers, embers wrapped in maple leaves, and an antibiotic birch fungus for medicine. He was also carrying a bone awl and panier, stone drills and scrapers, wood and antler tools for sharpening fine stones, and a sloe for flavouring food. He was better equipped than many modern climbers.

One only has to scrutinise Ötzi's clothes to realise their manufacture required painstaking dedication coupled with great skill. The 'trouser' tubes for his legs were made from goatskin. The incredible stitching on his clothes initially led to suspicions of a modern hoax. His cap, made from brown bear fur, was whip-stitched with fine, twisted thread made from animal sinew. Finally, his rainproof grass cape was similar to that worn by Alpine shepherds until the late 1800s. No one is sure what Ötzi was doing up there. He may have been a pre-Christian pilgrim, shepherd or outcast. Whatever the answer, there are few finer examples of a long-distance traveller. I would pick him as my patron saint.

While Ötzi trekked, I could drive high into the Alps towards Great St Bernard's Pass on an icy road, past towering walls of snow. Eventually my route was blocked by a house-sized heap of powder, so I switched to snow shoes and continued on foot along an ancient path between Switzerland and Italy, and headed to a refuge that has provided sanctuary for hikers and pilgrims for more than a thousand years.

Inside the sprawling Hospice du Grand-Saint-Bernard, its thick walls holding back tons of snow piled in drifts on all sides, there was a spirit of camaraderie among travellers who had arrived on the roof of Europe. I was given a bed, a bowl of thick soup, and, to my astonishment, a yoga session with a group of young American design students, most of them Mormons, on a tour of European holy sites and places that inspired great works of literature. We stretched, we strained, and then we paused for a few moments of meditation, to reflect on our journeys and our lives. Some of the students giggled, a few sobbed. I was struck by how utterly surreal it was to be at more than 8,000 feet, doing yoga and listening to the Sacred Chants of Shiva.

'It's kind of like what comes around goes around,' one of the students explained to me. 'Good karma and all that, right?'

I smiled at that comment. It struck me as evidence of one of the great joys of modern pilgrimage. Once upon a time in Europe you would only ever encounter like-minded Christians on your travels, because that's all there was. Now you mingle with the melting pot of all faiths and creeds, one of the great eye-opening joys of the journey, and you can experience the delight of hearing a Mormon embracing karma. In return for hospitality, the students did cleaning chores around the refuge, and that evening, after we had done the washing-up, I sat and chatted with the monks and the Mormons. I was impressed by how open-minded they were towards me. We talked about behaving ethically when you have no obvious faith, and lack a god to guide you. And then one Mormon said to me, 'Why not act as if God exists?'

I really liked that. I know there is a current belief that we should all do what we want when we want, taking our cue from the idea instilled by advertising that we're special and wonderful and unique. But sometimes what we need is to think a little bit more about the impact of what we do and say. Me definitely included. Whenever we step through our front door to meet the world, it's not a bad idea to act as if someone is watching.

When I'm getting cross about something and I can feel the red mist rising, a trick I use is to behave as if I'm being filmed, even when I'm not. The thought I'm on camera and being observed definitely encourages me to be a calmer and friendlier person than I often feel in my soul. It helps whether you're being cut up on the road, throttled by modern bureaucracy, or just talking to someone who is winding you up. If something prompts a rush to anger, just imagine you're being filmed and calm down.

But imagining ourselves being filmed shouldn't automatically lead to feeling we have to behave 'properly', whatever that means. Often it can lead to us behaving wonderfully improperly, being wild and free, and letting it all hang and dangle out. I use the idea I'm being filmed to help me behave more adventurously in many situations, to be on the pitch and not in the stands, so to speak. I want to know that if I watched the situation back in the future I'd be happy I wasn't a wallflower and I had some excitement and fun, or in a different situation, that I did the right thing and behaved kindly towards someone in a way I would approve of later.

It could take months for any medieval pilgrims who survived the Alps to trudge on to Rome. By the time they arrived many would have been exhausted, and then demoralised to find that the ancient city of which they had heard so much lay in ruins, while the River Tiber was a mosquito-infested swamp putting them at risk of malaria. Having endured malaria in Africa while following the equator, I can confirm it's no picnic. I have never felt so wretchedly unwell in my entire life. But pilgrims took the risk and headed to St Peter's because it was said to contain the finest collection of relics in the world, including the Ark of the Covenant, the tablets of Moses and even Jesus' umbilical cord and foreskin. Perhaps in some ways it's not that different from a modern pilgrimage to the Manchester United stadium, or Graceland, where 600,000 a year worship at the shrine of Elvis, the King. We still have that desire to touch and feel and commune with greatness.

Relics were also crucial to the medieval importance of Hagia Sophia in Istanbul, which I visited to understand the growth of pilgrimage after the city was called Constantinople and declared the new capital of the Roman Empire. Helena, the mother of the Emperor Constantine, went on pilgrimage to the Holy Land and brought back what was said to be a piece of the cross on which Jesus was crucified, and his crown of thorns. The relics were kept in Hagia Sophia and naturally the building became a magnet for Christian travellers. It can claim to be one of the most influential structures in human history. It is said a pagan prince from Ukraine was thinking of converting to either Judaism, Christianity or Islam but wasn't sure which to choose. He sent minions to investigate the religions. One visited Constantinople and reported back that upon entering Hagia Sophia he felt like he was in heaven. So the prince converted to Christianity. Ukraine followed and so, ultimately, did Russia.

I followed Helena to Israel and the Holy Land. Millions of pilgrims and travellers have trodden the same path. But it was in the 19th century that the line between pilgrimage and tourism really began to blur. In 1876 Thomas Cook, a highly devout Christian, published his guide book *Cook's Tourist Handbook to Palestine and Syria*. Cook took thousands of Victorians on tours of the Holy Land, and helped pioneer modern tourism. By the time I visited, a staggering half a million pilgrims were being baptised each year at the spot on the River Jordan where Jesus is thought to have received his blessing from John the Baptist. A local pastor was on call to perform a ceremony at 20 minutes' notice. I confess I wasn't tempted to join the queue.

Instead I headed to nearby Nazareth, where Jesus is said to have lived as a child, and visited an amazing open-air living history museum called Nazareth Village, which is spread across a large site and depicts life in the time of Jesus, with traditional first-century buildings, a carpenter's workshop, and volunteers playing and living the roles of villagers and crafters. Initially it felt rather bizarre, but as a historical theme park it certainly helped me to imagine life 2,000 years ago. The deeper benefits to some of those working there soon became apparent. I met an American called David, who was dressed as an ancient Nazarene and tended donkeys, sheep and goats. He began telling me about his life and how he'd had a drug overdose and at one point was actually dying in hospital. Clearly staying in the village was a form of therapy.

David was warm and friendly, and gave as good as he got when I gently teased him about the surroundings and what he was wearing. I helped as he fed the animals and sheared some sheep, and I confessed to him that although I didn't think I would be able to keep up the acting and the pretence if I lived there, it was obviously immersive and an exciting experience. David made a point I loved. He said pilgrimage needed to be woven into our everyday lives, so that 'all of life is an adventure'.

I completely agree we need to derive value and meaning from everything we do. David had a faith that meant he could take that one step further. No doubt that gifted an extra blessing, shape and focus. It meant David could feel he was still growing and learning whether he was shearing sheep, climbing mountains or exploring rainforests. Lucky chap.

I wanted to go to the heart of ancient and modern pilgrimage, so I drove down to Jerusalem. Millions of Christians, Jews and Muslims were visiting each year to worship in the holy sites of the Old City. An area of little more than a square mile is one of the most contested and controlled patches of land on the planet. Nowhere else has been at the centre of history for so long, and my visit to this impossible place had a profound emotional impact.

The last stretch of my journey was on foot along the Via Dolorosa, the route that Jesus is said to have taken while carrying his cross through the city to the site of his crucifixion. I joined Franciscan monks leading a procession along its half-mile course. As we all made our way through the narrow streets, I kept catching glimpses of a man dressed in biblical robes. He turned out to be a well-fed young American with a beard and long, centre-parted hair called James, who had been living in Jerusalem for six years. I wondered whether he might be suffering from Jerusalem Syndrome, a psychiatric condition afflicting people who come to the city and are so awestruck by its religiosity and power they can start believing they are the Messiah or an apostle. The delusion is surprisingly common and there are around 50 hospitalisations a year. One early case was an Englishwoman called Margery Kempe. In the 1400s she visited most of the major sites of Christian pilgrimage, but when she got to Jerusalem she kept falling to the ground in a series of dramatic fainting fits, accompanied by wild religious rants. I'm pleased to say that James modestly laughed off the idea he might be the saviour of humanity.

At that point in the labyrinth of alleys, a group of Nigerians from London came sailing along, full of excitement and praising the Lord, just as a gaggle of Armenians were coming the other way. The two groups each politely stopped and stepped aside for the other to go past, which meant nobody moved, so I sailed past with James dressed as Jesus. It was a little moment of human wonder.

I was getting ever closer to the Church of the Holy Sepulchre, by tradition home to the two holiest sites in Christianity, the site where Jesus was crucified and the tomb where he was said to have been buried and resurrected. The church, the fundamental heart of Christianity, sits in a neat little courtyard reached through an arch in an alley. Even with a large clutch of Israeli policemen observing everyone coming and going, it's impossible to overstate the aura of the Church of the Holy Sepulchre. Medieval Britons in particular believed the church was where the gap between heaven and earth was at its thinnest, and that it was a place of unlimited power where bodies could be healed and sins cleansed.

I entered the church and suddenly felt a strong sense of both sacred belief and the emotional tensions of the scores of pilgrims who were already inside. There was fervour in the air. We were all somewhere special. People were praying directly on the Stone of Anointing where Jesus is said to have been laid after he was crucified, rubbing their hands on it, wiping bits of cloth on it, putting candles on it, kissing it, just like ancient pilgrims did. Here in the holiest site for Christians was the final proof that many of us are just like our ancestors.

I could feel my nails dig into my palms as I entered the small chapel in the church called the Aedicule, and then ducked through another low doorway and into the tomb where Jesus was said to have been placed after his death on the cross, where he rose again and where Christianity was born. The tiny space, full of candles and flowers and Christian iconography, was key to the birth of a culture and a civilisation that has endured for two millennia. The shrine was the source of so much emotion and passion, so many paintings and so much music, so much joy, conflict and suffering. So much of human history could be traced back to that spot. To be there felt utterly overwhelming.

I had felt the power of the Holy Land, where every rock seemed to be imbued with potent energy. But it was the power of pilgrimage too. As I reached the climax of my journey I had a sense that I needed to feel a conclusion. I needed to be touched and transformed in some way by what I had seen and experienced. I was certainly imbued with a new respect for people of faith. My belief was renewed. But I was not feeling a religious conviction. What I felt was a powerful new belief in humanity. I felt such a deep sense of love and pity for us humans, with our unique capacity for warmth, creation and destruction. If I had to put a name to the set of principles that guide me through life, I would call myself a humanist. Though I don't always succeed, I strive to be a good person who leads a fulfilling life that impacts beneficially on others. I do not live by a religion or a religious book, and I set store by science and knowledge. I do not believe there is an afterlife. But that makes me believe all the more that we must make the most of this life, the precious existence we have been given.

Travelling around the equator had taught me about nature and conservation, the Tropic of Cancer about humanity and life on land, the Indian Ocean about our seas and oceans, and understanding pilgrimage was teaching me more about faith and the human spirit.

I thought back to the refuge at the top of Great St Bernard's Pass. When I asked him what he was doing on a pilgrimage, Ricky, one of the young American students I met at the top of the Alps said simply, 'I've got to get some meaning in my life.' It was an honest, unguarded line, the desire of many, and it captures the allure of the modern pilgrimage, for those of faith and those with none. Going on a pilgrimage, whether to Old Trafford, Memphis or the Holy Land, can provide a sense of purpose often lacking from life and much modern travel. So don't just leave pilgrimage to the pious. Get on the road, and head towards your own Jerusalem.

CHAPTER NINETEEN

The Grieving Room

Moving to Devon had transformed our lives. We were raising a beautiful baby son somewhere green and wild, and I could not have felt luckier. The strength of my love for Jake was unlike anything I had experienced before. Perhaps that ought to have been enough for me, especially as I had already faced the likelihood I would never be a father. But I still hoped for another baby. Maybe I was buying into the conventional idea of a nuclear family with two children. My feelings weren't helped when a friend said, 'You need to get on with having another. With one child you're just a couple with a kid.'

Those words rattled around inside my head. I realised nobody ever says, 'We have one child.' They always seem to say, 'We have just the one.' I was guilty of that as well. But more than anything, more than my desires, more than social or peer pressures, I wanted another child so Jake could have a sibling. When I started to imagine him growing as a child without a sister or brother, into his teens and then adulthood, I would literally start to sweat. I wanted him to have someone with him to share the journey, to support him whenever life was tricky or challenging. I started to fear that might not be possible, and found it really distressing.

His cousin Alice, and her brother Stanley, were both like siblings to him, and they had a beautiful bond whenever they were together. But my nagging voice said they had each other, and Jake needed a sibling of his own. Besides, being in a family of four was what I knew. It had come with lots of problems, and my relationship with my brother James could be tricky, but we had a shared sense of ownership over our childhood that I had always found stabilising. Now I know, as I look back, that I should have accepted what I had and learned to live in the moment and cherish the gift of one little lad. But I adored my son, and I felt I wanted more. For him, and for me. It's hardly unusual. I love giving love and feeling loved, and I felt I had more to give. I couldn't silence the nagging voice that said we should have another, and which meant we had to go through our fertility journey all over again.

Perhaps the impulse came from the same place that makes me a grafter. It doesn't just apply to my working life. My negativity translates into a desire always to be improving, to do better. In the past I've been able to use it as a superpower, to put a desire for more to good use. It helped me get out of my downward spiral as a teenager and lift myself up from nothing. I'm always trying to make the glass look less empty, even if that is so often how it still seems later. But at least one good thing about negativity as a driver and personality trait is that it can translate into action, and results. A determination to change and improve even transformed my fertility morphology, after all.

I cannot say Anya was quite as enthusiastic and committed to the idea of another child as I was. But she wasn't completely opposed. We decided to start trying, but after our past experience we thought we should go back and have some fertility checks, just to see what state we were in. Letters came back, and my readings and results were all acceptable. I had kept to my healthy regimen and was still looking lucky. Anya's results were not so hopeful. Nearly two years had passed since she first became pregnant and her age was now working against us. But we tried, naturally at first for a few months, and then using a form of assisted conception less intrusive than IVF. We were not very hopeful of success, and as we expected, nothing happened. I wanted us to try IVF, which I felt was our only real shot of conception, but Anya was still breastfeeding Jake and the drugs she would need to take would pass through her breast milk and into his little body. Which wasn't an option. She wanted us to stick with feeding him up, while I felt it was more important for him to have the chance of a sibling. We waited until months later when she had finished feeding, and then we started on IVF. Anya endured round after round of injections and tests, which was painful, difficult and upsetting, and none of it worked. Eventually, and completely understandably, Anya said she could not go through it again. So we gave up.

Anya felt that with one child, we already had more than nature intended. She was more disappointed for me than herself, or Jake. Personally I was in a much stronger place, emotionally, than when we were first trying to conceive. I had a gorgeous baby son, after all, who was cheeky and funny and brilliant. But for several months, only when I thought about it, I felt a cold gnawing sadness at the knowledge we had lost our final chance.

But then we had a little miracle. Despite the odds being stacked against us thanks to our age, we managed to get Anya pregnant, by the old-fashioned, tried and tested, natural route.

There was drama built into the day we found out. Anya's period was a few days late so she did a pregnancy test in the morning. A line was showing in the 'pregnant' window, but it was faint. We held our breath, and initially she planned to do another one in a few days' time. But we couldn't wait, so she did another test in the afternoon. It was a strong and solid line. That was at 4.15pm. We didn't have much time to take it in because at 4.30pm a cab came to take me to Heathrow, and I was off away travelling on another filming trip.

I was gone for three weeks, while poor Anya worked from home on the programmes, looked after a small child, and suffered terrible morning sickness. It was a lot to juggle. As soon as I returned we went for an early scan. We both felt nervous and tense, so had an immense sense of relief when the scan found the little foetus almost at once. It was less than a centimetre in length but we could hear its heart beating like the clappers. Overcome with emotion we kissed and hugged and floated home on air.

We began to make preparations stupidly early. I started rebuilding a cot. We had been given an expensive pram that, if bought new, would have cost as much as my first car. The arrangement had been for us to hand it on to somebody else but I apologised and said we were going to need it after all. It just seemed like it was going to happen, and a second child was the final piece of our personal jigsaw. There was a part of me that felt fate was smiling kindly on us. It felt right, like it was something we deserved. It never occurred to me anything could go wrong.

We went back for our 12-week scan. I was almost skipping on the way into the hospital, feeling convinced everything was fine. Anya had told me she thought something might be wrong, and her body had been sending her warning signals for the previous week. But my mindset was one of dumb confidence. Nothing could go awry. Besides, friends had reassured us everything would be fine.

We were greeted by two friendly ultrasound technicians waving magic wands around over Anya's womb, and soon we were looking at the outline of a baby with a gorgeous head. Its back was turned to us. We were all chatting away, and then the technicians tensed. They went quiet. The wand moved again. One of them spoke to Anya.

'Have you had any unexplained bleeding?' she asked.

With those words my world started to collapse. It was as if the walls began to fall away.

'I'm so sorry,' the technician said. 'There's no heartbeat.'

I couldn't stop myself. I howled. Anya and I gripped each other, and we cried.

Everything began to blur. The technicians were sympathetic, but it was a practised sympathy rather than a shock for them. I knew it was something that must happen frequently, to so many other couples whose hopes are destroyed in an instant. To people who have children, and people who don't. We were shown to a waiting room and told a doctor would come to see us. But really we were being shown to a room for grieving. It was a time for tears.

I tried to console Anya, and she tried to console and counsel me. We both kept saying to each other that we'd be OK, and, more importantly, Jake would be OK. But I felt devastated, for weeks and months. We'd lost our last chance to have another child and, more than that, I felt we'd failed Jake. It took time for me to find peace, and much of it was drawn from Anya and Jake. While she was pregnant Anya had been alone with Jake. She was aware that the special time where it was just the three of us would soon be over. She casually asked him if it would be nice if we had a little baby in the family.

'No,' he said. 'I'm happy.'

Whenever we asked if he'd like a brother or sister he would always say no. Not even a maybe. A no. He was only three but he was completely capable of expressing a feeling. Those three words – 'No ... I'm happy' – became something I clung to.

Anya may have mentioned one or two downsides of siblings. That you have to share toys. And attention. And he saw close friends of ours and their squabbling. Before her brother arrived when she was in her twenties, Anya was completely happy growing up as an only child, and she didn't share my desperation for more children and didn't have a feeling of guilt that we hadn't gifted Jake a younger sibling.

After the miscarriage, whenever we were with friends and saw their kids arguing I was always jokingly tempted to say to Jake, 'See, look how it is when you've got another.'

I didn't need to. I could see he was happy.

CHAPTER TWENTY

Mother Ganges

In the aftermath of our miscarriage, and while I struggled with profound feelings of loss, fate took me on the perfect journey for contemplation and healing. I began travelling along the length of the holy River Ganges, which rises in the western Himalayas and flows south and east across northern India.

Hindus worship the mother Ganges as a goddess of fertility and creation. The river has more than 100 names. It is the Daughter of the Himalayas, the Light Amid the Darkness of Ignorance, the Cow Which Gives Much Milk. Each name reflects the spirit and power invested in the river by those to whom it gifts life. The river is a force of creation, a goddess without form, providing water and irrigating fields for hundreds of millions. It makes perfect sense to celebrate and praise it, which is why making a pilgrimage to the Ganges is the supreme act for millions of Hindus. Many believe immersion in the waters of the Ganges washes away the sins of 100 lifetimes.

I had long been fascinated by rivers and the fundamental role they play in developing and defining countries and civilisations. So I jumped at the chance to make a series called *Sacred Rivers*, in which I journeyed along some of the world's great waterways: the Ganges, Yangtze and the Nile. Others we considered included the Congo, the Rhine, the Volga and the Mississippi. All offered a route into our culture and faith, and are a source of human stories galore. But none has quite the status of the Ganges, which has had more spiritual meaning imposed on it, and read into it, than any other river on the planet.

Travelling along the Ganges was just what I needed. It wasn't planned as a cathartic release from pain. We had begun plotting and planning the journey long before the desperate day when we lost our second child. Yet it turned out to be transformational. As I tried to understand what makes this river so holy for more than a billion Hindus, I found myself continuing the personal journey of learning I began with my *Pilgrimage* travels. My desire to know why people go on faith-based treks and journeys now deepened into a search for wisdom and enlightenment.

I did of course question whether it was right for me to go, and whether Anya was happy with me leaving in the circumstances. I certainly wouldn't have gone if I felt I was needed too much at home. But on a practical level we knew it was a project I had agreed to and needed to do. We also sensed a brief bit of space from the intensity of each other's emotions might be good for both of us. And just as when I went to Mogadishu after Jake's birth, Anya had the unwavering support of family and friends, especially Jake's grandparents.

In hindsight, India was the ideal place to draw my gaze away from my own navel. But as I travelled up into the foothills of the Himalayas I was operating on autopilot. Initially I found it harder to immerse myself in the experiences of the journey because I was wrapped up in myself, my feelings of negativity, and my heavy load of grief. I found it hard to move on. I was still thinking far more about what I couldn't have than what I had already.

I was to discover an India I had not seen while travelling along the shores of the Indian Ocean or the Tropic of Cancer. On those trips I had been a long way from a tourist trail, and often what I'd encountered was tremendous poverty. A third of the world's poorest people live in India, and on my previous trips I had found the suffering desperately upsetting. But for this journey I began in the town of Devprayag, a town little more than a village, but perhaps the most beautiful settlement I had seen in the entire country, clinging as it does to the side of the steep, forested hills around the perfect Y-shaped confluence of the narrow Alaknanda and the Bhagirathi rivers, which merge there to form the mighty Ganges. Temples and terraced houses painted yellow, blue, pink and green gaze down as the mighty mother Ganges joins and begins her journey across a basin covering nearly a third of India, where it waters the lands of around half a billion people.

At Devprayag, where the western Ganges, full of fresh glacial melt, gushes past high peaks and mountain villages, looking pristine-clean and deeply inviting, I met a baba, or holy man, who provides blessings for pilgrims. Ganesh Maharaj was one of many in India who have chosen to renounce worldly goods and live a simple life of contemplation close to the river. He meditates on its banks for hours every day. A smiling handsome man wearing a brightly coloured mohair jumper, Ganesh was so adept with his patter and so physically tactile, I couldn't quite tell if he was a genuine holy man or a charming cheeky seducer. We sat and talked in the cave where he'd been living for 12 years.

'We are holy men,' he explained with a beaming smile. 'We just have the clothes on our back. For the rest of our lives we are holy men. We are never again to do any job, any work. We just have a simple fire, good food, good sleep, good smoke, this is our lives.' He slapped my back and laughed appreciatively when I said it was a lifestyle that sounded appealing, and then at the river's edge splashed the crew and me with sacred water.

We set out on the road through spectacular scenery, the Ganges curling round corners far below us. Craig was filming this journey again, Dominic was directing, back in a country he loved, and we had a young assistant producer called Richard with us who had consumed masses of information about our sacred rivers, almost to the level of a PhD.

Given the sacred status of the river, it had been a slight shock for Richard when he discovered that hip young Indians were travelling up into the hills near Devprayag to go white-water rafting. We were keen to film this, but with a degree of discretion just in case anyone made a fuss that attracted complaints from militant Hindus outraged at any desecration of the Ganges. The rafting company had other ideas. For them our booking was a marketing opportunity, and they had raised colossal banners across the main road to welcome our TV crew.

'Hail, mother Ganges!' we all shouted to pacify and praise the goddess as we set off in yellow helmets and red life jackets, before I started swearing loudly when we had to paddle furiously through turbulent, swirling and churning water. It may have been sacrilege, but it was exceptionally good fun, and I was soaked by the holy water. Around me Indian tourists were flushed with excitement. Forty years ago few Indians were able to afford a holiday. But by the time I visited there were tens of millions of middle-class Indians, and on their holidays they were finding new ways to celebrate and enjoy the river.

We drove west for two hours to the city of Rishikesh. The Beatles put it on the map in 1968 when they visited an ashram, a sanctuary mainly for practising yoga and meditation, for some soul-searching and chanting, although Ringo was apparently less impressed than the other three. Hundreds of thousands of

Western travellers have since followed in their footsteps, seemingly lured by the belief, or cliché, that India is a holy place that can heal them, even as some perhaps overlook the grinding poverty around them. We had arranged for me to stay at Parmarth Niketan, the largest ashram in India, co-run by a Californian woman called Sadhvi who had arrived ten years earlier.

'Welcome home,' she said, with a warm smile, as I arrived after dark.

The ashram attracts hundreds of foreign visitors paying just a few pounds a day for a simple room and a chance to think and unwind and experience a completely different way of life. I'd barely set my bags down before I was taken down to the riverside to witness an aarti, where a large crowd of the ashram's visitors and residents gather on the banks of the Ganges to chant and pray. Beneath a pink temple-like structure standing above a terrace of steps, it made for a spectacular setting. In the middle of it I was introduced to His Holiness Pujya Swami Chidanand Saraswatiji, a short man in orange and pink robes with a rangy beard and a huge head of receding hair. He too welcomed me home.

When I look back at my photos and the footage from that early part of the journey, I fear I was a little too marinaded in scepticism. The negativity I brought with me on the plane had not yet been washed away by the sacred river. Perhaps my wariness was also something to do with British reserve too, and fear of the unknown. As I spoke to people in the ashram, my eyebrows arched just a little too high when they told me about the peace they had found, my conversation was too wry and my questions too loaded. I was even skeptical as the swami explained the power of holy Ganga to recharge our batteries, almost like a mobile phone. 'This place, especially, has become a powerhouse,' he said.

Early the next morning I joined prayer and meditation classes, wearing a white jumpsuit and what felt like a giant nappy. I sat cross-legged to meditate next to a middle-aged American woman with short grey hair. Afterwards she told me she had been in Rishikesh for a year and a half, practising yoga. She had no intention of leaving, having wound up her law practice, sold or given away everything she owned, and said goodbye to her children and parents.

'Why here?' I asked her. 'It's like a big energy vortex,' she said. I found it hard to square such conviction, even devotion, with the world on the streets of Rishikesh, where new age practices seemed to be commoditised as if it was a spiritual spa. You could seek emotional blockage treatment at one place and then next door in a café order a full English breakfast. But perhaps I was just a cynic. The ashram was home to several hundred local boys from poor and disadvantaged backgrounds who received an academic and spiritual education along with food and shelter. Another admirable campaign the swami was helping to lead were efforts to reduce pollution in the Ganges.

A clean-up was desperately needed, as I discovered when I journeyed on downriver to Haridwar, a bustling and brightly coloured city positioned where the Ganges fans out on to the northern plains. Unlike Rishikesh, which largely attracts Western visitors seeking enlightenment, Haridwar has long drawn Indian pilgrims and tourists from across the country who want to pay homage to the great goddess Ganga.

There's no central authority in Hinduism, no single founding text. It can be especially hard for an outsider to navigate and understand. So I linked up for a third time with the brilliant guide and fixer Abhra Bhattacharya. Over the years I had got to know him well. I first met him in West Bengal where government forces were battling a Maoist insurgency. In his Kolkata home his wife had served me carp fresh from the market and as an honoured guest I had the treat of sucking the eyes out. He was vital in Mizoram when I nipped over the border into Burma. Then he was my companion as I travelled up the east coast of the Indian Ocean. He had always been a generous fountain of knowledge and wisdom, but never more so than now, as he explained the complexities of Indian faith and Hinduism, a set of ancient beliefs allowing followers to create their own relationship with a multiplicity of gods.

Abhra and I followed the throng of Indian pilgrims down towards the crowded banks of the Ganges in Haridwar and nudged our way as politely as possible through to the front where Richard had been reserving two small spaces for us to sit down while we had been filming. Nobody seemed to mind. I squashed in tight next to a father holding a toddler on his lap. He shook my hand and smiled excitedly at me in the shared way we do when about to witness something special together. Priests in dark orange robes began making offerings of milk to the river. The crowd raised their palms to amplified chants of 'Hail, mother Ganges.' With darkness falling, pilgrims released offerings of flowers and candles into the river. We had bought our own natural bowl of petals and flowers for 100 rupees, less than one pound, and I waited patiently for a priest to bless them and then Abhra and I released them on to the water. The sight of flowers and candles floating off into the night made for a beautiful scene.

Abhra and I sat there at the river watching and sharing, while Craig and Dominic went into Haridwar to film more shots. Being with Abhra and among the crowd by the river, with water lapping at our feet, was inspiring. Abhra had already told me he was hoping somewhere along the Ganges we would bathe in the holy waters. It was a chilly night in Haridwar, but I could see a few men and women removing layers of clothing and preparing to go into the river.

'I'd like to go in,' I said to Richard. 'This feels like the right place.'

A look of mild panic spread across his face. Craig and the main camera were elsewhere. Unless something happens on camera, for all intents and purposes it never happened. He ran off to find them.

'Well if you're going in then so am I,' said Abhra with a defiant smile.

My main motivation was a desire for experiences, and perhaps the sacred emotions of the crowd also got to me. With hindsight it was also a wise tactical move to enter the water in Haridwar. The Ganges was already horrendously polluted by the time it reached the city, but east from there it was fetid. Any later in the journey and I might be bathing in a sewer.

Abhra and I both stripped down, and were getting close to the water's edge when Craig and Dominic returned and went straight into filming mode.

'For goodness' sake, Simon. Whatever you do don't get any of the water up your nose and least of all in your mouth,' said Abhra.

Wearing sarongs and holding on to thick chains attached to the stone steps of the shore, Abhra and I backed into the water, and then squatted down, immersing ourselves three times. It was freezing, bracing, and emotionally refreshing.

'All our past sins have been cleansed, even from previous lives,' said Abhra. 'Now it's the beginning of a new life, and a new journey for you.'

I managed to keep the water out of my mouth during the immersions, and then on my way out I slipped slightly on the bank and face-planted into the water, causing panic among my team who feared losing their presenter to cholera, diphtheria or some previously unknown disease. Back at our guest house I had a good hot shower and survived.

Three hundred miles to the south-east we entered the state of Uttar Pradesh and arrived into the industrial city of Kanpur. By this point the Ganges was suffering from an eye-popping level of pollution. The water looked muddier and dirtier, and the banks were knee-deep with rotting rubbish and plastic that was grazed by pigs and rats. But despite the evident filth leaching into the river, people were still washing and bathing themselves in the water and taking their own holy dip.

As we drove and walked through the streets of Kanpur there were cows everywhere, munching, walking, resting and dozing. Cows are revered in India because they are said to give milk freely, and it is taboo and even illegal to kill or injure them. Hence why drivers edge carefully around a cow if it is blocking the road. Yet India is among the biggest exporters of beef and leather in the world, and Kanpur is at the heart of a trade then worth around £3 billion a year. While sacred cows cluttered the streets, there were treated animal hides everywhere I looked, draped on railings and stretched out in fields. Most of them apparently come not from water buffalo, as the city's 400 tanneries claimed, but from cows that had been secretly slaughtered.

Whatever the source, the impact on the environment was colossal. To treat the hides, many tanneries used a cocktail of toxic chemicals including sulphuric acid and known carcinogens. The Indian Institute of Technology had found that waste water from tanneries contained dangerously high levels of arsenic and mercury, often flushed straight into the Ganges. Streams running into the river were piled high with pink toxic foam like mountains of killer candy floss. One environmental campaigner showed me a channel that pumped heavy metals, acids and dyes directly into the river. No wonder fish and turtle numbers have collapsed. Nothing could survive such a staggering level of pollution. In Kanpur, he told me, the Ganges was 'effectively dead'. The tannery owners were making so much money they had no incentive to clean up their act, while the state was far too corrupt and inept to do anything about it. Laws were ignored, money to fund clean-ups ended up in the wrong hands. Tanneries just tried to blame the pollution on other towns and cities along the Ganges.

Industry was killing the river, but so were people. One study discovered that bacteria from sewage in the Ganges was 12,000 times the permissible level for bathing. The reason was simple: hundreds of millions of Indians had no access to a toilet. I was starting to love both the Ganges and how it was venerated as the holiest of Indian rivers, but I couldn't square the faith on one hand with the fact it was being treated as an open sewer. It was a baffling contradiction that stayed with me as we journeyed on another 200 miles to the holy Hindu city of Varanasi, a place that was to be a major turning point in my life.

CHAPTER TWENTY-ONE

The Old Man and the Sadhu

Varanasi, also known as Benares, is a city unlike any other. It is one of the oldest inhabited cities in the world, a place of faith for 30 centuries, and is said to be as ancient as Babylon. The American writer Mark Twain, visiting in the 1890s, dubbed it 'older than history, older than tradition, older even than legend'. The same religious rituals have been practised in Varanasi's 10,000 temples, dedicated to the full panoply of gods and goddesses, for more than a thousand years and remain virtually unchanged.

Yet the full impact of Varanasi, known as the City of Light, was not revealed to me when we arrived late one evening in a four-wheel drive and picked our way through the throng of streets that tightened and narrowed as we drew closer to the cosy guest house where we spent the night. Before we went to bed, Abhra insisted we had to be up and out before dawn to watch the sun rise over the Ganges as it passes through the holiest city and bathers come to cleanse themselves of their sins and sufferings. I grumbled, but agreed.

It was still dark and bitterly cold when we picked our way down to the river along streets lined with the huddled sleeping bodies of beggars, rickshaw drivers and labourers. Abhra had hired a long wooden boat for us, and once afloat we hugged the western bank of the river's wide expanse as the current took us slowly downriver just as light began to creep over the horizon. Mist hugged the shoreline, so the city felt more like a ghostly rumour than a solid structure. It was ethereal.

Just as Varanasi began emerging into the daylight I began talking to the camera, trying to set the scene, as Craig Hastings captured both me and the emerging wonder of the ancient city. Then in the back of his shot an elderly man in ragged clothes hobbled down to the riverbank, turned, squatted and immediately began to visibly defecate on the ground right next to the river.

'I'm sorry, guys,' said Craig. 'I can't frame that out.' We turned the boat around and went back and tried for take two. Again, just at the point where I needed to start talking, two women came down the bank and began squatting. We had a brief team meeting and agreed that although I was all in favour of showing the reality of a place, and open defecation was an enormous problem in India that spoke of huge state failures, it might be a little inappropriate to show me entering the holiest city for the Hindu faith with people crapping right behind my head.

We went another hundred metres back upstream and hoped we would be third time lucky. But by now it was as if the lights were switching on and the whole of Varanasi was waking up for its morning ablutions. The banks of the Ganges were turning into a public convenience. But I spotted a slight pause in the flow and, giving my hair an obligatory ruffle, took the chance to deliver a few words. Normal service then resumed with a few weary labourers arriving and squatting at the river's edge. There was no time to go back for another shot, but I knew Craig would have worked his magic. We drifted around a small headland and the sun lifted above the horizon to reveal the miracle of Varanasi.

The sight was utterly breathtaking. On the west bank of the river was a dense network of decaying palaces and temples in every conceivable style, jostling and bumping for space with the many guest houses, in front of which were the ghats – flights of steps and stairs leading down and into the edge of the Ganges. One huge, tall tiered shrine in the shallows was leaning on its side like a listing old man. I felt like I had wandered through a museum full of empty, sterile rooms only to cross a threshold and be confronted by a vast painting, the work of a great master that compressed into it stories from the teeming narrative of human existence, each and every detail carefully slotted into its own segment of the canvas to convey an overall immensity of scope and scale. Everywhere I looked there was an absorbing detail to dive into, a busy little vignette to ponder. It was a panorama in which people prayed, scrubbed clothes, bathed, meditated, wailed, walked, talked and above all washed. Smoke rose from burning incense, and candles on lanterns swung on balconies that clambered up and up from the river's edge. I suddenly noticed huge stockpiles of wood lining the banks, more or less neatly arranged in high stacks or circular mounds, ready for use on funeral pyres slightly further down the river.

I found my first encounter with this living city of impossible age to be astonishing and overwhelming. Varanasi was instantly one of the most amazing places I had ever been. All the more because on the eastern bank of the river was emptiness. A legend suggests anyone who dies on the wrong side of the Ganges will be reborn as a donkey. Hence it was a flat, open land. It was almost as if every building had jumped to the other bank.

We moored and climbed out on to one of the ghats to take in more of the scene on foot. Abhra, who had spent eight years living in Varanasi, said he had something to show me. We walked through the streets and came to the iron gates of a simple hotel with rooms around a large courtyard and a huge tree at the centre providing shade. Unlike in most hotels, all the guests seemed to be elderly. It was a so-called death hotel, a place guests would never leave, a bit like the Hotel California. People stayed there not to convalesce, but to live out their remaining days in the hope they would die within the temple-lined pilgrim track that bounds Varanasi. The holy city is seen by Hindus as the last stop before nirvana. They believe that dying in Varanasi, or to have their ashes scattered in the river, would mean their soul could escape the laborious cycle of reincarnation and achieve 'moksha', or eternal liberation.

Some Hindus will go to great lengths to achieve moksha. Abhra introduced me to an elderly man called Manvodh Tripathi, who with his wife had retired from a life of farming and moved to the hotel to live out their final days. We found them sitting by a brazier in a long colonnade. She quietly busied herself with sewing and beading but listened while Manvodh talked. He was a striking figure in an orange dhoti around his legs, thick red jumper, a dark blue scarf wrapped over his head, a fake pearl necklace and a long beard tidied into a little bun.

'We can only die here if it is written in our destiny,' he said. But he seemed to be taking no chances. While his wife went back home now and then, Mr Tripathi had been in the hotel for 18 years. I told Manvodh that I had a terror of death, partly inherited from the culture in which I grew up. I don't fear pain or sickness or dying, I fear death. I fear the ending. I was having to confront this in Varanasi, because death was everywhere. He shrugged benignly. 'You should never be scared,' he said. 'From the moment you are born, death is part of life. They go together.'

Nowhere have I seen the end of our personal journey of life and death playing out more overtly, dramatically and explicitly than on the shores of the Ganges in Varanasi. Families go to great lengths to ensure their loved ones are cremated on the riverbank, thus securing their eternal salvation. Funerals are big business and the trade is run by members of the so-called 'untouchable' Dom caste who tend to the pyres. The story goes that the caste were once priests, but were cursed when one of them stole an earring from the wife of Shiva, one of the three central gods responsible for the creation, upkeep and destruction of the world, while she bathed in the Ganges. Shiva punished the Dom caste by condemning them to an eternity of burning bodies.

The job is said to be so despicable that Doms cry when one of their own is born and rejoice when they die. At the main cremation area next to the river, Abhra introduced me to the Dom Raja, a hereditary leader who is rumoured to have made a fortune controlling the funeral trade in Varanasi. He was a thick-set and well-fed man in his middle years, swathed in a white blanket. A somewhat remote figure, he was the only Indian I met who could not be coaxed to smile.

'It is a family tradition,' he explained of his profession, 'I see it as a duty. It doesn't upset me. It's my way of practising my faith as a Hindu.'

The Doms have a lot of practice. From a flame that priests say has been burning continuously since it was ignited by Shiva 3,500 years ago, 40,000 people were being cremated annually in Varanasi, consuming at least 20,000 trees. The Dom Raja said that people pay whatever they can afford, but the more they paid the better the quality and location of the funeral pyre. Sandalwood remains the most auspicious wood for a pyre, but costs more. The poor sometimes cannot muster the money to buy enough wood to entirely cremate a body, so the Doms focus on burning the main torso, and the remaining charred body parts are placed or thrown into the river with the ashes.

There was a hypnotic concentration of staggering sights as I stood next to the river in Varanasi watching this holy industry in action. Everything I could see was extreme, and impossible. It could have been any time in the past thousand years. I could have stood there for 100 years and still not been fully able to understand the full complexity and panorama.

Body after body, all wrapped in coloured shrouds and carried on bamboo litters, was brought down to the ghats by jogging, chanting men and bathed in the river. Shrouds indicate who was being cremated, with white for most men, and gold for an elderly man who has a good death. After immersion, bodies would be moved to a pyre of thick branches and chunks of firewood, with more placed on top of them. The eternal flame would be used to light a bundle of hay or a long stick with flammable rags at one end, and then that in turn was used to light the pyre. The chief mourner was often the dead man's oldest son. With other mourners he would circle the pyre five times, once for each element: fire, water, earth, air and ether. Women and especially widows were not permitted to attend for fear that they would throw themselves upon the flames. It could take between two and 12 hours for a body to burn, and it was considered bad karma for mourners to show grief during the cremation.

Moving among the throng were old beggars asking for money they would need to buy in advance the wood required to cremate their bodies after their death. Abhra explained that they had either been left there by their relatives or they had travelled to Varanasi under their own steam. Some were emaciated and clearly suffering terribly, but the pain they sought to alleviate was not pain in life but pain after death. Meanwhile people swam in the fetid water, while dogs and cows ambled about the banks. A dog darted past the mourners, rummaged at the edge of the fire and pulled out an arm. The most astonishing moment of the cremations I saw came when a chief mourner took a long heavy bamboo pole and with a careful thwack split the head of his father wide open, allowing the brain to pour into the fire and the soul to escape and fly free of the endless cycle of death. It was a dumbfounding thing to witness.

On the final stretch of my journey, the Ganges splits into two rivers and changes its name. One branch flows into Bangladesh and becomes the Padma, but I decided to stay in India and followed the River Hooghly, which flows through Kolkata towards a rendezvous with the Bay of Bengal. It was an auspicious time. Thousands of pilgrims were travelling to Sagar Island, where the river empties into the sea.

To get to the end of my journey I boarded a crowded ferry and headed out into the Bay of Bengal under bright sunshine. Looking at the other passengers, I was struck by the astonishing changes the country was experiencing. The population could soon surge past China to become the most populous nation that has ever existed, yet ancient beliefs were still thriving. The country has more than 3 million places of worship, but a shortage of hospitals and schools.

As the banks of the river receded into the distance, it was almost like we were heading out on to the ocean. I asked a lively old lady to explain her reasons for making the journey. She told me she was going to the point where the river meets the sea to meet God and bathe in the water. 'Ganga is India's number one god! You can do pilgrimages to other sites many times, but you must come here once,' she insisted.

I say my journey along the Ganges ended. But in a personal sense it never really ended at all. Having travelled down the river in the wake of traumatic loss, in Varanasi I learned two critical lessons that have stayed with me and deeply affect me to this day. They concern death, and they concern life.

The first took place in the death hotel. We had finished filming with Manvodh Tripathi, who had been waiting for his end in the city for 18 years. He looked into my eyes, and through Abhra he asked me a simple fundamental question.

'Where do you want to die?' he said.

The question was like a crack on the head. A moment of revelation. Nobody had ever asked me that. I had never directly thought about the question. There was no evading the subject in the death hotel. In that moment, and with those words, Manvodh made me accept something exceptional: knowing where you want to die helps to connect you to life. I needed to accept death more so I could embrace life. I needed to know where I want to die, because then I would know where I will be rooted. I will belong. I will be from 'somewhere'. Not 'anywhere'.

Where do you want to die? Where are you going to be buried? Death is the great decider of where or whether we have roots. The question might seem morbid, but in other cultures people calmly consider their answer from surprisingly early on in life. I cast my mind back to my first visit to Madagascar and deep conversations about death I had with my fixer, a wonderful young honey-voiced woman called Batsola Andrianjaka, who explained why Madagascans do not fear death the way we do in the West.

'This is a country where death is more important than life,' she had told me. 'Death is the chance for a humble human to become a powerful ancestor, someone respected and consulted by the living.' Youngsters like Batsola, and even teenagers, will spend time thinking seriously about where they want to be buried after they die. But not fearfully, because for them it is just another stage of life's adventure.

We can rail against death. We can find it upsetting, and we can be appalled by it. But we cannot cheat it. And we should not shy away from it. Because it is the very fact that death is the end, or at least a physical end for those of most faiths, that should lend shape to our lives and give them urgency. Death should encourage us to live our lives while we can, to enjoy and embrace our existence, to celebrate the magical and mystical fact that our collection of atoms has bundled together in a being with such an enormous propensity for love and existence.

The second lesson Varanasi taught me was about how to live. Early in the evening, after we had finished filming, I walked back down to the Ganges, through long alleys festooned with messy overhead wiring and string lights, past medieval shopfronts selling sweets, fruit, radios and fabrics.

There was a young man sitting by the burning ghats who to my inexpert eyes looked like a sadhu, a Hindu holy man. I wondered what he was watching. I paused about 10 feet from him. Not too close to be personal. I wasn't looking for conversation. But he turned his head towards me and seemed to nod just a fraction.

'Namaste,' I said to him.

'Namaste, and, good evening,' he said deliberately in English.

We turned back to the scene. It was a grand, epic, sweeping, ancient vista. A filthy young man wearing an even dirtier

AC/DC T-shirt was tending a huge fire with a long bamboo pole. Dark smoke from the pyres was all around.

The sadhu had a calm, intelligent air about him. He had short hair, the three white lines of the Tripuṇḍra hand-painted across his forehead, necklaces, wrist beads and a water bottle. He was wearing red fabric draped over one shoulder, leaving the other bare. He must have been freezing.

Below us three foreign tourists in tie-dye yoga pants were walking slowly along, snapping away on expensive SLR cameras, consuming the scene as they moved through it. They were taking photos of people while standing slightly too close to them, too close even for India, where life is lived in immediate proximity.

'And why are you here?' the sadhu said to me suddenly. Very direct, but smiling and polite.

'Oh, I'm just looking. Watching.'

'Ah. You have come here to observe?'

'Erm, I'm just trying to understand.'

He gave a little laugh and went back to watching the tourists.

'Looking, looking, looking,' he said softly, almost to himself. 'You are people in a labyrinth. Just be.'

He smiled at me.

He could see I was focused on his words. They were rolling around my head.

You are people in a labyrinth. Just be.

He needed to say nothing more. It was the essence of everything. The distillation of a thousand sacred texts and self-help manuals. Life can be a maze. Don't always look for something more. Enjoy the now. Live for the moment.

The sadhu began to shift to his feet.

'Thank you,' I said suddenly, almost without thinking.

He nodded to me slightly, and moved away.

I sat there for a while, watching bodies burning on the ghats. The lad in the AC/DC T-shirt tipped ashes into the sacred Ganges. Varanasi had become a place of pilgrimage and revelation.

The sadhu was so right. So many of us journey and search and struggle for something we think we need to have, rather than embracing and enjoying what we already possess. The sadhu was reminding me to cherish what fate had already gifted me.

I had one child and he was more than enough. He was a blessing and a life-affirming delight. I would quieten the voices that said I wanted anything more, that I needed more children. Jake was perfect.

That night, in our guest house well away from the ghats, where alcohol is banned, I drank cheap whisky with the team and we talked about what we had seen. I had been deeply affected. Like any Brit incapable of dealing with the emotional impact of the city, I got drunk. It doesn't take much. I'm a cheap date. Then I went to my room. I had a little cry. With the emotional lubrication of strong liquor, I wrote a short letter to my son. My only, beloved son. I felt I had to share what I was learning. But also I needed to pour out some thoughts, and some suggestions for his life. I so desperately want him to avoid the mistakes I have made.

It was a personal ramble, fuelled by whisky. But it also had meaning and raw emotion. I share it here now, partly in case it sparks a thought for someone else, and partly so Jake can't avoid it in the future.

My darling son,

I hope you never read this, or if you do I hope it's just because we're laughing about it as a bit of a joke. But if you do read this letter, it might be because something horrible has happened to me, and I don't want to leave you to make your journey through life without any thoughts or guidance from your dad.

I love you, Jake. I love you so much. I'm writing this while I'm on the road again, and I hate being away from you and miss you constantly when we're apart. Every moment not with you and Mum feels like a moment either wasted or not best spent. I am constantly wishing I could share with you the amazing, beautiful and upsetting sights and experiences I have on my travels.

You must must always remember that whatever I've been doing, and wherever I am, I'm wishing we were all together. I may never know whether I have done the right thing by being away from you for long stretches.

I go on my journeys because I love them and believe that in some tiny, tiny way they help people to understand more about the world. I try to balance the conflicting demands between us being together as a family, and being on the road doing my job and earning a living. I'm sure I don't get the balance right, and for that I'm sorry. But I know I've helped to give you the best mum you could possibly have in the world. I know you're safe with her. Look after her as you grow my darling son.

I can't bear any thought I might not be with you for the rest of my life. You are the point of my existence. Even in the first few years of your life, I've seen that you have such a fun, strong personality, and I hope and pray that I'll be able and allowed to watch as you grow and mature and stumble and fly.

Jake, whether I'm around or not, I'm sure you'll walk your own path in life. Forgive me for making just a few notes and suggestions for the road . . .

Dance like a wild thing. I've always been too proud, embarrassed and self-conscious to dance in public. I worried too much about what people would think. I regret it hugely. Try to avoid making my mistake. Dance yourself silly – nobody cares.

Most people I've met find happiness through discovering their purpose and meaning. Try to find yours. It can be almost anything. But life is so often a challenging maze. Love whatever you are, and whoever you are. Just be.

Trust people. Nothing is more important than friends and family. Cultivate your relationships. They all need tending and nurturing. The best friends are those who tell you what you really need to know.

Try to marry someone nicer than yourself. But you'll be lovely. Mum and I have a points system to help with our relationship. She will explain. Any relationship involves sharing and compromise. There is a huge value in giving up a bit of what you want to make sure someone else gets what they need.

Don't leave it too late to have children of your own. Mum and I did. We found each other in our 30s, and then waited a little too long to have you (in my view! Mum might disagree!).

You can't wait for something to happen, so be the catalyst. Remember just because we can't do everything doesn't mean we shouldn't do something.

Be adaptable. Try to become someone who can bend and flex for different situations.

If you want to be successful in your working life, try to do something you love. Then work hard, volunteer, say yes lots, be proactive, be imaginative, and have loads of ideas.

There is a real long-term value in study and hard work, even when that can be challenging or boring in the short term. People, advertisers, corporations will try to con you into thinking you can have overnight success in life. It's not true. Life is about grafting, staying the course, and luck.

When you're ready, watch the series The Century of the Self. *My favourite film is* The Battle of Algiers. *I read* Schindler's Ark *when I was about 14 and I found it extremely powerful, upsetting and moving.*

Travel is an incredible opportunity for profound experiences, but also for an education. There is such beauty and suffering out there in the world. Try to explore and understand both the light and the shade.

Some of the best advice I ever received was to take things step by step. Perhaps there will be a time when that helps you my darling.

You can work at confidence like a muscle. But start small. Eventually you will be able to confront your fears.

Be hungry for experiences. Don't waste a moment. When you're a bit older, use the fact we have to end as an encouragement to live your life to the full.

My darling Jake, you can ignore everything I've written. It's up to you. It's your journey.

Enjoy your life. I will love you for eternity.

CHAPTER TWENTY-TWO

The Ledge

Looking back on these experiences there are intense memories everywhere. Wherever I have been in the world, going around the middle of the planet once, twice, and a third time, exploring oceans, deserts, rainforests, rivers, and also closer to home in London and Devon, I see them all now as lessons in living that have given me strength and direction. With the time to reflect afforded by the pandemic, I have come to realise how critical and how profound my journeys have been for me.

I have always placed encounters with other people at the heart of my journeys. Before I had this chance to reconsider my travels, I thought I loved meeting our brothers and sisters and cousins on the road because I enjoy their stories and tales, and the thrill of making human connections.

Yet now I understand how each experience and impossible place, each moment of learning, has come directly from the people I have met, and those I travel with. They have taught me so much. Tuku who battled for turtles in India. The headhunter in Borneo who adopted me as his son. Marie in the Maldives. The elder of the Piedra Ni people in Colombia who stared into my soul. The brave journalist Javier Valdez Cárdenas, who lost his life in Culiacán. Fadli the Polisario officer who had not been home for 40 years. My Bangladeshi guide Tanjil. Cheery who courageously escorted me into Burma. Carlos the Mozambican defender of sharks. The three Kimberley croc hunters. The Mormon in the Alps who recommended I pretend God exists. What extraordinary people. What a privilege to have met them. When lockdown started to bite, I thought back to each and every encounter, and I drew strength from all of them. They were lessons in living that have given me immense purpose.

As for lockdown itself, that too has been a deep lesson for me. A great personal shock was how quickly the weeks and months ticked by. My travels have gifted me such variety, sometimes absurdly so. With so much packed in, life seems to roll by more slowly. A couple of days on a journey feels like a week. A week can feel as long as a month. It is almost as if when we head away on a trip we are sucked into a different time vortex, and when we return, exhausted, ecstatic and overwhelmed, feeling as though we have been gone for eons, just moments have passed back at home. Variety and travel lengthen life. When time started to pass too quickly during lockdown, I knew I had to inject more variety into my existence. I did something different every single day, even if it was mundane, like shopping in a different supermarket. I slept on the floor, as I often have on a journey. I had muesli for dinner and a shot of tequila with breakfast. I mixed things up, trying to replicate just a little of the variety conferred by travel. Even when the pandemic ends, and it will, I want to keep that variety in daily life.

The pandemic also helped me to think more about the future I would like for my lad Jake. As we tried, and failed, and tried again, to home-school him in a way where he actually learnt something useful and meaningful, like other parents I came into close contact with our system of education and the whole world of learning. It gave me a chance to apply what I've learnt on my journeys to what actually matters in the education we give our children.

I want Jake to study and be educated. I want him to stick at school and enjoy it, certainly more than I managed to do. But traditional school values and qualifications matter less to me than helping him to prioritise the value of experiences, and family, friendship, the natural world and even self-control.

In a society where education is valued as the overwhelming imperative for children, I place a higher priority on the value of time in nature, and the need to create lasting relationships with family and friends. However successful we are, our lives are less if we have nobody to share the journey with. Friendship, family and relationships are a reason *Why* to exist.

I especially want him to have more meaningful, real experiences, and I worry that children's lives are dominated by screens and the virtual world. Education now seems to rely on screens. Games, reading, coding, music, social media or an '80s-series box set are all available at the touch of a few buttons. Even when I hid the TV remote it turns out you can operate a television from a phone app. Many kids exist in a culture of endless and immediate screen gratification. They're bored? Chuck them a phone or a tablet. Of course it's easy for a telly type with one child to preach. But the instant screen solution cuts boredom out of their lives, which is a disaster, because boredom is key for developing our imagination. A child who is never bored has no space to dream, or to work up a solution to their predicament, and less reason to create.

Screens are helping to kill our desire for bigger, real experiences, which are how we grow, develop and mature. It is real experiences that gift the profound memories and encounters, and real experiences that help a child to start exercising their fear muscle and develop their physical and emotional confidence. I believe there's a risk of kids being trapped in a toxic mindset if trained to focus on short-term distractions rather than the real fulfilment of long-term goals.

In terms of self-control I'm a great believer in encouraging all of us, but children in particular, to learn the art of delaying gratification. That sounds puritanical, but really what I mean is avoid stupid distractions and short-term simple treats and focus on bigger prizes and greater rewards. So for me, at a very basic level, that means I only have the internet on for certain hours of the day, to reduce the constant pings of messages and alerts that can stop us focusing and enjoying the rest of real life.

I set a great deal of store by the lessons of the famous marshmallow test, which was shown to be a surprisingly accurate predictor of life chances, and whether a child would make a conventional success or failure of their existence. The experiment was first conducted in 1972 and led by a psychology professor at Stanford University. A child was shown into a room with nothing but a table, a plate and a marshmallow (or, if they preferred, a pretzel stick), and were told they could eat it there and then or wait 15 minutes and have two. The children who were able to wait almost invariably were the ones who made a success of their lives. They were tracked for years and their life outcomes were measured by a range of factors including exam scores, educational attainment, even body mass index.

Those who were able to delay gratification in the experiment, whether by humming, staring intently at their reward, looking at the wall or even picking their nose, were able to knuckle down and study, hold down lasting relationships, even put money into a pension. If we can teach our children to press the delay switch, to learn that better things come to those who wait, we will be teaching them a skill with rewards that can last a lifetime. It's not a lesson that's on the curriculum. But perhaps it should be.

The lockdown that started in early 2020 and continued on and off for more than a year certainly forced me to accept the delay of gratification. I was going somewhere wonderful, travelling the length of South America, and then I wasn't, and as I write these words I still don't know when it will be possible to travel freely again. Instead of my colleagues, the wonderful and supremely talented cameramen and directors in this book, my adventure companions have so often been my wife, son and our dogs.

Yes, dogs. Plural. During the summer of 2020 Anya and I decided to get Jake and Obi a friend. Everyone seemed to be in pursuit of a puppy. It was like a tulip craze only with pooches. Anya went to see one family with a litter to sell, came out to ring me and in five minutes two puppies went, including the one she had her eye on. Eventually a tan-coloured Belgian Malinois/German shepherd mix popped up and we swooped in. We didn't want to get a dog that could be bowled over by our bigger beast, so Obi had to give final clearance. He was taken to meet Lyla and they had a nuzzle and a play and got on well, although perhaps he didn't realise the plan was for her to become a permanent member of the family.

There is something uniquely wonderful about puppies. Obviously they get a little bit less cute as they grow, but the curiosity they're born with stays with them. They're always eager to know about the world around them, its sights, sounds and, above all, smells. They have the perfectly honed tool, a nose with more than 200 million receptors. For comparison, a human nose has 5 million. Their brain is a third the size of ours, but a third of it performs olfactory functions. It's their sense of smell, which can pick up on fear and grief, that helps make dogs such good companions. They infect us with their unconditional love and boundless enthusiasm for life, making us better people, more empathetic, more communal. That's certainly what my two dogs did for me.

A major part of the reason we picked Obi was because we had one child and I wanted a four-legged replacement sister or brother for my son. When we got Lyla we all agreed she would be another companion for Jake. But we also got her for me, so I had another creature to love, and to help stop me going mad. As much as anything else, and almost as much as my son, Obi and Lyla have become essential to my mental health. They are a powerful tonic and a psychological support. When I walk with them I spend almost the entire time with a grin plastered across my face, a big dopey intoxicated smile of love for the dogs, and pleasure because I get to share their joy and closer connection to nature. It's hard to be grumpy, let alone depressed, when you're around such excitement, such positivity, such unconditional trust and loyalty.

Lyla was a tonic, and not only for my family. Out on our little puppy walks, her impossible cuteness became a sort of free public medicine for all. When I'd bump into other people on walks, the fear of coronavirus would linger like a miasma depressing every socially distanced interaction. But then Lyla arrived, a small bundle gambolling and careering along with an outsized tongue and ears a-wobbling. She had the power to brighten any encounter. She was a tonic for everyone.

With two dogs to exercise, and with a need to inject more variety into daily life, I had to find new places to take them. I looked at paper maps and Google satellite shots, hunting for patches of forest. I followed advice I have given others, and upended a glass on a map of Dartmoor, centred it on my home, drew a ring around the rim, and explored every inch.

Which is how I found another secret spot, and impossible place. It is a patch of rarely visited ancient woodland, full of broadleaf trees including enormous old beeches. They grow among a scattering of rocks so huge they look like missiles hurled about by squabbling giants who have only just departed the battlefield. I love the animal paths that beckon in the woods, leading to mossy walls that run over the slopes, made of boulders weighing up to 100 kilos moved by prisoners during the Napoleonic Wars.

One day I was exploring the wood with Jake, my godson Elian and his sister Aurelia. They were racing along a narrow track in the forest, a long way from a main path, when suddenly they spotted a gap between huge towering rocks off to the side. It was full of thick brambles. Jake pulled out his heirloom knife and carefully cut a way through with a slow slicing action, then they squeezed their little frames up through the long cleft in a huge granite rampart, like a tunnel crevice between the rocks. The dogs followed. The kids called me to join them.

'It's like going through the cupboard to Narnia,' Jake shouted down.

It was a slightly tighter squeeze for me. But I made it through and clambered up to join them on top of the rocks on a secret ledge, a flat slab of stone smothered in spongy moss above the surrounding tree canopy with a view that stretches into the distance towards the colossal Haytor Rocks, a great icon of Dartmoor. The ledge feels like a viewing platform, the perfect stage for year-round nature watching, set under a wizened old oak that sends its long, low limbs out in all directions like messengers. I went back again and again to that ledge with the dogs to watch the seasons' progress, as the thick, lush green forest roof faded to golden brown and was then stripped away by wind and winter to reveal the trees' naked skeletons. It's a special place, best visited with special companions. What makes me treasure it all the more is that we live on such a crowded island, and in this secret wood I invariably see no one.

One day I was there alone with the dogs, and there was a perfect moment. On top of the stone slab stage, Obi stopped, then sat down, facing out. He doesn't normally pause. There's so much to do when you're an Obi. But he stopped, and he sat down, panting softly, and he looked out at the view, before turning to our new puppy, who was tearing around, almost saying to her: 'This is what we need to do, littler.' Then Lyla sat down next to him, and they looked at me, and Obi looked back at the view, and he sniffed the air. He took it in. It was a moment I utterly treasured. I needed to do the same. I sat down next to them, the three of us in a line, looking at the view. We all need to stop for a moment, sit down and sniff the air.

The dogs have taught me so much. They have shared something critical. How to be more present, more aware of nature, and to draw fulfilment from every exquisite moment it gifts us. This is the wisdom of dogs. They hate missing an outing or a walk. And when they are out and about they spend their entire time in the here and now. They are not distracted by the bleep of a message arriving on a smartphone. Theirs is a world of experiences, sights and especially smells. Not that they are creatures immune from distraction. Their entire walk can feel like a series of distractions. Squirrel! Stick! But they always remain within the experience, living in the present, and through their excited absorption in their immediate surroundings, they help to bond us more closely with the natural world.

I spent so much more time exploring locally during the dark months of the virus, on walks and treks that gifted me a new grounding, and a new sense of connection and contentment with my own land and island. I still have something worse, and better, than imposter syndrome. I don't believe I should be where I am, but I have delight and wonder at what I've done, and what I'm still able to do.

Jake and I were savouring the view from our secret ledge in late spring 2021, when there was a magical sound. At first my head doubted what my ears claimed to hear. But there it was again. No doubt. A cuckoo. A magical reassurance. The cuckoos of Dartmoor are flighty visitors. They spend a brief summer here before leaving our little island and travelling south, a long way south, on a circular trip of some 10,000 miles, to overwinter in the rainforests of the Congo. I find them an astonishing connection with the greater planet. The sound of them, I decided adamantly, was a lucky charm for a desperate traveller, a sign I will travel again. I will have the variety, and the experiences, that I love. We will get through this pandemic and endure to flourish again.

The secret ledge is one of my favourite impossible places, in a part of the world I never thought I could live, with a wife and child I never thought I could have. It is where I am happy to be. Forever. In answer to the question Manvodh in Varanasi asked me about death, where I want to die is out in nature. Don't let my life end in a hospital bed. Drag me out under a tree and let me look up at the branches and feel the roots ready to take me. After I die, my family can bury or burn me wherever they want. They can put me on a shelf or under a bed or do whatever they want or need with me. But if they want my guidance, the ledge is where I am happy to be scattered. Stand here on this rock one day, my son, this Dartmoor rock that you found, and scatter my ashes to the wind and the trees, the cuckoos and the moss. This is where I am at peace. This is where I feel I belong.

Lockdown taught me powerful lessons, about the need to harness and control negativity, and how I could find not just comfort and love but delight and excitement in the everyday, in my family, my home, and in Mother Nature. Looking back has helped me to realise I still have a powerful need for more experiences and more encounters. But now looking forward I feel it more as a desire than a desperation.

Sitting on the ledge I thought about the words of the young sadhu: 'You are people in a labyrinth. Just be.' Those words will always be a powerful reminder to me to enjoy where I am, and to accept who I am.

I know we all need to be encouraged to battle fear, conquer negativity, and embrace life, risk, opportunities and the glory of our world. Then we can all change, develop and transform ourselves.

Because we all need to go on journeys to impossible places.

Acknowledgements

Huge thanks go to Rupert Lancaster at Hodder & Stoughton for publishing this book, and also for suggesting, nudging and encouraging me to write it in the first place. They are a wonderful bunch at Hodder, and include Ciara Mongey, Cameron Myers, Veronique Norton, Alice Morley, Caitriona Horne and Libby Earland who sorted out the cover photograph, which was taken by Westley Hargrave.

Robert Kirby and Rosemary Scoular at United Agents were fantastic at prodding me to actually do something during the pandemic, rather than just moping around watching the news and thinking about R rates. Robert has been my book agent for more than a quarter of a century, and his colleague Rosemary, my television agent, for nearly as long. I thank them both and Natalia Lucas for their year-round wise counsel and support.

Jasper Rees was then magnificent at getting me to sit down, look back and talk about my journeys and experiences. At first I saw it as a challenge, then as therapy, in a good sense, but quickly I realised it was a huge opportunity. I have never spent enough time looking back, yet it so often helps us to see forward. Jasper and I talked endlessly about what should go in the book, and spent long hours together drafting and creating the initial shape and structure.

On my journeys a long list of wonderful people and guides in glorious and impossible places have gifted me astonishing experiences and taught me more about the world. Several of them took great risks. Only a few are mentioned by name in the text, and listing them all would take pages, but I especially want to thank Abhra Bhattacharya, Amit Vachharajani, Tanjilur Rahman, Jihan Labetubun, Hamdi Ould Med El Hassan, Marie Saleem, Said Chitour, Carlos Macuacua, Cheery, Gildas Andriamalala, Augusto Gazir Soares, Chicao, Juan Pablo Morris and Batsola Andrianjaka. Then there's all those I travelled with during the years covered in this book, often sharing spectacular experiences and thrills, or worked closely alongside and learnt from, including Sam Bagnall, Andrew Carter, Craig Hastings, Matt Brandon, Jonathan Young, Elena Cosentino, Dominic Ozanne, Chris Mitchell, Katharine Arthy, Marina Brito, Olly Bootle, Eric McFarland, Karen O'Connor, May Abdalla, Simon Frost, Will Daws, Darren Kemp, Rana Haddad, Tracey Gardiner, Susan Crighton, Phil Kingwell, Mike Smith, David Upshal, Fred Scott, Steve Grandison, Freddie Martin, Fiona Blair, Tim Hodge, Guillermo Galdos, Jason Gwynne, Fiona Cleary, Richard Pearson, Jane McMullen, Damian O'Mahony, Lizzie Abbott and others. They all deserve a massive thank you, as do the photographers who took several of the images in this book, including Anya, Ben Arogundade, Andrew Carter and Sam Bagnall. But they all just had to put up with me while we were away. My greatest thanks must go to my family and friends who kept me happy and level at home.

Anya, my wife, pal and partner, has travelled the world with me and been on our difficult personal journey, especially our path towards parenthood. She has been a rock, inspiration, buddy, motivation and wise guide. Nothing would have happened without her and everything good in my life is largely thanks to her. I owe her an eternal debt of gratitude and love.

My mum Cindy, brother James and his partner Elsa, and children Alice and Stanley, have all helped to keep my spirits up, while writing this book and during my long journeys, with notes and texts of support. I treasure every hilarious video message from you A & S. Thanks also to my godchildren Elian, George and Zeno. It is an enormous honour to be even a small part of your lives, and I am hugely proud of everything you do, everything you are and everything you will be.

But it is my son Jake who I must thank the most. This book would never have been written without his inspiration. *Journeys to Impossible Places* is partly meant to be a guidebook, apology and explanation for Jake. At ten years old, he's just embarking on his own journey. Writing this book has given me the chance to share my travel stories with him, explain where I've often been while he's been growing up, and pass on some of the lessons I've learnt from life and the thousands of people I've met around the world. From the outset I wanted to write this book directly to Jake. He is by far my proudest achievement, but for a long time he was also an impossible dream. Nothing else I have done comes close to the joy I feel at having you in my life, Jake. And for that I feel intensely lucky and grateful.

Simon Reeve
Dartmoor, Devon